INTERNATIONAL JUSTICE AND IMPUNITY:
THE CASE AGAINST THE UNITED STATES

INTERNATIONAL JUSTICE AND IMPUNITY

THE CASE OF THE UNITED STATES

edited by

NILS ANDERSSON, DANIEL IAGOLNITZER
DIANA G. COLLIER

First version published by Editions L'Harmattan, Paris, 2007
under the title *Justice internationale et impunité, le cas des Etats-Unis*
Edited by Nils Andersson, Daniel Iagolnitzer and Vincent Rivasseau
<http://www.editions-harmattan.fr>

CLARITY PRESS, INC.

© 2008 Clarity Press, Inc.

ISBN: 0-932863-57-4
       978-0-932863-57-7

Front cover photo: Goran Tomasevic
Baghdad burning from Iraq War Air Strikes
March 21, 2003
Translations: Daniel Iagolnitzer, Diana G. Collier

Library of Congress Cataloging-in-Publication Data

Clarity Press, Inc.
Ste. 469, 3277 Roswell Rd. NE
Atlanta, GA. 30305
USA
http://www.claritypress.com

TABLE OF CONTENTS

PREFACE

"Best wishes for a successful event,"
Message from former President Jimmy Carter
to the organizers of the September 2005 Conference

In September, 2005, an international conference on the international issue of impunity for war crimes and crimes against humanity was held at the Palais Bourbon (Assemblée Nationale) in Paris. Confronted with the US policies, its "war on terrorism" and its disastrous impact on global efforts to deepen and entrench the rule of law, the Association for the Defence of International Humanitarian Law, France (ADIF), in cooperation with the International Federation of Human Rights (FIDH), assembled leading human rights intellectuals, historians, lawyers and NGO representatives from the United States, Europe, Latin America and the Middle East, to spearhead international civil society's response to this threat, for the well-being and positive development of humankind.

As is clear for everyone, both then and since, international justice cannot be credible if, on the one hand, persons responsible for crimes committed in African countries, from Congo to Darfur, are rightly prosecuted, while at the same time powerful countries benefit from a quasi total impunity. The United States is not the only powerful State responsible for war crimes. However, its case is emblematic. Since it is the world's foremost economic and military power, a permanent member of the UN Security Council, and purports not only to be a great democracy but a nation engaged in the spread of democracy worldwide, the United States should provide the world with the best example of the observance and practice of human rights. It is instead responsible for some of the worst war crimes of these last decades, torture, inhuman treatment, intense bombardments causing grave civilian losses…

The United States record in relation to the very international law that it supposedly helped to establish is terrible. It did not ratify some of the most important treaties of humanitarian law, neither the 1977 Geneva Protocol I which represented a major advance for the protection of civilian populations in armed conflicts, nor the Statute of the International Criminal Court nor various treaties prohibiting some weapons. Nor does it respect other treaties it ratified, such as the 1949 Geneva Conventions, or the 1968 Non Proliferation Treaty whose Article 6 obliges it to engage in good faith in negotiations towards nuclear disarmament, nor does it respect the Charter of the United Nations which prohibits wars of aggression.

All speakers at the conference have agreed to further pursue their efforts to combat impunity through their contribution to this book, which is a new English language edition of that previously published by Editions l'Harmattan in Paris in 2007. The various viewpoints and ideas expressed during the conference on what can be done are reiterated, and updated as needed, here. The analyses presented denounce the successive US governments from those responsible for Hiroshima and Nagasaki to those responsible for the crimes committed in Indochina and Latin America and those for the crimes recently committed in particular in Iraq and in Guantanamo. Different viewpoints on some topics and different approaches will be found in the various contributions, written under the sole responsibility of their authors. But a strong consensus appears on the need to struggle against impunity and a number of proposals to do so will be found in these pages.

We hope this book will contribute to a redoubled global effort to shed light on and curtail the criminal reality of impunity, which slanders and destroys any meaningful law of nations, and leads only to humankind's descent into chaos, worldwide.

We hope it will be, in that way, a small complementary support to all those people in the United States who courageously struggle to change present US policies and to whom we express our deepest respect, including all those who participate in massive protests against the wars launched by their governments, as well as those eminent personalities who try to advance a different orientation by US policies. We particularly thank in that respect President Carter, who has expressed courageous opinions in various domains and has supported our 2005 conference, and Ramsey Clark, former Attorney General of the United States, whose contribution opens this book, who has for so many years acted against the policies of successive US governments and most recently, for the impeachment of the present US president, George W. Bush.

Nils Andersson, Daniel Iagolnitzer and Vincent Rivasseau
Organizers of the 2005 Paris Conference
and Diana G. Collier
Editorial Director, Clarity Press, Inc.

Acknowledgments

Besides contributors to the book, it is a pleasure once again to thank the two honorary presidents of the conference, Theo Van Boven, eminent lawyer and UN Special Rapporteur, and Pierre Vidal-Naquet, historian and eminent French personality whose death in 2006 has been a great loss for all of us. We would also like the thank the chairpersons of the conference:

Hugo Ruiz Diaz Balbuena, expert and professor of international law (Paraguay)

Roger Bille, Mouvement de la Paix (France)

Mireille Fanon-Mendes-France, Initiatives pour un autre monde (France)

Julio Fernandez, journalist (Spain)

Richard Labévière, chief redactor, international department, Radio France International (France)

Gustave Massiah, ATTAC, vice-president and AITEC, International Association of Technicians, Experts and Researchers, president (France)

Malik Ozden, permanent representative of CETIM, Centre Europe-Tiers Monde, at the United Nations (Switzerland)

Eric Rouleau, journalist, former ambassador (France)

Dominique Tricaud, lawyer, French Helsinki Committee for Human Rights, general secretary (France)

RAMSEY CLARK

IMPUNITY FOR POWER IS THE LAW OF THE JUNGLE

Impunity is such an inadequate word for the problem of power being able to do what it wants with people without accountability. We always complain about Pinochet and impunity, and about how many presidents of Guatemala enjoyed impunity. What we're talking about is whether it is possible to have all people equally accountable under the law. We tend to assume that the law is good and right, and that if we could get everybody under the law, everybody will be living happily ever after. So I feel a need, in trying to talk here rationally about an irrational subject, to observe, first, that the law that we want all to be accountable to has to be worked on some, constantly, and all the time.

An easy illustration of the problem is an observation of Anatole France in *The Red Lily*, where he said that the law in its majestic equality prohibits the rich as well as the poor from sleeping under bridges, from begging in the streets, and from stealing bread. But it is not bringing about a very good world, mainly because Louis XVI doesn't sleep under bridges very often, and doesn't need to steal bread (he eats cake), while others starve. You have to work to have a higher awareness, to constantly improve the law, to make it just. There won't be much difference between arbitrary power and the rule of law until you do. With a benevolent despot, the people may be better off than in a system where the despot himself may be accountable, but everyone is suffering under a law that is not adequate to human needs.

That's why the more profound thinkers and observers on the question of international law have always begun with the proposition that you have to identify the purposes of law, and not simply accept the law as it is—or you will always be in trouble. That's why Hugo Grotius, the first major European to address the problems of war and peace, said that it is this care to preserve society that is the source of all law. When we read what he says about that standard, we see that he is talking about the human condition: not merely fairness, good health, opportunity, and all the rest. A couple of centuries earlier, Ibn Khaldun, who was an incredibly wise and learned scholar, said the same thing, in greater detail. So it is hardly a secret. When we talk about impunity concerning the major issues of our time, it becomes clear that we not only need to put power under the law, but we also need to provide a law that protects us from the dangerous world that technology has created. Oppenheimer once observed that "We scientists too have known sin", but he obviously enjoyed it. He never did anything, or anything adequate, to address the threat that that sin that scientists enjoyed posed to life on the planet. We have to do that, as we struggle to bring everyone under the law.

George Bush, by his every act, makes it clear that he thinks he is, and ought to be, above the law. If you take the nuclear issue, you see that he wants the United States, at least, to be exempt from the Comprehensive Nuclear Test Ban Treaty; he doesn't intend to comply with the test ban treaty. President Kennedy, the first president that I served, the first to appoint me to government, was a dominant force in the promulgation of the test ban treaty. George H.W. Bush (I've known him since he ran for Congress down in Texas, I knew his father, who was a United States Senator) brought the United States online and agreed to a test ban. A test ban is hardly the whole answer to nuclearism—of course some fools would use them without testing them—but it inhibits anyone with some intelligence from using nuclear weapons, because you don't know if the thing will go off, whether it will work if you send it, whether it will explode and kill a lot of other people. And if it fails to do that, then all those missiles from the other people may come raining in on you, and they may work.

The Non-Proliferation Treaty, to me, was the most important of all the efforts which occurred in government under President Johnson. You rarely hear an expression of the concept of the treaty: the treaty was really an abolition treaty, and its concept was to prevent any additional country from acquiring military uses of nuclear power. But there was a quid pro quo. At that time, we thought there were six nuclear powers, and in consideration for the rest of the world agreeing not to develop nuclear weapons, the nuclear powers had to agree—not that they would simply be restrained in their use—but that they would work towards the elimination of nuclear weapons in each of their own countries. When the NPT was signed by a nuclear power, it had the immediate obligation to design a program for elimination of its own nuclear weapons. I have to say that from the moment the US signed it, it was in violation of the treaty, because it never intended to begin the elimination of its own nuclear arsenal.

We talk about the arrogance of power—think of the arrogance of George Bush destroying Iraq on a false allegation—false, I believe, because it was well known that not only was Iraq not developing nuclear weapons, but that of all the countries in the world, it was least capable of threatening the United States in any way. It had had the daylights bombed out of it in 1991. In 42 days there were 110,000 aerial sorties, the Pentagon says, from its aircraft. That's one every thirty seconds. They dropped 88,400 tons of bombs, the Pentagon says. That's the equivalent of seven and a half Hiroshimas, but dispersed more democratically, because they spread them everywhere around the country, not just making seven and a half big holes in the ground. It was an assault on civilians and civilian life. It killed—we've had a huge debate in the United States—100-150,000 people outright.

Sanctions are far deadlier than nuclear bombs, and yet people of good will wanted to look at the sanctions as an alternative to violence. I was in Iraq every year under the sanctions which were put in place—and you have to wonder whether it was a coincidence—on Hiroshima Day, August 6, 1990. With due respect for human life, they could have either waited a day, or done it a day before. So did they intend the symbolism? The sanctions killed and killed. The UN Food and Agriculture Organization in 1996 said a million and a half Iraqis had died as a direct result of the sanctions.

Sometimes a blockade can really pull a country down. In the Peloponnesian War, Athens, as a sea power, could bring Mylos to its knees by naval blockade because they couldn't get anything in there, and those islands don't have a lot of water on them. And after about 6 months, they had to surrender. Lots of the men were killed, many were taken to other colonies. The island grew tall trees that made good ship masts. And of course we found Venus de Milo there, which shows that some goodness and human expression could come from that place. But it was pulled down completely by a blockade.

Cuba has been under a unilateral blockade by the United States. The United States happens to be right there, and it has lots of ships. For how many years? Even with the UN General Assembly voting year after year to condemn the United States blockade, and with the votes often 129 to 2. On a bad year it might be 117 to 7. The overwhelming majority of world opinion is against it.

The FAO also said that half of the million and a half people who died in Iraq were children under the age of five. And that is the occasion on which Madeline Albright was asked about it on a major US TV program called 60 Minutes by Leslie Stahl, an internationally known correspondent, one of the best known in the United States… She's got the FAO report in front of her, and she's read from it. She's also gone down the same corridors with cameras, the same hospital corridors that I was going down year after year, and she's gone to pediatric wards. There would be the mother sitting on the bed with the child as they always do. They didn't catch it, but it happened two or three times while I was there—the child would die. You'd look at the child and think, how can that child still be alive. And when the child died, the wail of the mother ... in a culture that doesn't have our peculiarities, totally uninhibited, wailing because her baby's gone... Stahl asked the then-Ambassador to the United Nations from the United States about it, and she infamously replied that it was a price *the US* was willing to pay.

Albright has been responsible for many things like resolutions to create illegal tribunals. The UN Charter contains no power to create a criminal tribunal. As anyone who has studied the history of the United Nations, remembers World War II, thinks about San Francisco, and looks at the words of the Charter would know—there would have never been a United Nations if they had tried to put within that document the power to create an international criminal tribunal, because none of the victors of WWII would ever submit themselves to the risk that they might be held accountable before that court.

But when you want to pursue enemies, when you want to demonize a whole country, when you want to check one side, when you want to make it seem that world opinion says that *these are the villains*, then you create a special ad hoc criminal tribunal. After all, equality is the mother of justice. Witness the Rwandan Court. Every person accused by the Rwandan Court has been a Hutu, and every witness against them has been a Tutsi... In the Arusha Accords where the United Nations had tried to work out a resolution of the Rwandan disputes (Hutus being 85 percent of the population, Tutsis being 15 percent or so, and the Twa being one or two percent), Faustin Twagiramungu had been the consensus of all the parties to be the prime minister. But then after the invasion of Rwanda—we don't hear much about this, Rwanda is one of the great tragedies of our time, it didn't have to be, at all—who becomes the first prime minister—Paul Kagame, the former intelligence minister of Uganda because the Tutsis held power in Uganda for seven years. They invaded from there. Faustin Twagiramungu says, and there is no question about it, how can you have 15 percent of the population, which is less than a million, and have a million casualties, while 85 percent of the population have—more Hutus were killed than Tutsis.

The tragedy of Yugoslavia was that Yugoslavia was created on an idea, the idea was peace, and the essence of the idea was that if you don't bring the peoples of the Balkans and their countries and nations into some federation, they will keep on fighting like they always have. If you look at the Vance-Owen plan for Bosnia, Vance being former US Secretary of State and Owen being the former Foreign Minister of the UK—they made poor Bosnia look like a checkerboard. They were doing the very thing that leads to violence. It was the essence of our problem with civil rights—segregation: this idea that you can solve problems by violence or by segregation. Prisons are solving problems by segregation and execution—if you think you can solve it that way by killing somebody—which is what they do with war. So here's poor little Bosnia, they're going to put all the Muslims in these squares, all the Orthodox or Eastern Christians will be in these squares, all the Catholics or westerners will be in those squares. But you learn about Bosnia, you read *The Bridge On Drina* by Ivo Andrich, and you will see that the people were learning to live together from the Ottoman and from the Austrian Empire, with all their different religions.

Now we have Balkanized the Balkans beyond compare, and who's held accountable for it? One party, really, is demonized—the Serbs—and we're still balkanizing the Balkans. And what is the UN doing now? It's trying to work out a federation for that part of Europe. Ninety percent of all economic activity and interchange of the six republics of the former Yugoslavia was inside the country. They're not viable individually. They were the only economy that survived the collapse of the eastern bloc. They were the only country that, right between the east and west, maintained some kind of independence. And in my view, they were the country more than any other, that was the inspiration for the Non-Aligned, which in the Cold War was one of the best chances that we had to avoid mutual assured destruction.

But to get back to Bush and his audacity. He crushes Iraq on the false statement that they are preparing to develop a nuclear weapon. Even if they were, you can't attack them. But they weren't. And they had been bled down to where they could barely stand. It's true that the privileged had plenty to eat. But I'll tell you, if they weren't able to accomplish anything during the sanctions period of 12 years, they did one thing better than I've ever seen it done in any place, and that is, that they shared the basic foods, and without any corruption. The government acquired a monopoly of seven basic staples and gathered it all in, and allocated special rations for special needs: infants, children, pregnant women, nursing mothers, and so on. It distributed these through all the little local markets. Every family had its bi-monthly ration, every family as far as I could tell, and I was driving up and down the country every year. You'd go to the market to see who hadn't gotten any, and why. But you never heard a person saying—and the idea that repression caused that is absolutely absurd, because people would be standing in line—"I didn't get my ration, my child's hungry". Everybody was getting their rations. I was at war too, we had rations, ABC, butter, sugar and gas, and everybody was cheating – selling their butter rations, selling their sugar rations, selling gasoline rations and all the rest. I'm not saying everybody was corrupt, it's just the way it works in our society. But here in Iraq, where there was life and death, somehow or other they were able to carry that out.

While destroying this country—again—on the claim that they were developing weapons of mass destruction, Bush was pushing for, and got Congressional approval for, three new generations of nuclear weapons—a clear violation of the Non-Proliferation Treaty and a clear and present danger to life on earth. As we were told yesterday by a Nobel Laureate, these are weapons that would be used. There's enough common sense to know that you just can't use a weapon, even a small weapon like the atomic bomb that was dropped on Hiroshima, or the slightly larger one that was dropped on Nagasaki. It's too big. It kills too many people. A lot of people get upset about it. You can't use them—except in dire conditions. What you want is something that can be more precise. So they want a bomb that can take out these six blocks in Fallujah. (I used to call Fallujah the modern Guernica. Now I think of it more as a latter-day Warsaw.) So you don't have to send guys in, some of whom get shot—not many in comparison to what you're doing, a couple of thousand by now. You just take this tactical nuclear weapon and *pooof*. They want one that will penetrate bunkers. So with an armory or bomb shelter, you don't have to send one in to try to open it up, and another one down the same hole to get there... Or take the Al-Rashid Hotel. They thought Saddam Hussein was going to be at a meeting at the Al-Rashid, and as usual, who gets killed? Some guy mopping up the floor right outside, and a maid downstairs; two people got killed when they hit the Al-Rashid. You get this bomb that will do whatever you need, that will go through whatever is there, and you do it.

The world barely has the will to use its voice, to say: you can't do that. The people of the United States are barely aware of it, and don't consider it any of their business. I have always loved mayors, but let me tell you, the mayors of the United States are totally detached from this sort of power. Totally detached. The only possible threat that they face is, I'll run against that Congressman. Every once in a while, a mayor gets big enough that he can run against a Senator. Or run for governor. Governors are totally detached. Their power over this sort of thing—they don't even know about it. The concentration of power in a handful is intense. And the handful are individuals, with their own ideas. Don't think Wolfowitz doesn't have his own ideas. I went to the University of Chicago because I thought it was a place of high intellectual curiosity and the desire to know. Wolfowitz got out there for some other reason, with the institution, and developed his own ideas about these things. Accountability is not anything that they don't sneer at.

Perhaps the most obvious and blatant activity by the United States, or perhaps any other country in history, to show its intention never to be accountable—has to do with the history of the International Criminal Court. I'm an idealist, so I can't be taken very seriously. I have always believed that you have to have an international court if you want peace. It has to have authority and power and jurisdiction to hold all leadership accountable for international crimes. I started working on that in 1969.

The US fought that in every way. It participated in the drafting, and so weakened the court in its charter or mandate that it is barely able, with full support of the international community, to address problems that are urgent in international criminal law. Four or five important times, the United States said, well if you change the language this way, we may sign. Changing the language that way cut out 20 percent of the utility or meaningfulness of the court. And then they said well, we may not be able to sign, but change it this way. And they brought it down until it was extremely weak but better than nothing. Finally we got more than 120 nations signed on as of the first of July, 2002. The court was ratified; the number of nations necessary for it to be ratified had come into force.

So now the US has gotten more than 100 countries to sign bilateral treaties with the United States, such as the Philippines. The Philippines has had some history with the United States militarism, let me tell you. Over the past 100 years, the dominant factor of their daily life has been US militarism. There was a time when 6,000 families, chosen by auction, had the privilege of living by scouring the garbage from Subic naval station, and their standard of living was almost three times that of the Philippine people as a whole. In other words, you come in for a raffle, or however they finally chose, and if you were one of the lucky ones, you got to participate in salvaging from US garbage at one naval base. The Clark air force base is the same.

A million people died in the Philippine-American war. You don't find reference in our history books to the Philippine-American war. It's called the Spanish-American War. We sailed into Manila Bay and shot up a bunch of ships. The Spanish folded in no time, but it was five years later before the Philippine-American war was over. Eight hundred thousand people died from dengue fever. There are documents in the Senate of the United States in which Colonel Liverpool, I think it was, asked General Smith for an interpretation of an order made to kill all of the men on the Island of Negros. Now Negros could feed the Philippines and beyond. It was a marvelously fertile island, and even to this day produces a major part of the agricultural export of the country. It's in the hands of four or five people, and the children on that island suffer from malnutrition. General Smith answered, "All of the men over the age of twelve."

There are ditches in which you can see the bodies of what our soldiers called "little niggers" —that hateful racial word.I come from the South, east Texas itself. When Texas was part of the confederation and slaves existed, they couldn't exist in West Texas because you'd have to feed them, and there wasn't any agriculture, and any labor for them to do.

They didn't want a slave out there, they had enough trouble feeding their own families. But they called the Filipinos "little niggers". No accountability.

Now 100 nations have signed bilateral treaties with the United States in which they agree that they will not surrender any American citizen to an international criminal court. It's pretty amazing. Here we have whatever processes a particular nation has for signing a treaty, necessarily involving the highest foreign policy leadership, agreeing to impunity for the United States.

The Nuremberg Judgment is rarely thought about, rarely read, and the whole process is generally discredited in popular opinion—the West likes to feel it was justice and others like to feel it was power. But there were a lot of scholars, a lot of intellectual power, and a lot of hope and good will, there. I sat in the trial for two days—I was 18 years old, a United States Marine Corp corporal. I watched the process and thought it was good. The Judgment said that the supreme international crime is war of aggression. Every initiative in that time was a war of aggression, beginning at least with Poland. The court found Poland was the first aggression. There were explanations for Czechoslovakia and Austria—they wanted in; one was in the Munich Treaty, you can't say that's an aggression because you've signed the treaty. The war of aggression is the supreme international crime.

It's almost impossible to look at the attack of the United States on Iraq without seeing that it is the supreme international crime. There is a process in the United States Constitution designed to address this. The American people have the power, if they have the understanding, desire and the will. It's called impeachment. Of all the provisions in the Constitution, it involves the greatest number of references and the greatest intricacies, completely provided for, in seven separate parts of a very short constitution. And what it is designed to do is to protect the country from criminal conduct by public officials who can't be prosecuted in office, some of them, and to guarantee the power in the people, through their elected representatives. The sole power of impeachment is in the House of Representatives; the trial is in the Senate. We've got to remember that President Nixon had been impeached, and had made a head count of the Senate when he resigned, and had the promise from Gerald Ford that he would be pardoned. The power of pardon is with the president, and that relieved him of any concern for accountability, granted him impunity for anything he might have done. Which is peanuts: I mean, there's the Democratic National Committee, and some jerks break in and try to steal some secrets, when it's clear that Nixon is going to win by a landslide, anyway. You've got to remember that Bill Clinton was impeached, 107 to 117 on the major vote. There were three grounds that he was impeached on. It was cheap politics—not a high crime or misdemeanor—fooling around with a young woman.

George Bush has committed the supreme international crime, and that's only one. We've got a list of fifteen. There's a major impeachment movement in the United States. Tomorrow there will be a rally in Washington, and there will be a major impeachment meeting, there. It's hard work, let me tell you, hard rock mining. We've got over 600,000 signatures for impeachment, people who've put their name, and their social security numbers on the line. The integrity of the constitution of the United States requires it for there to be an impeachment. Article 2, Section 4 says that the president, vice-president or other civil officers of the United States shall be removed from office upon impeachment for and conviction of high crimes and misdemeanors. Whether it will happen or not, I don't know. Whether it ought to happen is as clear to me as anything can be. But we've got miles to go.

That is a very temporary and minor remedy. All the pictures from Katrina reminded me of everything that I learned in twenty years on the ground in the civil rights movement in the United States—that we have this huge impoverished third world standard of living of people, who have no rights, who don't even have conditions of living that are bearable. It breaks my heart to see those on TV, but I've seen them before. The pictures there that have to be looked at are between the troops that finally arrive nine days later to give help, and the people. What do they do? They go in, in the same military squads that they go into Fallujah, or Ramadi, or out in Anbar, or anywhere. These guys have got these heavy automatic rifles that can fire 600 rounds a minute, they've got on steel helmets, and they're going down, one guy's looking at the back, doing this jumping stuff, they go around the corner, they jump like that. It's New Orleans, Louisiana, *in the United States.* Where we're finding dead bodies, people who can barely move. They come in the door and they smash it, just like they're going to kick it through. That's the mentality: the culture of violence. It's staggering. Look at our movies. Look at our games for children. Look at the toys that mothers are proudest of acquiring when they first come out.

The African American culture has produced, I think, our greatest music. It's almost like their painkiller. One of our most powerful African American musicians of recent years, a man named Marvin Gaye, singing soul and blues—I was listening yesterday to the mayor of Hiroshima, and it brought to mind his greatest song, called "Save the Children". The last line is: save the babies. Marvin Gaye was murdered by his own father when he was about 45 years old. It's not that Marvin Gaye was such a protector of children, but that African Americans know how endangered their children are, and how important it is to save them.

Article 1, Section 2 of the United Nations Charter states that the first principle of the United Nations, its founding principle, is the sovereign equality of all states. I think that needs to be extrapolated in international law to the sovereign equality of all peoples, and the protection of the fundamental rights of every man, woman and child on earth, and the dignity of each. And the best expression I've ever heard of came from a person who, statistically, had no right to live very long—a full-blooded Zapatec Indian from Oaxaca, Mexico. His parents died when he was still an infant. He became a lawyer, he became twice the president of Mexico, he fought the French a couple of times. (We ought to remember Haiti when we think of wars of aggression... Then, we recall that four months before Aristide was forced from Haiti by the United States, George Bush said on television, "Aristide has to go". Aristide is one of the most moral leaders of modern times, he's trusted by the Haitian people, he's been voted in by a huge majority. They trust him, he's lived among them, he was one of them. He was born in poverty, maintained a vow of poverty. He was a priest. The United States can't stand him because he won't do what they say.) In the lobby of the United Nations outside the General Assembly, there's a big stone from Mexico. Every nation gives a gift. Inscribed on it is a message, from the writings of Benito Juarez: "A respect for the rights of others is peace."

In a sense, I think that applies mother to child, wife to husband. Inter-family, inter-social, international. If the rights are right, and they are respected and enforced against any violator, you may find peace.

PART I

FROM HIROSHIMA
TO GUANTANAMO

TADATOSHI AKIBA

TOWARDS THE ABOLITION OF NUCLEAR WEAPONS

It is an honor for me to be given this opportunity to address the Association for the Defense of International Humanitarian Fundamental Law. I am especially grateful for this opportunity because never has your role been more important. I believe that the world is being forced to choose between the rule of law, which is basically your concern, and the rule of power, that is, the rule by force and violence. Perhaps it is too mild to say we are being forced to choose. Perhaps the rule of law is being forced upon us, and how to change that situation seems to be one of the greatest problems we face today. As defenders of international humanitarian laws, I do hope that you will take the lead in publicly asserting that democratic rule of law is the proper basis, as a matter of fact, the only basis for international relations. I also hope that you will support the International Court of Justice and take a strong, public, high-profile action or stand condemning nuclear weapons as immoral and illegal. I'll refer to this a little later.

First, let me explain what the Mayors for Peace is all about. It is a UN-accredited NGO based in Hiroshima. It was created in 1982 by an initiative of the mayors of Hiroshima and Nagasaki. The purpose was certainly to work toward the abolition of nuclear weapons, but in the beginning, the role was focused on the educational aspects of our purpose. Recently, we have become more active, and as a proof of what we have done I can give you some figures. Before I left Japan a few days ago, we had 1,055 city members in 112 countries and regions. This number has increased dramatically just since I left for Europe on Sunday. With the enthusiastic participation of the Italian cities I just visited, we now have more than 1,200 members. I think this great growth will probably continue. Our members include Beijing, London, Paris, Moscow, New Delhi, and Jerusalem—all the nuclear-weapon-state capitals except Washington and Islamabad.

In 2003, we launched a campaign which we called the 2020 Vision, or the Emergency Campaign to Abolish Nuclear Weapons. We primarily focused on the NPT Review Process, leading up to the Review Conference itself, which was held in May this past year. But today I want to tell you more about what we intend to do in the course of campaigning to abolish nuclear weapons by the year 2020. The name "2020 vision," actually sometimes people reverse the order saying, "Vision 2020," but the name really does not matter. What important is that we have set the year 2020 as the target year by which we intend to make this world nuclear-weapon-free. Now this year, 2005, is the 60th anniversary of the atomic bombings of Hiroshima and Nagasaki. The number 60 has a special meaning in Asian cultures, especially in China and Japan. It is the number that brings the cycle of nature and the humanity back to the original form. So at 60 years we go back to the origin of whatever we are engaged in and try to create a new cycle of activities based on a history of 60 years. And that is exactly what I would like to do here today. I'd like briefly to go back to the point of departure, August 6th, 1945.

If you have never been to Hiroshima, I'm sure it is hard for you to imagine. Even if you've learned through books, photographs and listening to the testimonials of the *hibakusha*, I believe it is still worthwhile to come to Hiroshima and go through the A-bomb museum and talk to the survivors and other citizens as well. Doing so will give you an added dimension of understanding of why we have to continue our struggle to rid the world of nuclear weapons.

First, let me briefly again describe the devastation. Within a half-kilometer circle from the hypocenter, 99% of our population died immediately. Some of them simply evaporated, but 99% died within a few days. I say 99% instead of 100% because we know for a fact that there were a few people who survived. The survivors were not outdoors or on the ground level. They were in a basement or shielded by an unusually heavy wall, and therefore miraculously survived. Some people use this fact to insist that being at the center of the explosion of the bomb was not all that dangerous. But that is not true. 99% died instantly. That's what we really have to understand.

Within 1 kilometer from the hypocenter, people were burned badly through all layers of skin, with the heat reaching internal organs and muscles. As far away as two kilometers, people were bombarded with fragments of flying glass, and radiation was certainly still a devastating force within this range. Then, within 20 to 30 minutes, a conflagration engulfed the entire city. If you were trapped in the house or had no way of escaping quickly, you were burned to death by the fire. Then, the black rain started falling within a few hours. With the bomb and the fire, the entire city was destroyed. By the following day, as you have seen in the pictures, the entire city was gone. People who actually saw that happen, who went through that experience, describe it as hell itself. We human beings have not developed a vocabulary sufficient to describe what actually happened. And that is one of the reasons it is so difficult for us to convince everybody that this kind of tragedy and suffering must never be repeated.

It is also important for us to notice here a point that often escapes our consciousness. Our *hibakusha*, that's the Japanese word for the survivors of the atomic bombings, were very young at the time. The average age of *hibakusha*, surviving victims of the atomic bombing, is seventy-three this year. And since I am a mathematician I can do the subtraction very well. Seventy-three minus sixty is thirteen. So the average age of the people who actually went through the bombing and are living right now, at the time their age was thirteen. These were children who were victims of this incredible and illegal, heinous weapon of mass destruction. And through these years, they have tried to live with that experience and tried to somehow come to terms with this experience. And their conclusion is very simple. This is the expression I hear from these people most often, that is, "No one else should suffer as I did." No one else. The important thing is that "no one else" includes President Truman, Paul Tibbets, who brought the bomb to Hiroshima, the scientists who created the bomb, and everyone else on Earth. And that precludes the possibility of retaliation or revenge. This is the important message. This is a future-oriented message that we would like to share again with you and with the rest of the world. And another important point is that when the *hibakusha* talk about "no one else suffering as we did," that emphasis is definitely, if not consciously, on the children.

This message for peace, this message of non-repetition comes from the hearts of people who were children at that time, thirteen years old or fourteen years old. Thus, they are, in effect, saying, no child should never go through this experience. And that is why in this year's Peace Declaration, I took this message further to say that we should adopt, "Thou shalt not kill children," as the axiom of highest priority for humanity in the 21st century. And that is why Mayor Delanoë of Paris, when he promised that he would hold the A-bomb exhibition in the City Hall of Paris, which is going on right now and which will last until the end of September, that is why Mayor Delanoë placed the emphasis on the children. He wants children to understand the message. The message of those children is to be shared by adults in an artistic, cultural fashion, which I'm sure is very persuasive. If you haven't had a chance to see it, I hope you will go to City Hall and look at this wonderful exhibition.

Now, I would like to briefly mention that the *hibakusha*, after going through this experience, have worked tirelessly to rid the world of nuclear weapons. Their voices have spread gradually, and for some time, we have sometimes had reason to believe that their wish was coming very close to reality. As a matter of fact, in 1989 when the Berlin Wall came down, we thought that most of the problems of the world had been solved. Even in

Hiroshima, we thought the day was approaching in which the world would finally get rid of nuclear weapons. But as you all know, as we all know, we were wrong. Since September 11th, the world appears to be obsessed with violence and revenge. But perhaps the greatest shock of all to the people of Hiroshima was the American Nuclear Posture Review that came out in 2002. That document announced in black and white that, first of all, the United States has no intention of getting rid of nuclear weapons. The second point the Posture Review made is that the United States will be engaged in creating more technically advanced means of killing people with nuclear weapons that will be usable. That is, instead of simply utilizing nuclear weapons as a means of deterrence, they will start manufacturing bombs and other devices of mass destruction for the purpose of actually using them. And the third, and the most important point I believe, is that they clearly stated their intention to use those weapons in combat. This is certainly the antithesis of what Hiroshima and the *hibakusha* had been saying. So we really had to do something about this.

We turned to the Mayors for Peace to solve this problem together with the citizens of Hiroshima. And the Mayors for Peace, together with civil society, NGOs and friendly governments, launched an emergency campaign to ban nuclear weapons or the 2020 Vision, as I mentioned earlier. The purpose of this 2020 Vision is to abolish all nuclear weapons by the year 2020, but there is an intermediate goal. That is, we'd like to have a universal nuclear weapons convention signed by 2010. That's only 5 years from now. However, that is the first step. We already have a model nuclear weapons convention. It may not be necessary to explain that a nuclear weapons convention really means a treaty that prohibits the use or manufacturer or anything that has to do with nuclear weapons, and there is a good model nuclear weapons convention developed by the NGOs and experts in this field. All the United Nations officials and interested governments need to do is to read this document and simply sign it, and that should be done within five years.

But let me explain what sorts of things we ought to be doing in these five years. Initially our strategy was to focus on NPT Review Process. We participated in the Preparatory Committee Meetings and the Review Conference itself, which was held in May this year. However, as you all know, the result was not satisfactory. And the reason is, I believe, quite simple. The NPT Review Conference, as well as the Conference on Disarmament regularly held in Geneva, which has the task of developing an action program for the decisions taken by the NPT Review Conference, must make all decisions based on the consensus rule. That means that if a single country objects to even the tiniest point in the procedure, nothing happens. As a matter of fact, nothing has happened for these five years, and nothing happened in the Review Conference in May.

Therefore, we intend to shift our attention to the original spirit of the United Nations. By the way the United Nations itself will be celebrating its

60th anniversary this year, and October 24th, UN Day, will be the focus of all of this. However, in the meantime, we will be working with mayors around the world, NGOs and government officials from many countries to make the process work in our effort to revive the NPT process. This is also our effort to find new ways of utilizing the power behind United Nations, that is, the power of people. For example, in April 2004, we brought 19 mayors from around the world to attend the Preparatory Committee Meeting of the NPT. The New York City Council was enthusiastic about our presence in New York City, so they declared April 28th to be Nuclear Weapons Abolition Day. The New York City Council worked with us to send this message to the rest of the world. That led us to redouble our efforts toward the May Review Conference this year.

The New York City Council was not the only body that worked enthusiastically with us. The 2020 Vision has been well received and has been amplified by the participation and endorsement, cooperation and new branching out of ideas stemming from it in many different ways. The European Parliament formally endorsed the 2020 Vision last year, as did the US Conference of Mayors, the US National Conference of Black Mayors and many city councils and NGOs including IPPNW and IPB. Peace activists, who have really done a great job in changing the consciousness of the people around the world, all came around to endorse our 2020 Vision.

Now, let me briefly expand on the US Conference of Mayors. This is an organization of American mayors. The membership count now is 1,183 and the only condition for an American mayor to join this organization is that the city must have a population larger than 30,000. So this organization endorsed the 2020 Vision unanimously, and I was really surprised to find out that this organization has taken this stand since 1984. But as you know, that organization of mayors, just like any other organization, has different areas to concentrate on depending on the time, the environment and everything else. But the US Conference of Mayors has decided that this is a priority issue that they will be involved in during the coming few years.

So to the May Review Conference this year, we brought a delegation of 167 city representatives including 51 mayors. On May 1st, we helped to lead one of the biggest anti-nuclear demonstrations in New York in 20 years, bringing 40,000 people to march through the streets of New York and ending in a rally in Central Park. Our allies collected 6 million signatures demanding the abolition of nuclear weapons. However, these efforts were not enough for us to achieve the goal of activating the Review Conference itself. That is why I mentioned earlier that we have to find a new way of pursuing and accomplishing our goal.

Our 2020 Vision Campaign for this coming year will be done at every possible level we can pick up. First of all, we will be lobbying at UN level, the governmental level including diplomats, government officials and so forth.

That's the regular sort of channel that, whenever anybody thinks about international issues like disarmament, that is the level we usually concentrate on. But that is not all. We will also work at the local government level and the citizen level. That's where the Mayors or Peace can play a large role.

We intend to work on the grassroots level, and that is the level where NGOs and many activists, including most of you, I assume, are extremely effective. That's where the people's energy and voices and resources are. But the Mayors for Peace want to be a bridge to help that energy and that creativity and the desire to create a new better world get to the top level of international diplomacy and international bureaucracy so that together we can accomplish our goal.

I will tell you more about this campaign and what we want to do during this year, but before I do, I would like to answer one question, which is, why mayors? Nuclear weapons are an international issue, and we have been asked this many times by journalists especially, they want to know what mayors can do. But I think that the journalists should be answered quite honestly with facts, and I think we should have answers when citizens also ask us why mayors. One simple reason is that when a nuclear war occurs or nuclear weapons are used, it is the cities that will suffer. And as mayors, we have the responsibility to protect our citizens from any harm. We have to protect their lives, their property and welfare. That's what mayors are chosen for. That's our job. So we have to think about the possibility of a catastrophe such as a nuclear attack. After all, many world leaders are saying that a nuclear weapon could be used by terrorists, so we have to think about this. And our conclusion is that the only way we can protect our citizens from nuclear attack is to prevent nuclear attacks from happening. And the only permanent way to prevent nuclear attacks is to get rid of nuclear weapons.

That is our conclusion, and that is why many mayors have been joining this organization. However, that is not the only reason. The history of the world, and especially the history of Europe, shows that it is the cities that have been the engines of economic, cultural, political, educational, religious and other human development. In other words, it is the cities that actually create civilization. It is the cities that actually are responsible for maintaining our civilization, and the time has come for cities to start speaking up.

We are the closest governmental organizations to the citizens. Our political philosophies as mayors of cities really do not come from abstract ideologies. Our primary job is to make sure that our cities are run smoothly. We have to take care of the everyday needs of our citizens. We have to collect the garbage. We have to repair bridges, and it may sound absurd, but these routine needs are the basis of our thinking. We are closest to the hearts of our citizens. Mayors know their citizens, and citizens know us. That is why we are concerned about our citizen's lives, honestly and sincerely.

And perhaps even more important, cities do not have or want or need any means of mass destruction. We do not have armies. There is no point for us to even think about utilizing brute force to solve inter-city problems. Hiroshima could not possibly benefit from launching a war on Tokyo, Osaka, or Paris or Florence or anywhere. It is in our best interest to work together with these cities, cooperatively, exchange our young people, hold cultural events, and visit each other. We have to cooperate to make sure the future will be richer and brighter for our younger generations, to give their creativity a chance to blossom, and to let businesses bloom.

That is why we are involved in this. We mayors are the ones that will determine the future. Let me give you a couple of examples of how things can be done. In the US-Japan City Summit, which was held in Hiroshima in November last year, former mayor, Jeremy Harris of Honolulu made an interesting comment. He said that the US Federal Government does not want to sign the Kyoto Protocol to reduce CO_2 emissions. However, he pointed out that if all of the cities in the United States, or if not all, if most of the cities in the United States created their own standards for CO_2 emissions, and if most of them achieved their reduction goals, that would be the equivalent of having the Federal Government of the United States signing the Kyoto Protocol and actually implementing it. The cities actually have the power to accomplish important goals that we set ourselves.

Another example is New Zealand. New Zealand was suffering from a high rate of unemployment. Then most of the New Zealand mayors got together and, without the help of the National Government, they actually solved the unemployment problem. These two examples are probably enough to convince you that we are serious about working with our citizens to solve not only local problems like garbage and unemployment, but such important international problems as protecting the environment. Certainly, preserving humanity for the coming centuries is just as important as any of the problems I have mentioned.

Based on this thinking, we intend to launch specific activities for the coming year. Let me mention three of them in reverse chronological order. The first one is July 8th, 2006. That is the tenth anniversary of the advisory opinion of the International Court of Justice. That ruling is extremely important, and we will help to organize a huge event in The Hague on that day. Perhaps even larger than the demonstration you held right before the Iraq war. We have to show that we are serious about the content of the advisory opinion. We are contemplating whether it is possible to bring lawsuits against those countries that refuse to enter good faith negotiations to get rid of nuclear weapons. If it is possible illegally to do so, we have to arouse world public demand for such action. So July 8th next year will be very important.

Prior to that, June 23rd through June 28th, there is going to be the World Peace Forum in Vancouver, Canada. That is one of the main events next year for all peace activists. Peace workers will gather to report on what they have accomplished and what new strategies they could adopt to accomplish our goal, the goal of creating a sustainable peace throughout the world.

The most immediate activity I would like to ask you to focus on is October 24th, United Nations Day, and UN Disarmament Week, which means the one week period starting October 24th. Just about that time, we will be trying to focus the world's attention on the First Committee of the United Nations. As I mentioned, we have to utilize mechanisms within the United Nations that reflect majority opinion. And the First Committee of the United Nations, which is in charge of disarmament and security, can do its job using majority rule, if necessary. So it is that Committee that we would like to have the world focus on. If that Committee, with leadership coming from some of the nations and government officials who share our values, proposes to create a special committee mandated to enter serious negotiation toward the goal of creating and maintaining a nuclear- free world, then we will be in business. So we would like to focus on the First Committee to encourage it to create that special committee by a majority, if necessary, and make sure that there will be enough countries to support such a move. To help this process, we need to have the world's public opinion raised to a very high level. We need all the governments and diplomats to actually listen to the majority voices of the world.

Let me explain, in case you are doubtful, that we are really the majority. The media tends to give the impression that the goal of the abolition of nuclear weapons is just a fringe opinion of a small number of people, just Hiroshima and Nagasaki. But that is not true. Even within the United Nations framework, more than half of the countries have actually signed treaties declaring themselves nuclear free, and bound by these treaties, they have agreed not to have the nuclear weapons. Nuclear-weapon-free-zones exist in several areas in the world, and that area is expanding. So we already have the majority within the United Nations clearly on the side of getting rid of nuclear weapons.

The problem is that this majority voice is not the will of the United Nations. But as I proposed, we do have a mechanism we can utilize to ensure that this majority opinion becomes the will of the United Nations. In poll after poll, the majority voices of the world actually are for the elimination of nuclear weapons. Even in the United States, in an AP poll taken this spring, 66% of Americans actually said that they favor eliminating nuclear weapons. This result is very significant because it came in answer to a four-part question. The question was, "What is the best way to prevent the proliferation of nuclear weapons?" Answer no. 1: only the United States should have nuclear weapons. Answer no. 2: the United States and its friends should have nuclear weapons. Answer no. 3: the status quo, those countries that have nuclear weapons can keep them but no other countries should have nuclear weapons. Answer no. 4: no country should have nuclear weapons. Now, given these four choices, and if American citizens were asleep, they would probably choose one of the first three. After all, they include the United States as one of the countries allowed to own nuclear weapons. And yet, 66% chose no. 4, and that percentage I'm sure is much higher in the rest of the world. We would like to conduct an actual statistical survey to show by numbers that this is indeed the case. We would like to have the data in front of us. But at the same time, we have been fed the idea that we cannot do anything about this. Most citizens say, "That's an international problem. We ordinary citizens don't have anything to do with it. I have no means of going to the United Nations and making a speech." But that's where all of you come in. We have to make sure that our voices are united, and united for the single purpose of creating a much better world without nuclear weapons. If we are united, I think we can accomplish the goal. So it is very important for us to unite with each other.

In general, I think we are separated from our own feelings. We are separated from the knowledge that the majority of the people want the same thing we do. We are separated from the knowledge that within the United Nations, there is a mechanism by which the majority opinion can be respected. We are separated from the knowledge that the majority of the countries in the United Nations actually would like to work with us. We are separated from our own emotions about what should or should not happen to our children. We are separated from our own ability to act. We are told that there is nothing we can do. "Nuclear weapons are good for us. Listen to us, we are the leaders, se we will solve all the problems." We are separated from thinking independently, utilizing our heads.

We have to bring all of these things together, bring ourselves together, and unite. And as leaders who defend international humanitarian fundamental law, your role is greater than ever. As mayors, our role in representing the true voices and feeling of our citizens is also growing. We have to work together to accomplish the goal of abolishing nuclear weapons.

I talk to many *hibakusha* who are in their seventies now, who were teenagers or children in 1945. They all agree it's wonderful that mayors throughout the world are doing this. Actually, I really wanted to show these *hibakusha* what happened in Florence. I was one of the few representatives from Hiroshima in Florence, when 80 mayors from all over Italy, even 5 from Sicily, came to Florence to join or activate their membership in Mayors for Peace and start doing something. I really wanted to have some of the *hibakusha* who have died working for the cause to see that their cause has been understood. Their voice, their childlike voice, has been heard, and something is really going to happening. I wish I could show them the support that has been created. It is important that we mayors work together in a similar fashion to mobilize and represent our citizens' voices, and ADIF will lead us from the point of view of the law governing the international scene from the humanitarian point of view. Based on the accomplishments of the past great movements and many other important events in the world actually prove to us that when we put our strengths together, when we unite to work for the common goal of a brighter future, we can actually accomplish it.

So, I hope 2020 will be a year to celebrate. We really must keep this promise. One thing that many of the aging *hibakusha* have said is, "Mayor, it's a wonderful idea to accomplish the abolition of nuclear weapons by 2020. Establishing a specific the date is very important because that will give us concrete guide as we try to actualize our idea and ideals. But 2020 is too far away for us. Can't you make it 2015 or 2010? We may not be alive in 2020. So we really have to make the nuclear-free world happen before 2020 if possible, and 2020 at the latest. Seeing your faces here today, talking to the mayors and citizens of Italy, France, Paris, and seeing those people who came to the exhibition where I met yesterday with Mayor Delanoë, and the many, many more people who have been supporting the *hibakusha* cause, I believe we can accomplish this goal. So, please, let's work together, and please help me retire happy in the year 2021.

SAMIR AMIN

THE GEOSTRATEGY OF CONTEMPORARY IMPERIALISM

1. From permanent conflict of imperialisms to collective imperialism

In its globalized deployment, imperialism was always conjugated in the plural, from its inception (in the XVIth century) until 1945. The conflict of imperialisms, permanent and often violent, has occupied, due to this fact, as decisive a place in the transformation of the world as class struggle, through which the fundamental contradictions of capitalism are expressed. Moreover, social fights and conflicts of the imperialisms are closely articulated and it is this articulation that determines the course of really existing capitalism. I also point out that the analysis that I have proposed in this respect differs vastly from that of the "succession of hegemonies".

The Second World War ended in a major transformation with regard to the forms of imperialism: the substitution of the multiplicity of imperialisms in permanent conflict by collective imperialism combining the ensemble of the centers of the world capitalist system (simply, the "triad": the United States and its external Canadian province, Western and central Europe, Japan). This new form of imperialist expansion went through various phases of its development, but it remained all the time present. The eventual hegemonic role of the United States, whose bases will have to be specified as the forms of its articulation with the new collective imperialism, must be located within this perspective. These questions pose problems, which are precisely those that I would wish to point out here.

The United States drew a gigantic benefit from the Second World War, which had ruined its principal combatants—Europe, the Soviet Union, China and Japan. It was thus in a position to exert its economic hegemony, since it concentrated more than half of the global industrial production and exclusively held new technologies that would shape the development of the second half of the century. In addition, it alone had a nuclear weapon—the new "absolute" weapon. This is why I situate the break announcing the end of the war not at Yalta, as is often said (at Yalta the United States did not have the weapon yet) but at Potsdam (a few days before the bombardment of Hiroshima and Nagasaki). At Potsdam, the American tone changed: the decision to engage in what was going to be the "cold war" was made by them.

This double absolute advantage was nevertheless eroded in a relatively short period of time (within two decades) by double recoveries, economic for the capitalist Europe and Japan, military for the Soviet Union. It will be remembered that this relative retreat of US power at the time gave rise to a flowering of discourse on "American decline", and even an ascent of alternative hegemonies (Europe, Japan, later China...).

Does this new collective imperialism thus arouse a "definitive" (non-conjunctural) qualitative transformation? Does it inevitably imply a "leadership" of the United States in one way or another?

2. The project of the ruling class of the United States: To extend their military control over the whole planet

This project, which I will describe without much hesitation as overweening, even crazy, and criminal by what it implies, did not come out of President Bush Junior's head, to be implemented by an extreme right junta, seizing power through dubious elections.

It is the project which the ruling class of the United States has unceasingly nurtured since 1945, even though its implementation evidently passed through ups and downs, encountered a few vicissitudes, and was here and there checked, and could not be pursued with the consistency and violence that this implied in certain conjunctural moments like that following the disintegration of the Soviet Union.

The project always rendered a decisive role to its military dimension. It was conceived after Potsdam, as I pointed out, and founded on nuclear monopoly. Very quickly, the United States conceived a global military strategy, dividing the planet into regions and allocating the responsibility for the control of each of them under a "US Military Command". I refer to what I wrote on this subject even before the collapse of the USSR, and on the priority position occupied by the Middle East in this global strategic vision. The objective was not only "to encircle the USSR" (and China), but also to draw up means for making Washington the ruler in the last resort of all the regions of the planet. In other words, it extended the Monroe Doctrine to the whole planet, which effectively gave the exclusive right of managing the ensemble of the New World to the United States in accordance with what it defined as its "national interests".

The preferred instrument of the hegemonist offensive is therefore the military. US hegemony, which in turn guarantees the hegemony of the Triad over the world system, therefore demands that its allies like Great Britain and Japan agree to follow in the American wake, acknowledge the necessity of doing so, and acknowledge it without any emotional crises or any hand-wringing over "culture". But that means that all the speeches that the European politicians feed their audiences about the economic power of Europe have no real significance. By grounding itself solely on the terrain of mercantile disputes, with no project of its own, Europe is beaten in advance. Washington knows that very well.

The project implies that the "sovereignty of the national interests of the United States" is placed above all the other principles controlling the political behaviors that we regard as "legitimate" means; it develops a systematic mistrust towards all supranational rights. The ruling class of the United States proclaims openly that it "will not tolerate" the reconstitution of any economic and military power capable of questioning its monopoly of domination over the planet, and for this purpose, it gave itself the right to lead "preventive wars". Three principal potential adversaries are targeted here.

In the first place is Russia, whose dismemberment, after that of the USSR, constitutes henceforth a major strategic objective of the United States. The Russian ruling class does not appear to have understood this until now. It seems convinced that after having "lost the war", it could "win peace", as had Germany and Japan. It forgets that Washington needed the recovery of these two adversaries in the Second World War, precisely to face the Soviet challenge. The new conjuncture is different, the United States no longer having a serious competitor. Its option is then to permanently and completely destroy the ravaged Russian adversary. Will Putin understand this and facilitate Russia's coming out of its illusions?

In the second place is China, whose expanse and economic success worry the United States, whose strategic objective remains, here too, to dismember this large country.

Europe comes in third place in this global vision of the new masters of the world. But here the North American establishment does not appear anxious, at least so far. The unconditional Atlanticism of a few (Great Britain, as well as the new servile powers of the East), the "quicksand of the European project" (a point to which I will return), the converging interests of the dominant capital of the collective imperialism of the triad, contribute in the effacement of the European project, maintaining it in its status of "European wing of the US project". The diplomacy of Washington has managed to keep Germany on its track; the reunification and the conquest of Eastern Europe even seemed to reinforce this alliance: Germany would be encouraged to reclaim its tradition of "thrust towards the East" (the part played by Berlin in the dismemberment of Yugoslavia by the hasty recognition of Slovenian and Croatian independence was its expression) and, as for the rest, induced to navigate in Washington's trail. Is there a reversing of steam in progress? The German political class appears hesitant and could be divided as far as its strategic choices are concerned. The alternative to the Atlanticist alignment—which seems to have wind in its sails—calls, in counterpoint, for a reinforcement of Paris-Berlin-Moscow axis, which would then become the most solid pillar of a European system independent of Washington.

3. The economic and political management of the new imperialist system under US leadership

The instruments for that management were created after World War II and eventually reformulated with a view to meeting new challenges.

The main instruments, with respect to the economic dimension of the management of the system, are the WTO, the World Bank and the IMF while the G7/8 and NATO undertake its political and military management.

The World Trade Organization (WTO) was established precisely to strengthen these "advantages" of transnational capital and establish their legitimacy for the ruling of the global economy. The so-called "rights of industrial and intellectual property" are conceived with a view to perpetuating the monopoly of transnationals, guaranteeing their super profits and creating additional enormous obstacles for further autonomous industrial development in the peripheries. Similarly the offensive of the WTO aiming at integrating agriculture in the global deregulated open market will simply destroy any attempt by countries of the South to ensure food security, and further throw into poverty hundreds of millions of peasants in the South.

The logic which commands these policies of systematic overprotection of northern monopolies denies the validity of the dominant discourse with respect to the advantages of the so-called "free trade, free access to markets". These policies contradict brutally that discourse, which is therefore nothing but simply "propaganda", i.e., a lie. That logic is clearly formulated in the strategy of the WTO aimed at developing an "international business law" which is given priority over any national legislation. The scandalous project of a "Multinational Agreement on Investment", prepared in secret by OECD countries, is part of that plan.

Other institutions of the global system also play some role in that framework, while only supportive of G7 overall strategies. That is the case, for instance, of the World Bank. This institution, often pompously presented as the major "think tank" formulating strategic choices for the global economy, is certainly not that important. The World Bank is hardly more than a kind of Ministry of Propaganda for the G7 in charge of producing slogans and discourses, while actual responsibility for making economic strategic decisions is reserved to the WTO, and for political decisions, to NATO. The International Monetary Fund (IMF) is more important, albeit not as much as is usually said. As long as the principle of flexible exchange rates governs the international monetary system and as long as IMF is not accountable for the relations between major currencies (dollar, mark-euro, yen), the Fund operates only as a kind of supreme currency authority for the South, governed by the North.

These institutions—and particularly the G7 and NATO—are there to replace the UN family, which is invited to submit, or it will be marginalized and perhaps even dismantled.

4. Collective imperialism of the Triad and hegemonies of the United States: Their articulation and their contradictions

Today's world is militarily unipolar. At the same time, some fissures seem to become apparent between the United States and some of the European countries with regard to the political management of a global system so far united on the principles of liberalism, in theory at least. Are these fissures only conjunctural and of limited range, or do they portend some lasting changes? Thus, it will be necessary to analyze in all their complexity the logics that command the deployment of the new phase of collective imperialism (North-South relationships in the current language) and the specific objectives of the US project. In this spirit I will approach succinctly and successively five series of questions.

• Concerning the nature of evolutions which have led to the constitution of the new collective imperialism

I suggest here that the formation of the new collective imperialism finds its origin in the transformation of the conditions of competition. Only a few decades ago, the large firms fought their competing battles essentially over national markets, whether that of the United States (the largest national market in the world) or even those of the European states (in spite of their modest size, which handicapped them in relation to the United States). The winners of the national "matches" could perform well on the world market. Today, the size of the market necessary for gaining an upper hand in the first cycle of matches approaches some 500-600 million "potential consumers". The battle must thus be launched straightaway on the global market and won on this ground. And those who perform across this market then assert themselves more within their respective national terrains. Thorough internationalization becomes the primary setting of the activity of the large firms. In other words, in the pair national/global, the terms of causality are reversed: earlier, the national power commanded the global presence and today, it is the reverse. Therefore the transnational firms, whatever their nationality, have common interests in the management of the world market. These interests are superimposed on the permanent and mercantile conflicts, which define all the forms of competition specific to capitalism, irrespective of what they are.

The solidarity of the dominant segments of the transnationalized capital of all the partners in the triad is real, and is expressed by their rallying to globalized neo-liberalism. The United States is seen from this perspective as the defender (military, if necessary) of these "common interests". Nonetheless, Washington does not intend "to equitably share" the profits of its leadership. The United States seeks, on the contrary, to reduce its allies to vassals and thus is only ready to make minor concessions to junior allies in the Triad. Will this conflict of interests within dominant capital lead to the break-up of the Atlantic alliance? Not impossible, but unlikely.

• *Concerning the place of the United States in the world economy*

General opinion has it that US military power only constitutes the tip of the iceberg, extending the country's superiority in all areas, notably economic, but even political and cultural. Therefore, submission to the hegemony that it asserts would be impossible to circumvent.

I maintain, in counterpoint, that in the system of collective imperialism, the United States does not have decisive economic advantages; the US production system is far from being "the most efficient in the world". On the contrary, almost none of its sectors would be certain of beating competitors in the truly free market dreamt of by liberal economists. The US trade deficit, which increases year by year, went from 100 billion dollars in 1989 to 500 billion in 2002. Moreover, this deficit involved practically all areas of the production system. Even the surplus once enjoyed by the US in the area of high technology goods, which stood at 35 billion in 1990, has now turned into a deficit. Competition between Ariane rockets and those of NASA, between Airbus and Boeing, testifies to the vulnerability of the American advantages. Faced by European and Japanese competition in high-technology products, by Chinese, Korean and other Asian and Latin American industrialized countries in competition for banal manufactured products, by Europe and the southern cone of Latin America in agriculture, the United States probably would not be able to win were it not for the recourse to "extra-economic" means, violating the principles of liberalism imposed on its competitors!

In fact, the US only benefits from comparative advantages in the armaments sector, precisely because this sector largely operates outside the rules of the market and benefits from state support. This advantage probably brings certain benefits for the civil sphere in its wake (the Internet being the best-known example), but it also causes serious distortions that handicap many production sectors.

The North American economy lives parasitically to the detriment of its partners in the world system. "The United States depends for 10 per cent of its industrial consumption on goods whose import costs are not covered by the exports of its own products", as Emmanuel Todd recalls. The world produces, and the United States (which has practically no national savings) consumes. The "advantage" of the US is that of a predator whose deficit is covered by loans from others, whether consenting or forced. The means put in place by Washington to compensate for deficiencies are of various kinds: repeated unilateral violations of liberal principles, arms exports, a search for greater profits from oil (which presupposes systematic control over the producers—one of the real reasons for the wars in Central Asia and Iraq). The fact is that the essential part of the American deficit is covered by contributions of capital from Europe, Japan and the South (from oil-rich countries and comprador classes of every country of the Third World, the poorest included), to which are added the additional sums brought in from servicing the debt that has been forced on almost all the countries on the periphery of the world system.

The growth of the Clinton years, vaunted as the result of a "liberalism" that Europe was unfortunately resisting, was in fact largely fake, and in any case, non-generalizable, depending on capital transfers that meant the stagnation of partner economies. For all sectors of the real production system, US growth was not better than that of Europe. The "American miracle" was fed exclusively by a growth in expenditure produced by growing social inequalities (financial and personal services: the legions of lawyers and private police forces, etc). In this sense, Clinton's liberalism indeed prepared the conditions for the reactionary wave, and later victory, of Bush Junior.

The causes of the weakening of the US production system are complex. They are certainly not conjunctural, and they cannot be corrected by the adoption of a correct rate of exchange, for example, or by putting in place a more favorable balance between salaries and productivity. They are structural. The mediocrity of general education and training systems, and a deep-rooted prejudice systematically in favor of the "private" to the detriment of the public service, is one of the main reasons for the profound crisis that the US society is going through.

One should, therefore, be surprised that the Europeans, far from drawing the conclusions that observation of the deficiencies of the US economy forces upon one, are actively going about imitating it. Here, too, the liberal virus does not explain everything, even if it fulfils some useful functions for the system in paralyzing the left. Widespread privatization and the dismantling of public services will only reduce the comparative advantages that "Old Europe" (as Bush qualifies it) still benefits from. However, whatever damage these things will cause in the long term, such measures offer dominant capital, which lives in the short term, the chance of making additional profits.

• *Concerning the specific objectives of the project of the United States*

The hegemonic strategy of the United States is within the framework of the new collective imperialism. The target is simply to establish the military control of the US forces over the planet. This would guarantee to Washington a privileged special access to all the natural resources of the Earth, and through it, would subordinate the allies and submit Russia, China and the Third World to the status of dependent states.

The "(conventional) economists" do not have the analytical tools to enable them to understand the paramount importance of these objectives. They are heard repeating ad nauseam that in the "new economy" the raw materials coming from the Third World are destined to lose their importance and thus it is becoming more and more marginal in the world system. In counterpoint to this naïve and hollow discourse, the *Mein Kampf* of the new administration of Washington ("The Project for a New American Century"), admits that the United States works hard for the right to seize all the natural resources of the planet to satisfy, in priority, its consumption requirements. The race for raw materials (oil in the first place, but as much for other resources too—water in particular) has already recovered all its virulence. All the more since these resources are likely to become scarce, not only by the exponential cancer of the wastage of Western consumption, but also by the development of the new industrialization of the peripheries.

Moreover, a respectable number of countries from the South are destined to become increasingly important industrial producers as much for their internal markets as in the world market. As importers of technologies, of capital, also as competitors in exports, they are destined to push down on the global economic equilibrium with an increasing weight. And it is not a question only of some East Asian countries (like Korea), but of immense China and, tomorrow, India and the large countries of Latin America. However, far from being a factor of stabilization, the acceleration of capitalist expansion in the South can only be the cause of violent conflicts, internal and international, because this expansion cannot absorb, under the conditions of the periphery, the enormous reserve force of labor which is concentrated there. In fact, the peripheries of the system remain the "zone of tempests". The centers of the capitalist system are thus required to exert their domination over the peripheries, to subject their peoples to the pitiless discipline that the satisfaction of its priorities requires.

Within this perspective, the American establishment has perfectly understood that, in the pursuit of its hegemony, it has three decisive advantages over its European and Japanese competitors: the control over the natural resources of the globe, the military monopoly, and the weight of the "Anglo-Saxon culture" by which the ideological domination of capitalism is expressed preferentially. A systematic bringing into play of these three advantages clarifies many aspects of US policy, in particular the systematic efforts that Washington exerts with regard to the military control of the oil-producing Middle East, its offensive strategy with regard to Korea—taking advantage of this country's "financial crisis"—and to China, its subtle game aiming at perpetuating divisions in Europe—while mobilizing to this end its unconditional British ally—and at preventing any serious rapprochement between the European Union and Russia. At the level of global control over the resources of the planet, the United States has a decisive advantage over Europe and Japan—not only because the United States is the sole international military power, and thus no strong intervention in the Third World can be led without it, but more because Europe (excluding ex-USSR) and Japan are, themselves, steadily divested of essential resources from their economy. For example, their dependence in the energy sector, in particular their oil dependence with regard to the Gulf, is an actuality, and will remain so for a considerably long period of time, even if it were to decrease in relative terms. By militarily seizing control of this region through the Iraq war, the US has demonstrated that it was perfectly conscious of the utility of this pressure medium, which it brings to bear on its allied competitors. Not long ago, the Soviet power had also understood this vulnerability of Europe and Japan; certain Soviet interventions in the Third World had aimed to remind them of it, so as to induce them to negotiate on other grounds. Evidently the deficiencies of Europe and Japan could be compensated for in the event of a serious Europe-Russia rapprochement ("the common home" of Gorbachev). It is for this reason that the danger of this construction of Eurasia becomes Washington's nightmare.

The military control of the planet is—in last resort—the means for the USA to pump tribute to its benefit through the use of political violence. This pumping should replace the "spontaneous" flow of capital which makes up for the US deficit—the main reason for the vulnerability of US hegemony. The target is therefore not to "open the markets on an equal basis for all" (that rhetoric is left to the neo-liberal propagandists). Neither is it, of course, to promote democracy!

• Concerning the conflicts that place the United States and its partners in the Triad opposed to each other within this framework

If the partners in the Triad share common interests in the global management of collective imperialism implied in their relationship with the South, they are certainly not less in a serious potential conflictual relationship.

The American superpower sustains itself due to the capital flow that feeds the parasitism of its economy and society. The vulnerability of the United States constitutes, therefore, a serious threat for the project of Washington.

Europe in particular, and the rest of the world in general, will have to choose one of the following two strategic options: to invest the "surplus" of their capital ("or savings") from which they arrange for financing the US deficit (consumption, investments and military expenditures); or conserve and invest this surplus at home.

The conventional economists are ignorant of the problem, having made the hypothesis (which is nothing but nonsense) that as "globalization" has abolished the nations, the economic figures (saving and investment) cannot be managed any more "at national levels." It is a matter of tautological reasoning where the conclusions at which one wishes to arrive are implied in the very premises: to justify and accept the financing of the US deficit by others since, at the world level, one finds indeed a savings-investment identity!

Why is such ineptitude thus accepted? No doubt, the teams of "scholarly economists" who encircle the European (and also Russian and Chinese) political classes of the right as well as of the electoral left are themselves victims of their economic alienation, which I term the "liberal virus". Besides, through this option, in fact, the political judgment of large transnational capital is expressed, which considers that the advantages obtained by US management of the globalized system on behalf of collective imperialism prevail over its disadvantages: the tribute which is needed to pay Washington for ensuring permanence. Because it was a tribute, after all, and not an "investment" with a good guaranteed return. There are some countries qualified as "poor indebted countries" which are always constrained to ensure the servicing of their debt at any price. But there is also a "powerful indebted country" which has the means to devalue its debt, if it considers it necessary.

The other option for Europe (and the rest of the world) would thus consist in putting an end to the transfusion in favor of the United States. The surplus could then be used on the original spot (in Europe) and the economy could be revived. Because the transfusion requires a submission of Europeans to "deflationary" policies (an improper term in the language of conventional economics) that I call "stagnationist"—so as to release a surplus of exportable savings, it makes a recovery in Europe—always mediocre—dependent on an artificial support from that of the United States. The mobilization of this surplus in the opposite direction for local employment in Europe would permit the simultaneous revival of consumption (by rebuilding the social dimension of economic management devastated by the liberal virus) and investment— particularly in new technologies (and financing their research), even military expenditure (putting an end to the "advantages" of the United States in this field). The option in favor of this challenging response implies a rebalancing of social relationships in favor of the laboring classes. National conflicts and social struggles are articulated in this way. In other words, the contrast between the United States and Europe does not fundamentally oppose the interests of dominant segments of the capital of various partners.

The neo-liberal option of Europe, reinforced by a so-called "apolitical" management of its currency (the Euro), does not help the continent to move out of stagnation. It is an absurd choice, perfectly convenient for Washington, which manages its currency (the dollar) differently, with political sense! Along with an eventual exclusive control of the US over oil, this management permits what I call the "oil-dollar standard" to be the only international currency of last resort, while the Euro remains a subordinate regional currency.

The political conflict which may develop between Europe (or some of the major European states) and the USA is not the product of major divergences between dominant capital. I locate this conflict elsewhere, in the domain of what could be called "national interests" and/or in the inheritance of different political cultures, which I discussed at length elsewhere.

• *Concerning the questions of theory that the preceding reflections suggest*

Complicity-competition between the partners in collective imperialism for control over the South—the plundering of its natural resources and submission of its people—can be analyzed from different angles of vision. I will make, in this respect, three observations, which appear major to me.

First observation: the contemporary world system that I describe as collective imperialist is not "less" imperialist than its precedents. It is not an "Empire" of "post-capitalist" nature. I have proposed elsewhere a criticism of ideological formulations of the "disguise" that feeds this fashionable dominant discourse.

I am referring here to the so-called "post modernist" theses which invite a renunciation of any attempt to act and "change the world", to the benefit of a day-to-day adjustment to those changes produced by the deployment of capitalism. Hardt and Negri aligned on that thesis—which is the permanent discourse of American liberalism ever since —in a perspective— naïve in the best of the hypotheses—that the world will change to the better by its own logics.

Second observation: I have proposed a reading of the history of capitalism, globalized right from its origin, centered on the distinction between the various phases of imperialism (of centers/peripheries relationships). There exist of course other readings of this same history, in particular that which is articulated around the "succession of hegemonies".

I have some reservations with regard to this last reading. Primarily and essentially because it is "western-centric" in the sense that it considers that the transformations operating at the heart of the system, in its centers, command the global evolution of the system in a decisive, and almost exclusive, manner. I believe that the reactions of the people of the peripheries to the imperialist deployment should not be underestimated, for they provoked the independence of Americas, the great revolutions made in the name of socialism (Russia, China), the re-conquest of independence by the Asian and African countries. I do not believe that one can account for the history of world capitalism without accounting for the "adjustments" that these transformations imposed even on central capitalism itself.

Further, because the history of imperialism appears to me to have been made more through the conflict of imperialisms than by the type of "order" that successive hegemonies have imposed, the apparent periods of "hegemony" have been always extremely short and the said hegemony very relative.

Third observation: internationalization is not synonymous with "unification" of the economic system by "the de-regulated opening up of the markets". The latter—in its successive historical forms (the "freedom of trade" yesterday, the "freedom of firms" today)—always constituted the project of the dominant capital, only. In reality this project was almost always forced to adjust to exigencies that are not the concern of its exclusive and specific internal logic. It thus could never be implemented except in some short moments of the history. The "free exchange" promoted by the major industrial power of its time—Great Britain—was effective only during two decades (1860-1880) which was succeeded by a century (1880-1980) characterized at once by the conflict between the imperialists and by the strong de-linking of the countries known as socialist (starting from the Russian revolution of 1917, then that of China) and, more modestly, the populist nationalist countries (the era of Bandung for Asia and Africa from 1955 to 1975). The current moment of reunification of the world market ("free enterprise") inaugurated by neo-liberalism since 1980, extended to the whole planet with the Soviet collapse, probably is not destined to experience a better fate. The chaos which it generates—a term by which I have described this system since 1990—testifies to its character of "permanent utopia of capital".

5. Derailing the USA, Israel, and their allied countries on the front line (Palestine, Lebanon, Afghanistan, Iraq, Syria, Iran).

The USA project, supported by its allied subordinates from Europe and by Israel, consists in establishing US military control all over the world. The "Middle East" has been chosen as the "first impact" target for four reasons: (I) there are the most plentiful oil resources in the world, and its direct control by the USA army would grant Washington a privileged situation and would make its allies—Europe and Japan—and its possible rivals (China) depend on it in terms of oil supplies; (II) it is located in the heart of the ancient world and would be suitable for a permanent military menace against China, India and Russia; (III) it is undergoing a stage of weakness and confusion which assures the aggressor at least an easy short-term success; (IV) in that region there is an unconditional US ally, Israel, which has nuclear weapons.

To the countries on the front line, the aggression brings about a situation of destruction (the first four countries) or threat (Syria and Iran).

The aggression against Lebanon

Israel's aggression against the people of Lebanon (July-August 2006) is part of Washington's plan for the whole region. The offer to liberate the two Israeli soldiers captured on the territory of Lebanon against Lebanese detained in Israel after their having been highjacked in Lebanon was therefore perfectly legitimate. The terrain for the aggression had been prepared by a UN resolution requesting the evacuation of the Syrian forces from Lebanon and the "disarmament" of Hizbollah, following the assassination of Rafik el Hariri, on which full light has not been thrown. The USA and Europe insist on the integral application of that resolution, while they have always neglected any demand for the implementation of resolution 242 which demanded the evacuation of occupied Palestine since 1967, as well as having forgotten the illegal annexation of Golan. The double standard is more than visible.

Washington aims at establishing its total military control over the whole region, disguising the real target with talks on exporting democracy there, associated with a neo-liberal order facilitating the plunder of its oil resources. Washington has also embraced zionist phantasms: the partition of the region into micro-states based on ethnicity and religious differences, with Israel exercising a kind of protectorate on them, in company with the US.

The implementation of the plan is well advanced: Palestine, Iraq, and Afghanistan have been destroyed and occupied; Syria and Iran are openly threatened after Lebanon. Nonetheless, the failure of the project is visible: the resistance of the peoples is growing, Lebanon has given a lesson in unity by supporting its freedom fighters, defeating, in that respect, the expectations of Tel Aviv, Washington and the Europeans. With rudimentary armaments, the Lebanese resistance has been able to create serious problems for the over- equipped Israeli army, fed by the US air bridge from Diego Garcia (here appears the real role of the US bases throughout the planet). The Lebanese resistance having now proved its capacity to defeat the Israeli aggressor, all the efforts of the United States and of Europe are now concentrated on disarming it, in order to facilitate a "brilliant victory" for the next aggression of Israel! It is therefore time now to repeat that the right of peoples to prepare themselves for any intervention by the imperialists and their agents by keeping themselves armed is an undeniable right.

Afghanistan

Afghanistan reached its peak in modern history during the so-called "communist" Republic. It was a modern enlightened despotic regime, which favored education for children of both sexes, against obscurantism, thus strengthening the decisive basis of the society. Its "agrarian reform" was essentially a set of measures aiming at the reduction of the tyrannical power of the tribal chiefs. The support—at least implicit—by the majority of the citizenship allowed a possible success of that already oncoming evolution. The propaganda conveyed both by the Western media and by political Islam presented that experience as a "communist atheist totalitarianism" rejected by the Afghan people. Indeed, like that of Ataturk in his time, the regime was far from "unpopular".

It is not surprising at all that its supporters, at least in its larger fractions (Khalq and Parcham) called themselves Communists. The paradigm of the achievements by the Soviet peoples of Central Asia (despite any criticism and the autocratic practices by that system), in contrast to the permanent British imperialist social disaster in the neighboring countries (India and Pakistan), had led the patriots here and in many other regions to acknowledge what a big obstacle imperialism was to any attempt at modernization. The invitation to intervene, sent by some fractions to the Soviets as an attempt to get rid of the others, has really had a negative impact and mortgaged the possibilities of the national-popular-modern project.

Specially, the USA, and generally speaking, its allies of the Triad, have been the stubborn adversaries of the Afghan parties of modernization, communist or not. They were the ones who mobilized the obscurantist forces of political Islam, the Pakistanis (Taliban) and the warlords (the chiefs of tribes, neutralized by the so-called "communist regime"), and gave them training and weapons. Even after the Soviet withdrawal, the resistance of the government of Najibullah to the assaults of the obscurantist forces would have probably not been defeated without the Pakistani military offensive which came to support the Taliban, stimulating chaos, and the reconstitution of the forces of the warlords.

Afghanistan has been devastated by the military intervention by the USA, its allies and agents, particularly the Islamic. A reconstruction will not be possible as directed by these actors, a power hardly concealed by a clown with no roots in the country, encouraged by a Texan transnational where he had been an employee. The salvation of the fake "democracy" claimed by Washington, NATO and the UN is nothing but an attempt to legitimize their "presence" (occupation, indeed). It had always been a white lie; it has become a mean farce.

There is only one solution to the Afghan problem: that the foreign forces leave the country and that all the powers are forced not to give financial support and weapons to their "allies". To those good souls showing their fear that the Afghans tolerate a Taliban dictatorship (or a *warlords* dictatorship), I would answer that the foreign presence was and still is the best support for such a dictatorship! Also, the Afghan people went in a different direction—maybe the best one—in those times when "the West" did not participate in their issues. The civilized West prefers obscurantist despotism over enlightened autocracy, as it is less dangerous for their own interests!

Iraq

The US armed diplomacy aimed at literally destroying Iraq long before finding an excuse to do so. First when Kuwait was invaded in 1990, and then after September 11, an event cynically and hypocritically manipulated by Bush junior following the Goebbels' principle ("repeating a lie enough times, causes it to become true"). The reason is simple and has nothing to do with the discourse that proclaims the "freedom" of the Iraqi people from the (real) bloody dictatorship of Saddam Hussein. A major part of the world's oil resources lie under the Iraqi soil. Besides, Iraq would succeed in training scientific and technical cadres capable, due to their critical mass, of supporting a consistent national project. This "danger" had to be eliminated by a "preventive war", something the USA has given itself the right to start whenever and wherever it finds it suitable, with no respect for the international "law".

Beyond this sample of common evidences, there remain a series of serious questions: (I) How could Washington's plan so easily mount the façade of a brilliant success? (II) What is the new situation created for the Iraqi nation? (III) How do the different components of the Iraqi people face this challenge? (IV) What solutions can the Iraqi, Arab and international democratic and progressive forces provide?

The defeat of Saddam Hussein could be foreseen. Facing an enemy whose principal advantage lies in its capacity to inflict genocide by means of unpunished air bombing (while attending nuclear use) there is only one effective answer the peoples can give: to deploy their resistance on their invaded soil, as the Lebanese people have proved. Now, Saddam´s regime devoted its efforts to eliminating the means of defense the Iraqi people could use, by systematically exterminating every organization or political party (beginning with the communists) that had taken part in the modern history of Iraq, including the Ba'ath itself, one of the main actors in this history. What must be surprising under these conditions is not that the "Iraqi people" had allowed the invasion without fighting, nor even that certain behaviors (such as the supposed participation in the elections called for by the invaders, or the upsurge of fratricidal struggles between Kurds, Sunnite Arabs, and Shiite Arabs) which seem to indicate the possibility of an acceptance of defeat (as was calculated by Washington), but rather that the resistance on the battlefield grows stronger every day (in spite of the serious weaknesses this resistance has), that this has made it impossible to install a servile regime capable of assuring a facade of "order", and that the failure of the Washington project has been demonstrated to such an extent. The fact that the tamed United Nations has recognized such a fake government does not change the truth; it is neither legitimate nor acceptable.

However, the military occupation has nonetheless created a new situation. The Iraqi nation is really threatened, whether it be by the Washington project, which is unable to assert its control over the country (and plunder its oil resources, which is its main priority) by means of a government with a "national" appearance as an intermediary, which can only be pursued by destroying the country. The division of the country into at least three "States" (Kurd, Sunni Arab and Shiite Arab) could, from the very beginning, have been an objective of Washington, together with Israel (in the future the archives may reveal that). At present, "civil war" is the card constantly played by Washington when trying to legitimize its ongoing occupation. Permanent occupation was—and still is—the objective: it is the only means for Washington to guarantee its control of the oil. Assuredly, one should not believe Washington's "declarations" of will, like "we will leave the country once order is restored". Let's remember the British said nothing from 1882 onwards but that their occupation of Egypt was "provisional" (it lasted until 1956!). Meanwhile, every day the USA destroys a bit more of Iraq by all means, including the most criminal: the country, its schools, its factories, its scientific capacities.

The response by the Iraqi people to this challenge does not seem—at least, up to now—suitable to the extreme severity of the circumstances. That is the least we could say. Why? The Western media repeat again and again that Iraq is an "artificial" country, and that the oppressive domination of the "Sunni" regime of Saddam over Shiites and Kurds is the origin of the inevitable war (that only the prolongation of the foreign occupation could put a stop to). The "resistance" in that case would be limited to some Islamist pro-Saddam cells of the Sunni "triangle". It is only with great difficulty that so many lies can be put together.

After World War I, it was difficult for the British colonization to face the Iraqi people's resistance. In full conformity with their imperialist tradition, the British created an imported monarchy and a class of landowners to help maintain their power, and gave Sunni Islam a privileged position. The Communist party and the Ba'ath were the main organized political forces which undermined the power of the "Sunni" monarchy, which was hated by everyone—Sunnites, Shiites and Kurds. The violent confrontation between both forces, the focus of attention between 1958 and 1963, ended up with the victory of the Ba'athists, which the Western powers celebrated with relief. The communist project potentially implied a democratic evolution, while the Ba'ath did not. The Ba'ath was a nationalist pan-Arab and unitary by principle, admiring the Prussian model for the construction of German unity, recruiting among the small modern laicising bourgeoisie, and hostile to the obscurantist trends of religion. It became, as it was possible to expect, a dictatorship that was only half anti-imperialist, in the sense that, according to the conditions and circumstances, a compromise could be accepted by the two partners (Ba'athist power in Iraq, and American imperialism in the region). This "deal" encouraged the megalomaniac hopes of the leader, who believed Washington would accept him as its main ally in the region.

Washington's support for Baghdad (with its provision of chemical weapons) during the criminal and absurd war against Iran between 1980 and 1989 seemed to make that believable. Saddam could not imagine that Washington was lying, that the modernization of Iraq was unacceptable to imperialism, and that the decision to destroy the country had already been taken. Once in the trap (Saddam had been allowed to annex Kuwait, indeed an Iraqi province that the British imperialists had detached in order to make it one of their oil producing colonies), Iraq suffered sanctions for ten years designed to bleed the country and pave the way for the glorious conquest of the wasteland by American troops.

One might accuse all the successive Ba'athist regimes, even that of the last stage of its decay under the "direction" of Saddam, for everything but for having stimulated the religious conflict between Sunnis and Shiites. Then, who is responsible for the bloody clashes that today have the two communities at each other's throat? For sure, one day we will know how the CIA (and undoubtedly the Mossad) organized many of these massacres. Yet it is true that the political desert created by Saddam's regime and his example in terms of opportunistic methods without principles "stimulated" the candidates in power to pursue the same pattern, often protected by the occupiers, sometimes maybe naïve enough to believe they could "use" the occupiers. The candidates in question, whether "religious" leaders (Shiites or Sunnis), paratribal headmen, or notoriously corrupt "businessmen" exported from the USA, never had real roots in the country. Even those religious leaders the believers respected had no political program acceptable to the Iraqi people. Were it not for the void left by Saddam, their names would have never been mentioned. Against this new "political world" built by the imperialism of liberal globalization, will other political forces, authentically popular and national, eventually democratic, have the means to reconstitute themselves?

There was a time when the Communist Party provided the focus for the best produced by Iraqi society. The Communist Party was based all over the country, was the most widespread among the intellectuals, particularly those of Shiite origin (in my opinion Shi'ism produces revolutionaries and religious leaders, and seldom bureaucrats or compradores!). The Communist Party was authentically popular and anti-imperialist, hardly inclined to demagogy, and potentially democratic. Is it now doomed to definitely disappear from history, after the Ba'ath dictatorships massacred thousands of its best militants, the USSR collapsed (something it was not prepared for), and some intellectuals thought it was acceptable to come back from exile in the vans of the American troops? That is not impossible, yet it is not "inevitable". It is far from being so.

The "Kurdish" problem is a real one, in Iraq, Iran, and in Turkey. But on this issue we should remember that the Western powers have always put into practice, with the same cynicism, the rule of double standards. In Iraq or Iran, the repression of the Kurds' claims has never reached the degree of violence (military or by the police) of that of Ankara. Neither Iran nor Iraq has denied the existence of the Kurds, as Ankara did. However, Turkey has been forgiven, and is a member of NATO—an organization of democratic nations, as the mass media remind us, in which that outstanding democrat, Salazar, got involved as a founding member, as did those no less unconditional supporters of democracy, the Greek colonels and the Turkish generals!

The Iraqi popular fronts constituted around the Communist Party and the Ba'ath in the best stage of their history; each time they exercised the responsibilities of power, they always found terms of agreement with the main Kurdish parties, which have always been their allies.

The "anti Shiite" and the "anti Kurdish" acts of Saddam's regime are a truth: Saddam's army bombed the region of Basra after their defeat in Kuwait in 1990; gas has been used against the Kurds. Yet these actions came in "response" to the maneuvers by Washington's armed diplomacy, which had mobilized the sorcerer apprentices who were pressed into seizing the day. They were no less criminal a diversion, and especially stupid, the likely success of what Washington called for being extremely limited. But is there anything else we could expect from a dictator such as Saddam?

At the same time, the powerful image of resistance to the foreign occupation in these conditions seems something "unexpected", almost a "miracle". This is not the case. The elementary reality is simply that the Iraqi people as a whole (Arab and Kurd, Sunni and Shiite) hate the occupiers and have been aware of their daily crimes (murders, bombing, massacres, tortures). We should then expect a United Front of National Resistance (call it as you please), self-defined as such, that publishes the names, lists of organizations and parties involved, and their common program. To date, this has not occurred, particularly because of all the preceding reasons related to the destruction of the social and political fabric brought about by the dictatorship of Saddam and that of the occupiers. But whatever the reasons, this weakness is a severe handicap, which favors divisive maneuvers, encourages the opportunists, and throws confusion into the objectives of liberation.

Who will overcome these weaknesses? Communists must be willing to make it happen. Militants—already present in the field—make their difference as opposed to those "leaders" (the only ones the mass media seem to know!) who do not really know what route to take and attempt to give an appearance of legitimacy to their "alignment" with the collaboration government, while pretending to complement the actions of the armed resistance!! However, many other political forces, according to circumstances, could take initiatives aimed at the creation of that front.

Still, despite its "weaknesses", the Iraqi resistance has already derailed (politically speaking, not militarily speaking yet) the Washington project. This is precisely what worries the Atlantists of the European Union, its faithful allies. Washington-subordinated associates fear the defeat of the USA because that would strengthen the capacity of the peoples of the South to have the globalized transnational capital of the imperialist triad (US, Europe and Japan) respect the interests of the nations and peoples of Asia, Africa and Latin America.

The Iraqi resistance has made proposals that could avoid a dead end and encourage the USA to leave the wasps' nest. It proposes: (I) the constitution of a transitional administrative authority supported by the Security Council; (II) the immediate cessation of actions by the resistance, and of interventions (military and police) by the occupation troops; (III) the departure from the country of military and civil foreign authorities within 6 months. The details of these proposals appeared in the prestigious Arab magazine *Al Mustaqbal Al Arabi*, published in Beirut, in January 2006.

The European mass media's total silence about this message demonstrates, from this perspective, the solidarity among the imperialists. The European democratic and progressive forces should oppose this strategy of the imperialist triad and support the proposals by the Iraqi resistance. Leaving the Iraqi people alone, as it faces its enemy, is not an acceptable choice: it entails the dangerous idea that there is nothing to expect from the West and its countries and, in turn, stimulates unacceptable—indeed, criminal—practices in certain resistance movements.

The stronger the support to the Iraqi people from democratic forces in Europe and the world, the sooner the occupation troops will leave the country; the stronger will be the possibilities of a better future for that martyred people. The longer the occupation remains, the darker will be the future after its inevitable demise.

Palestine

Since the famous declaration of Balfour during World War One, the Palestinian people have been victims of a colonial project involving the implantation of a foreign population, which allots to them a fate similar to that of the "Redskins", a matter as much ignored as recognized. This project has always been supported unconditionally by the imperialist powers dominating the region (first Great Britain, then the USA) because that country, foreign to the region and created in such a manner, could be nothing other than unconditionally allied, in turn, with the continuous interventions aiming at the submission of the Arab Middle East to the imperialist capitalist domination.

This is an understanding, for all the peoples of Africa and Asia, which is self-evident. As a result, for the peoples of these two continents, the assertion and the defense of the rights of the Palestinian people are spontaneously united. In contrast, in Europe the "Palestinian problem" brings about a division caused by the confusion encouraged by Zionist ideology, which usually finds favorable echoes there.

Today more than never before, in conjunction with the American "Greater Middle East" project, the Palestine people's rights have been abolished. For all that, the PLO had accepted the plans of Oslo and Madrid, and the roadmap designed by Washington. It was Israel who openly rejected to sign, who put into practice an expansion plan even more ambitious! The PLO was in turn weakened: it would be fair to say it naively believed in its adversaries' honesty. The support given to the Islamic adversary (Hamas) by the Israeli authorities—at least at first—the chain of corrupted practices performed by the Palestinian administration (obviated by the "financial donors"—the World Bank, Europe, many NGOs) would lead—it could be foretold (and it was possibly desired)—to the electoral success of Hamas, a complementary excuse immediately used to justify unconditional support for Israeli politics "whatever they were"!

The Zionist colonial project has always been a threat, both to Palestine and to the neighboring Arab countries, evidenced by its interest in annexing the Egyptian Sinai, and its effective annexation of the Syrian Golan Heights. In the "Greater Middle East" project, a special place is given to Israel, to the regional monopoly of its military nuclear equipment, and its role as "obligatory partner", using the fallacious pretext that Israel had "technological capacities" of which no Arab country was capable! (thus demonstrating the spontaneous racism of the imperialist ideologues).

Our intention here is not to suggest analyses concerning the complex interactions between the struggles against Zionist colonial expansion and the conflicts and political choices in Lebanon and Syria. The Ba'athist regimes in Syria resisted in their way the demands of the political powers and Israel. That this resistance had equally been useful to legitimize more questionable ambitions (the control of Lebanon) is undeniable. On the other hand, Syria carefully chose its "allies" among the "less dangerous" in Lebanon. It is known that the resistance to Israeli moves in South Lebanon (including the deviation of water) had been led by the Lebanese Communist Party. The Syrian, Lebanese and Iranian powers collaborated in order to destroy this "dangerous basis" and substitute that of Hezbollah. The murder of Rafik el Harriri—far from being clear—apparently gave the imperialist powers (United States in the forefront, France behind it) the chance for an intervention with two objectives: making Damascus accept a definite alignment to the group of servile Arab states (Egypt, Saudi Arabia)—or, at least, eradicate the remains of degenerated Ba'athist power—eliminate the remains of the capacity to resist the Israeli moves (demanding the "disarmament" of Hezbollah). Their rhetoric on "democracy" can be quoted in this context, if it is useful.

At present, defending the legitimate rights of the Palestinian people is a primary duty for all democrats, worldwide. Palestine is at the center of the greatest conflicts of our times. Accepting the Israeli plan of destroying the whole of Palestine and its people would be the same as denying these peoples their first right: the right to exist. Accusing those against the completion of such project of "anti-Semitism" is unacceptable.

Iran

It is not our objective to make the analyses that the "Islamic revolution" calls for. This is the way it defines itself and how it is usually seen by political Islam, or by "foreign observers", i.e. the announcement and starting point for an evolution that in the end should comprise the whole region, in fact, the whole "Muslim world", then rebaptized as "the *umma*" ("nation", which it has never been). Or was it a unique event, particularly because of its combination of interpretations of Shiite Islam and Iranian nationalism?

From the point of view we are interested in, I will only make a couple of comments. First, the political Islamic regime in Iran is not in its roots incompatible with the integration of the country into the world capitalist system as such (the principles on which it relies accord with a vision of a "liberal" management of economy). Second, Iran is a "strong nation"; in other words, its best components, if not all of them—popular classes and leaders—do not accept the integration of the country as a dominated nation within the world system. There is an obvious contradiction between these two dimensions of the Iranian reality, and the second explains those trends of the foreign policy of Teheran showing a will to reject foreign commands.

It is Iranian nationalism—strong and, in my opinion, historically positive—that explains the success of the "modernization" of the scientific, industrial, technological and military capacities begun by the successive regimes of the Shah and Khomenism. Iran is one of those rare states of the South (together with China, India, Korea, Brazil, and maybe some others, but not many more!) which enjoys the conditions to have a "national bourgeois" project. Whether the completion of that project is, in the long run, possible or not (and this is my opinion) is not the focus of this presentation. Today such project exists; it is there.

Because Iran constitutes a critical mass capable of attempting to impose itself as an independent partner, the USA decided to destroy the country by means of a new "preventive war". As we know, the "conflict" takes place in the area of the nuclear capacities Iran has been developing. Will not this country, the same as any other, have the right to become a military nuclear power? Do the imperialist powers, and their puppet Israel, have any right to aim at controlling a monopoly of the weapons of mass destruction? Can we believe the rhetoric according to which the "democratic" nations will not use such weapons whereas the "rogue states" could? When will we hear that such "democratic" nations are responsible for the bigger genocides of modern times, including that of the Jews, and that the USA already used atomic weapons, and rejects a general and absolute prohibition to use it? Unfortunately, the European are aligned to the Washington project for aggression against Iran.

As a conclusion

At present, three groups of forces are involved in the "political conflicts" operating in the area: those that claim a nationalist past (but are nothing but the corrupted and degenerated heirs of the bureaucracies of the nationalist-populist earlier stage), those who belong to the political Islam family, and those that tend to emerge related to "democratic" demands compatible with the liberal management of the economy. None of these forces is acceptable for a left thought aware of the interests of the nation and the popular classes. In fact, the interests of the comprador classes dominate in these three "families". Trying to "get involved" in their internal conflicts, searching for the alliances with this one here or that one there (preferring the established regimes so as to avoid the political Islamic alternative, or looking for an alliance with some Islamic movements so as to get rid of the regimes) is doomed. The left should keep on supporting the struggles in those areas where it finds its own place: in defending the economic and social interests of the popular classes, democracy, and the consolidation of a national sovereignty, as inseparable targets. All democrats of the world should support the chances of the progressive forces and, in the same spirit, condemn without limits any intervention by the USA, NATO, Israel, the tamed United Nations, and their allies in the region.

The "Greater Middle East" is nowadays essential in the conflict that pits the imperialist Center against all the peoples of the world. Encouraging the possibilities of all the avant-gardes worldwide is conditional on derailing the Washington project. Without this, the avant-gardes would be extremely vulnerable. That does not mean underestimating the importance of other struggles in other parts of the world—Europe, Latin America. It just means that these struggles should be inserted into a global perspective, contributing to derail Washington's interests in the region chosen as its criminal target number one.

Conclusion: The Empire of Chaos and Permanent War

The project of US domination—the extension of Monroe doctrine to the entire planet—is disproportionate. This project, which I have designated for this reason as the Empire of Chaos since the collapse of the Soviet Union in 1991, will be fatally confronted with the rise of growing resistance of those nations of the old world who are not ready to be subjected to it. The United States then will have to behave like a "Rogue State" par excellence, substituting international law with recourse to permanent war (starting with the Middle East, but aiming beyond that to Russia and Asia), slipping on the fascist slope (the "Patriot Act" has already given powers to the police force, equal to those of Gestapo, with regard to foreigners—"aliens").

ABRAHAM BEHAR

THE ELIMINATION OF NUCLEAR WEAPONS THROUGH INTERNATIONAL LAW, AMERICAN BLOCKAGE, AND THE FAILURE OF THE NPT

I must explain, before embarking on this article, why we doctors are obliged to intervene in the politico-legal field, which is completely outside our competence: the IPPNW shares in this consensus view: in the event of a use of atomic weapons, there is no curative treatment for our patients. In fact, we will go up in smoke with them. As a result, only prevention remains, and thus, as is the rule for public health, the obligation for practitioners to embark outside their field of competence to explain and to act before events lead to the usage of atomic weapons.

It is in this spirit that we broach the issue of American unilateralism, within the prism of its consequences for the survival of our planet or, otherwise put, under the aegis of the genocidal threat of nuclear weapons.

Even if these premises are of long standing, even if Democratic administrations have contributed in their manner to putting into place the global aggressive strategy of the United States, it's the Bush administration which bears theoretical and practical responsibility for the "national security strategy" adopted by Congress in September, 2002.

1. The first step: The U.S. National Missile Defense Program, 2001

This concerns putting into place an anti-missile shield capable at best of intercepting 30 percent of nuclear missiles which would be launched against the United States. In fact, it concerns a selective protection of military targets on domestic territory, to the detriment of civilian targets, which then become simply collateral damage. Ever since the adoption of this program by the Bush administration, all the experts have stressed the unreality of this project, its colossal cost, and its weak credibility. Its practical interest would be the increase in federal disbursements to the friends of Dick Cheney and Donald Rumsfeld, such as Martin-Marieta, Lockheed and Boeing. Surpassing the identical anti-Star Wars bluff of Ronald Reagan, we now understand that this concerns a drastic change in the fundamentals of U.S. strategy as it concerns defense, for the NMD presupposes:

1.   The rejection of all international treaties—because these prevent the realization of this strategy; the first victim has been the (anti-ballistic) ABM treaty, unilaterally revoked by Bush. We already know that all the other treaties will remain unratified or be revoked in turn.

2.   The total enthrallment of all "allies": this is necessary in order to put in place a global network of radar detection stations connected to the American anti-missile network, placed under the exclusive control of the Americans. This vassalization, preceding the coalition for the war in Iraq, concerns on the first level Great Britain, Greenland and then Denmark, and to a lesser extent, Australia and Taiwan. The other allies, who manifest some semblances of independence, must be neutralized one by one, beginning with Canada, reticent in the face of its new status as the first receptacle of collateral damage, since missiles coming from Russia and China via the North Pole would be destroyed in Canadian skies. From this period, one can sense the change in attitude towards Europe with its loyal countries, that is to say, those under the American diktat, and its reticent countries. This new distribution of the cards is coming into being state by state, and thus outside of NATO or the European Union. Notably, from the commencement, two countries refused this American logic at NATO on May 29, 2001, Germany as represented by J. Fischer, and France by H. Vedrine.

3.   The increasing contradictions between this strategy and the official defense strategy of the United States.

If the officially proclaimed target is "rogue states", how can it be pretended that Libya or Iraq is capable of sending hundreds of missiles against the United States?

If China and Russia have returned to being official enemies, how can this designation be rendered compatible with the efforts agreed to, to support Putin and his "democracy"?

It was becoming urgent, even before the events of September 11, 2001, to redefine the fundamentals of American defense in the context of the 21st century.

2. The Confirmation: "The National Posture Review", 9 January 2002

This is the present doctrine of the United States, seeking absolute invulnerability for its interests and for its soil. In this design, certain fundamental principles have had to be abandoned:

• Since the Cold War has ended, the MAD doctrine (mutually assured destruction) has, too. There is no longer a single technologically advanced enemy, a partner/adversary in the arms race, but multiple enemies, large or small states, rogue or other singled-out states, who are treated as of the same genre as non-state enemies, the terrorists. The immediate consequence is the end of dissuasion, the end of the balance of terror, and the end of nuclear arms as a central element of defense: "Nuclear arms must be sized to the lowest level possible considered compatible with the security of the United States".

• The former policy of deterrence is dead, giving way to the new "credible" deterrence, consisting of a triad unabashedly mixing nuclear and conventional arms:
1. Systems of offensive forces, nuclear and non-nuclear. We will see that this composition is at the origin of the concept of "pre-emptive war", that is to say, preventive war.
2. Active and passive systems of defense, including anti-missile defense with the shield described above.
3. An infrastructure of integrated defense, totally renewed and more reactive, integrating command, control and information capacities reinforced and adapted to new forms of threats.

· This new doctrine proposes to hold all military options open, and to finish with all taboos. As a result, it's necessary to modernize the nuclear arsenal by eliminating 6,000 warheads which presently are useless, and from them, making 1700 new ones, to be carried by three classic components, land, sea and air, capable of being integrated within the triad. It's also necessary to bring up to speed non-strategic nuclear arms usable on the ground for specific targets like "bunkers". It's necessary to resume nuclear testing, and to accelerate setting up the anti-missile shield. It's necessary to resume production of fissile material, breaking down old warheads and creating new factories for making, for example, titanium. And finally, it's necessary to preserve and develop the American stockpile of chemical and biological weapons.

· One might summarize this doctrine by four key words:
  o Deter. This is a message for all aggressors, real or imagined, to prove to them that America has all the means to counter them, and that its anti-missile system dooms all attempts to failure.
  o Dissuade. This message is for all future competitors, to convince them that an arms race with the United States is in vain.
  o Assure. This is addressed to the good allies who accept to place themselves under American military protection, and thus under the orders of the president of the United States.
  o Defeat. A warning to the enemies large and small, who will be destroyed, whatever they do.

3. Preventive War

This concept replaces that of proportionate response to all attacks coming from nuclear countries. Preventive war gives to the sole political power, that is to say, to the President of the United States alone, the decision to strike *first*, no matter what country, outside of all international control, and without consulting its allies.

It is understandable why the Americans systematically reject international treaties (ABM, an end to nuclear testing, treaties prohibiting the circulation of fissile materials, etc.) and why they have fundamentally modified the deal as it concerns nuclear weapons. In the last analysis, it matters little if this or that country endows itself with nuclear arms. What matters is the target being designated by the states. If this is local, as in the case of India, Israel or Pakistan, or even to the limit of Korea, the Bush administration ignores it. But if it concerns a threat, real or supposed, for the United States, then the triad turns towards this country. All the conditions were thus assembled prior to 2005 to torpedo the Nuclear Non-Proliferation Treat (NPT).

4. The Foreseeable Failure of the Nuclear Non-Proliferation Treaty

This treaty is based on a double movement: on the one hand to prevent non-members of the atomic club from acquiring nuclear arms. To realize this, the five member countries of the atomic club agreed to furnish technological aid for the construction of nuclear reactors. On the other hand, to engage in a plan for simultaneous and controlled disarmament of the five atomic powers, having as objective since 1995, "the total elimination of nuclear arms". To this dynamic should be added an effort to have the three non-signatory nuclear powers, India, Israel and Pakistan, sign, and thus invite them to disarm. If one follows the reasoning of Canadian Senator, Douglas Roche, president of the "middle power initiative", the mechanics of the failure, or in other words, the profound reasons for the arrest of this double process, is the following:

· For the five members of the club, and in the wake of the new American nuclear posture, the deactivation of nuclear warheads means a simple transfer for other arms, since a nuclear arsenal remains a major component of their defense strategy, which does not plead in favor of the elimination of atomic weapons. Further, the American concept of "usable nuclear weapons", such as the decision to perfect new arms, is in contradiction to a real disarmament. Finally, the fragilization of accords or treaties by the United States and their replacement with reversible and non-verifiable bilateral accords sounds the death knell to the logic of the NPT.

· For the non-nuclear powers signatory to the treaty, the demonstration of the pacific substance of "give-give" is a failure. The exchange of nuclear technology for energy against the refusal to undertake a military strategy is an absurdity. *All the countries* who have or want to have atomic arms have passed by the same route: acquisition of nuclear technology, camouflaged by pacific attestations, is the condition sine qua non for feeding a military program. Behind the pacifist rhetoric, these states construct their arsenal undisturbed. This reality explains the anti-NPT tactic developed by Iran and Egypt at the United Nations. This tactic is simple: since the United States has a strategy of defense including nuclear arms, offensive as well, no resolution concerning "horizontal proliferation" can be received; the NPT no longer has the function of control and sanction in this domain. This result has led the Brazilian, Sergio de Queiroz Duarte, president of the session, to speak of "the fiasco of the NPT". Since the control and surveillance of the UN based on international law has broken down, there remains only the American threat of "preventive war" against (certain) proliferating countries. We have entered into a period of major risk of conflicts unleashed by the United States, conflicts eventually nuclear.

5. A Concrete Example: The Case of Iran

The military nuclear program of Iran: the facts. This program has a very long history, which we might list by dates:

· In 1967, Iran bought a reactor of 5 MGW from the United States for

Teheran. The Shah of Iran then re-enforced the technology with the aid of the West and, starting in 1974, with the aid of India.

- In 1979, Ayatollah Khomeini suspended the nuclear program.

- In 1981, after the destruction of the Osirik (French) reactor in Iraq by Israel, Iran again took up its nuclear program, establishing a nuclear plant at Bushehr with the aid of China and Pakistan.

- In 2002, a heavy-water station is operationalized at Bushehr. At the same time, at Arak near the village of Qom, ultracentrifuges are implanted (to enrich uranium) as well as at Natanz, near Istaphan, with a plutonigene heavy-water reactor, a method to produce tritium, a light element necessary for the fusion compartment of a hydrogen bomb.

The Iranian government openly recognizes the solid foundation of the accusations of the Vienna agency of the United Nations and declares it is pursuing the enrichment of uranium 235 and of plutonium 239 of military grade as well as of tritium, to endow its missile launchers with a nuclear fuse.

What is the problem? Iran is a signatory to the NPT and intends to remain so, despite its program (which is a unique case, insofar as North Korea withdrew from the treaty). Its contention of energy needs is not very credible; the country is overflowing with gas and oil. The construction of a plant some thousands of kilometers from major cities like Teheran and Tabriz makes the international community even more skeptical. We have here a very good example of nuclear proliferation promoted by the failure of the NPT.

In this context, we are confronted with two strategies: On the one hand, that of Europe, which bases itself on law and the United Nations. But alas, this strategy has failed. Iran no longer believes in the European Union. On the other hand, that of the United States: according to Richard Heinberg, the real reason for the intervention of the United States has nothing to do with the nuclear question. The real reason concerns preventing this country from founding a regional petroleum exchange, intended to become operational in March 2006. This exchange would permit the purchase of Iranian oil by exchange, and in a currency other than petro-dollars. If this initiative succeeds, the United States is in great financial danger because, eventually, a collapse of the American dollar, taking into account the American foreign debt, is possible. The months ahead will enlighten us on this threat of preventive war, necessarily leading beyond conventional means. (An American invasion and occupation of Iran is hardly plausible.) This is the question of the day at the Pentagon.

6. Conclusion

American unilateralism doesn't only have political, juridical and social impact; it is also the source of a real threat to the inhabitants of the Earth, and thus a threat to their life. In our role as doctors, we are sworn to protect them.

In the face of this danger, the only response, the single lever at our disposal, is that of public opinion in general, and that in the United States, in particular. As an alumni member of the Russell Tribunal, I have seen American public opinion impose peace in Vietnam. Confronted with the disaster of the Iraq occupation, faced with the rescue disaster in New Orleans, this public opinion is capable of stopping the dark designs of the Bush administration.

Our medical prescription is simple: do everything to aid, encourage, and support the American people in their difficult march towards the light, towards the end of the nightmare put in place by their president.

ENDNOTES

1   NMD, *Medecine et guerre nucleaire,* 16, No. 2, 2001.
2   IPPNW communications plan draft, Vancouver, April 12, 2001.
3   George Lee Butler, "A wake-up call", *Fourth World Review* 108/109, 2001.
4   Brice Smith, l'arme nucleaire utilisable contre-attaque, IEER, No. 26, 2005.
5   Nuclear posture review report, <http://www.globalsecurity.org> 8 January 2002.
6   La nouvelle doctrine americaine, medecine et guerre nucleaire, 17, No2, 2002.
7   Douglas Roche, *Disarmament Times*, 28, No. 2, 2005.
8   J. Jayantha, R. Rydell, *Multilateral Diplomacy and the NPT.* UNIDIR, ISBN, 92-9045-170-X, 2005.
9   *Medecine et guerre nucleaire,* 17, No. 3, 2002.
10   *Medecine et guerre nucleaire,* 20, No. 1, 2005.
11   Richard Heinberg "Iran/USA the tyrannical war is it possible?" NEXUS, No. 39, July-August, 2005.

RUDOLPH EL-KAREH

THE AMERICAN POLITIC IN THE MIDDLE EAST

FORCE, IMPUNITY, LAWLESSNESS

"Whatever form justice may take,
it will have to satisfy President Bush."
The White House, December 8, 2001

"The very existence [of post-modern Europe] depends
on the renunciation of the politic of force."
Robert Kagan, Of Paradise and Power

"In the world of men, the arguments of law
only have weight to the extent that the present adversaries
dispose of equivalent means. If this is not the case,
the strongest take as much as their strength makes possible
while the weakest can only bow down..."
Thucydides, History of the Peloponnesian War

Since September 11, 2001, the United States has proclaimed itself the arbiter of good and evil on a planetary scale. For all that—and in appearance, paradoxically—despite the legalism which dominates, to an almost pathological extent, the mechanisms of its social and internal functioning, violation of the law has been a constant in its foreign policy. It has progressively imposed a unilateralist politics which has permitted it to use and abuse force, in contempt of the entirety of rules issued by the United Nations. It has tried, and tries incessantly, to transform the accumulation of its violations of international law and its practices outside the law, into new rules. The contortions permitting the exclusion of the prison at Guantanamo from American jurisdiction, the refusal to accord the protection of international conventions to prisoners, the casuistries permitting the dehumanization of detainees at Abu Ghraib in Iraq and justifying torture, are only recent examples.

But these examples are embedded in ongoing dynamics, and are certainly not twists of fate or flashes of lightning in a serene sky. How can one dissociate these American violations of international law from an earlier more global stage. The demonization of the United Nations, and then the co-optation of the organization, reduced to its administrative or technical apparatus, is one of these expressions. The permanent blackmail exercised at the Security Council over the past fifty years of its existence is another, as revealed in a recent study by two Harvard economists, Ilyana Kuziemko and Eric Werker, published in the *Journal of Political Economy,* titled "How Much is a Seat at the Security Council Worth: International Aid and Bribery at the UNO".

The willingness to destroy international treaties is another—from the Kyoto Protocol to multilateral accords on nuclear arms, the bypassing of the Conventions on chemical, biological and conventional weapons, not counting the willingness to empty the International Criminal Court of its substance. This effort at sapping international law found its culminating point in the invasion of Iraq, in contempt for all the international laws. It is clearly rooted in an historical and structural dynamic whose objective is to systematically denounce and discredit the European belief in a United Nations viewed as the sole source of legitimacy for the use of force among states.

It is notably in the Middle East, and surrounding the question of Palestine, that the United States has systematically instituted impunity in the face of violations of international law. The American ambassador at the United Nations in the middle of the 1970s, Daniel Patrick Moynihan, has thus congratulated himself in his memoirs, for having rendered "totally ineffective, on the instruction of the State Department, all measures taken by the United Nations". The violation of international law and the work of sapping the United Nations were not only infractions of its Charter, of which the United States was one of the principal authors, but also contravened Article 6 of the American Constitution considering this as an integral part of the "supreme law" of the country.

In the Middle East, one could schematically consider that the United States had led, during the Cold War and in a systematic manner since the June 1967 war, a deliberate politic of paralysis of the application of UN resolutions. The end of the system of blocs leads them today, inter alia, to the prevention of adoption of resolutions, to the utilization of the Security Council towards adopting texts decked out with the seal of international legality but transformed into tools of formal "legalization" of unilateral imperial policies. In the terms of American historian Paul Kennedy, "The United

States doesn't position itself on the international scene according to the criteria that it pronounces: democracy, the spirit of justice, tolerance, respect for human rights ... to speak truly, an empire has no allies, only vassals."

The neo-conservatives' conquest of power has thus found a bed made to their measure, and has erected as a principle that which, previouly, corresponded to actual practices, but practices which could not be avowed or claimed openly. One of their most influential theorists, Richard Perle, was able to publicly affirm, since then, that the destruction of the Iraqi nuclear reactor at Osirik "was a pertinent example of the legitimate use of force". Impunity in the face of an illegal and illegitimate use of force and the violation of the rules of international law leads to the theorization and legitimization of practices that are outside the law. It supports the notion of "preemptive war", a veritable judicial heresy, introducing a sort of preeminence to "the preemptive law of violence" as a judicial norm. This concerned the occurrence of a practice introduced as normal by the state of Israel, but considered a violation of international law. After the impunity resulting from the biases and paralyses of United Nations resolutions, this violation of the rule is being erected as a norm in the framework of the "new global struggle against terrorism" launched by the Empire. The United States no longer finds itself associated with the state of Israel simply by common interests, but now by a common conception, and closely linked regarding the use of force in international relations.

The distortion between the principles of international law and its application is supported equally by two weights and two measures, as another norm of international relations, elaborated by the British ideologue, Robert Cooper, longtime counselor of British Prime Minister Tony Blair, then a European functionary. It's backed up by his conception of the necessity of a new imperialism (cf. *La fracture des nations* [The breakup of nations]). Elaborated in the context of the invasion of Iraq, this theory serves to consolidate the ideologues of the American adventure, and it is not surprising that strong intellectual convergences would become manifest between Robert Cooper and Robert Kagan.

The UN ambiguities have themselves prepared the terrain for the present great drift, and the trivialization of impunity in the face of violations of the law. As was stated in 1991 in a premonitory manner by the jurist, Gerard de la Pradelle in the *Revue d'Etudes Palestiniennes* (N41, Fall 1991), "the Security Council remains mute in the face of many violations of international humanitarian law [and] has not seriously tried to impose the application of those principles which it has ceaselessly called to mind ...(...) It is to be feared that, over time, principles regularly affirmed and still totally unapplied will lose all sense of value. Furthermore, the institution which indefinitely tolerates such a number of illegalities, as serious as they are flagrant, risks finding itself completely discredited. Finally, especially if its powerlessness is selective, the entire system composed of the law and the institutions charged with imposing respect for it will appear as the toy of certain states, instead of subservient to the United Nations Charter, whose purpose is to serve the peoples of the United Nations."

The discrediting of the United Nations has not slackened in its pace, and is reaching abysmal levels. Blackmail, including against personnel close to its secretary-generals, has become the norm. The departing Secretary-General, Kofi Annan, had to face this bitter experience when he was summoned in November 2002 by six highly-placed American functionaries to the New York apartment of American diplomat Richard Holbrooke, the architect of the destructive war in Yugoslavia, as was reported at the time by *The New York Times* and the *Herald Tribune*. The steps it was proposed that he take were clear: he should bend to the injunctions of Washington, or the plot rigged against his son would proceed to its conclusion. Several weeks later at a conference held in Madrid, the United Nations endorsed the conceptions and definitions of terrorism put forward by the group in power in Washington. A deliberate confusion between the right to resistance and terrorism was agreed to. The day after September 11, 2001, the Israeli Foreign Minister, Eliahu Ben Eliezer, brutally declared, "What has changed is that today, we have killed fourteen Palestinians, and the world has not budged."

Violations of the rules, practices outside the law transformed into norms, blackmail in diverse forms, impunity and transgression have progressively become the norm. Investigation of the war crimes committed in Jenin was prevented due to direct American intervention. The publication of a report on the first massacre in Qana in Lebanon in 1996 (105 civilians killed in a UNIFIL camp in the South of Lebanon) cost the Secretary-General of the time his re-election. Boutros Boutros-Ghali received direct orders from Washington to bury the report of the international commission of inquiry establishing Israeli responsibility for war crimes, but overrode them, driving Madeleine Albright, then US Secretary of State, into a furor. Ten years later, the massacre of 54 civilians in the same locality and eighteen members of the same family at Beit Hanoun in Gaza met with the same impunity.

The United Nations mission led by Nobel prize-winner, South African Archbishop Desmond Tutu, was turned back by Israel. Washington had beforehand used its right of veto at the Security Council to prevent the adoption of a resolution condemning the massacre, and calling on the Quartet to relaunch the roadmap, because, to cite Condoleeza Rice, "the resolution was not conceived to contribute to the cause of peace." This was the forty-fourth veto used by the US aimed at protecting Israel.

In the meantime, Security Council resolutions implicating the state of Israel have remained dead letters. From 1948 to 1967, resolutions 106,

111, 127, 162, 171 and 228 have been without result. Subsequent to the war of June, 1967, the following resolutions concerning Palestine have been without effect: 237, 242, 248, 250, 251, 252, 256, 259, 265, 267, 271, 298, 446, 452, 465, 468, 469, 471, 476, 478, 484, 487, 497, 573, 592, 605, 607, 608, 611, 636, 641, 672, 673, 681, 694, 726, 799, 1052, 1322, 1402, 1405, and 1435.

Resolutions concerning Lebanon have met the same fate. These are: 262, 270, 279, 280, 285, 313, 316, 317, 332, 337, 347, 427, 444, 450, 467, 498, 501, 509, 515, 517, 518, 520, 587. In all of these texts, the terms aggression, violation, attack, premeditation, are repeatedly used.

Impunity and breaking the law under American cover has equally taken on a flagrant character in the progressive destruction of the entire institutional, political and juridical plan resulting from the Conference of Madrid and the Oslo Accords. While this undoubtedly concerned the degeneration of a political process, it remains the case that it couldn't have taken place without American protection and good will, including American transgression of rules which it, itself, had forged. The Israeli assault and the kidnapping of Ahmed Saadat, secretary general of the PFLP, at the beginning of 2006 constitutes a case in point. He had been incarcerated in Jericho according to an accord drawn up and guaranteed by the United States, the Quartet, the UN and Great Britain. Furthermore, the prisoner was under the direct guard of the US and Britain. The military personnel of these two countries received the order to withdraw only minutes before the Israeli assault. The American and British authorities, as well as the international component, thus violated their own regulatory framework.

But the ultimate occurred—last but not least—in the summer of 2006 in Lebanon. The war of 33 days in the summer of 2006 gave rise to new flagrant violations of international law, reinforced by an as yet unequalled impunity, adding to a situation that was already deeply scandalous. Let's examine the facts.

The State of Israel and its army, in a war of aggression launched against Lebanon on July 12, 2006, committed war crimes and crimes against humanity as characterized by articles 7 and 8 of the Statute of Rome of the International Criminal Court. Lebanon was made the target of a generalized assault "committed as part of a widespread or systematic attack directed against any civilian population, with knowledge of the attack" (Article 7.1 of the Statute). As for war crimes, they were "committed as part of a plan or policy" (article 8.1) as was publicly revealed July 15th by Alex Frishman, the military commentator of the Israeli daily, *Yedioth Ahronoth*, as well as by Seymour Hersh in *The New Yorker* of August 14, 2006.

Among the most flagrant acts, according to UNIFIL reports, was the dispersal of more than 1.4 million cluster bombs—prohibited by international conventions in civilian zones—on inhabited zones in the south of Lebanon, which threatens, according to the UN, the lives of thousands of Lebanese civilians. The deputy secretary-general of the United Nations, Jan Egland, stated, "What is shocking and totally immoral is the fact that 90 percent of these bombs were dropped during the last three days of the conflict, when we knew that a resolution [of the Security Council] was going to be adopted, when we knew that there was going to be an end... Each day, people were crippled, wounded or killed by these arms". The Belgian Minister of Defense, Andre Flahaut, announced that Belgian soldiers were equipped with radiation detection equipment, which re-enforced the accusations of the Lebanese government concerning the use by the Israelis of depleted uranium bombs, while the head of mission of Handicap International confirmed that "the entire south is covered with these submunitions [which are] like a minefield, only much more pernicious, scattered throughout the trees, gardens, fields, homes, on the roofs, everywhere".

Amnesty International considered "Israel's assertion that the attacks on the infrastructure were lawful is manifestly wrong. "Many of the violations identified in our report are war crimes, including indiscriminate and disproportionate attacks. The evidence strongly suggests that the extensive destruction of power and water plants, as well as the transport infrastructure vital for food and other humanitarian relief, was deliberate and an integral part of a military strategy" according to Kate Gilmore, Amnesty's Executive Deputy Secretary-General. The use of prohibited arms also violates article 8.2xx of the Statute of Rome, which qualifies as war crimes, "employing weapons, projectiles and material and methods of warfare which are of a nature to cause superfluous injury or unnecessary suffering or which are inherently indiscriminate in violation of the international law of armed conflict". The illegal blockade launched against Lebanon, the destruction of its transportation infrastructure, the deliberate destruction of trucks carrying foodstuffs and medications has also violated clause xxv of article 8.2, which considers as a war crime "intentionally using starvation of civilians as a method of warfare by depriving them of objects indispensable to their survival (...)".

Each day and each night carried its portion of violations of international humanitarian law, and to cite only these few examples:

> • "Willfully causing great suffering or serious injury to body or health" article 8.2.a.vi (the massacre of civilians, of which the most symbolic was that at Qana, not counting those on Chyah, Marouahine, and Aitaroun, to name a few);

> • the "extensive destruction and appropriation of property, not justified by military necessity and carried out unlawfully and wantonly" article 8.2.a.iv (the case, by no means

exclusive, of the southern suburb of Beirut and numerous villages of the south);

• "Intentionally directing attacks against personnel, installations, material, units or vehicles involved in a humanitarian assistance or peacekeeping mission in accordance with the Charter of the United Nations", article 8.1.b.iii (the case of the four officers of the UN Observers' Mission killed during the deliberate bombardment of their observation post in Khiam on July 26th, the helicopter operation against a hospital in Baalbeck, the destruction of a convoy of ambulances dispatched by the United Arab Emirates, etc.;

• the act of "using... the military insignia and uniform of the enemy" article 8.2vii (case of the aborted helicopter operation in the district of Baalbeck-Hermel where Israeli commandos dressed in the uniforms of the Lebanese army, moved around in vehicles bearing its colors which had been unloaded from helicopters...);

• the act of "[i]ntentionally directing attacks against buildings devoted to religion..." article 8.2.ix (case of the destruction of several mosques and the historic monastery of Deir Mimas...).

To escape criminal responsibility, the State of Israel resorted to a massive use of military censorship, and in particular took up the old argument which it had used in its invasion of Lebanon in 1982, the pretext that it was not attacking Lebanon, but rather the PLO, which permitted it to claim the inapplicability of the Geneva Conventions because the PLO could not, according to it, be considered as a "contracting party" of the Geneva Conventions because "it wasn't a state", nor as a "party to the conflict". That argument was demolished and Israel was forced to apply the law of Geneva. Already, at this time, the PLO was being presented as a "terrorist organization" and Israel was speaking of the "presence" of its armed forces as "a factor in the restoration of Lebanese sovereignty and freedom". This argument was taken up again in 2006, made more weighty by the pretense of contending it was serving as "a tool for the application of Security Council resolution 1559".

In other words, the State that had been the object of heavy condemnation of the Security Council, that had been openly pilloried by the International Court of Justice (The Hague) for the construction of its so-called "separation" wall, presented itself under the American umbrella deployed in the Middle East since the American invasion and occupation of Iraq, as "the tool" (cf. Ehud Olmert) of international law (Security Council resolution 1559). Morally and politically speaking, it was scandalous.

Furthermore, trying once again to escape its criminal responsibility, Israel added that it was not attacking "Lebanon", but rather "Hezbollah". That will do nothing to prevent its pursuit for war crimes. If its posture of 1982 was juridically inept, it is *a fortiori* so in the present instance. For that, it suffices to recall that Hezbollah is a Lebanese party profoundly associated with the institutional life, parliamentary and governmental, of Lebanon, and that, in the ministerial declaration of investiture by the Sinoria government, it is clearly stipulated that "the government considers that the Lebanese resistance is the true and natural expression of the national right of the Lebanese people to liberate its land and to defend and protect its liberty in the face of Israeli aggressions, threats, covetousness, as well as the expression of its inalienable right to strive to bring to completion the liberation of its territory". The entire state apparatus (ministries, army, police, civil defense, etc.) and the very numerous forces of civil society participated in a multifaceted resistance to this aggression. The Lebanese political and institutional problems change nothing in this regard.

Under the pressure of the American authorities, and notably that of Secretary of State Condoleeza Rice, and of John Bolton, then American ambassador at the UN, the Security Council committed two major violations of UN and Charter rules, of which it, along with the General Assembly, is the guardian and servant. For the first time in the history of the institution, it strove to delay the adoption of a resolution calling for a ceasefire in order to permit the aggressor (the State of Israel) "to finish the job", to use the odious terms of George W. Bush. And when the Israeli failure became flagrant, the Security Council gave birth to a veritable logical, political and military heresy, since, for the first time in the history of modern conflicts, it demanded a "cessation of hostilities" to emerge from a "ceasefire", and not the reverse.

What Resolution 1711 is, is a suit sized to measure to ensure the impunity of the aggressor. This is perfectly inscribed in the ideological matrix and imperial politic of the two weights and two measures. The creation of tribunals appears to echo it. Instead and in place of the International Criminal Court, a tool for the application of a common law bitterly contested by the United States, the latter seeks to put in place selective jurisdictions according to the circumstances, starting with the "tribunal" put in place by the first proconsul of occupied Iraq, Paul Bremer III, to judge the vanquished. Bremer has taken care to exclude from the field of justiciable action the aggressions undertaken by the Iraqi regime against... non-Arab states, such as Iran. This would permit it to conceal American responsibility in the war of aggression unleashed against this country in 1980. The precipitous elimination of a dictator under these conditions provides the opportunity to get rid of an embarrassing witness.

The evident bears repeating here, that the real restoration of law and the end of selective impunity can only come to pass through a return to international common law. This is not at all a "menu a la carte". It concerns an indivisible whole. It is on this sole condition that international relations, notably in the Middle East, will find the routes to peace and to justice.

MONIQUE CHEMILLIER-GENDREAU

IMPUNITY AND MASSIVE BREACHES OF HUMANITARIAN LAW IN VIETNAM

Spreading of chemical products was knowingly carried out by the US army during the Vietnam War (1951-1971) and led to a humanitarian and ecological disaster that is still not well-known and remains unpunished to this day. There have been hundreds of thousands of victims of these methods of war. I will first present the basic data for this instance, which strikingly illustrates the insufficiencies of what is called humanitarian law and, beyond that, the crisis of international law.

I. The Case of Agent Orange in Vietnam

Toxic chemical products were spread by US military forces on the territory of Vietnam (center and south regions) between 1961 and 1971, according to recent figures which have been upwardly revised.[1] These products, called defoliants at that time, contained various percentages of dioxin (those with the highest concentration of dioxin are known under the name of Agent Orange). They were mainly spread by aircraft (19,905 flights between 1961 and 1971) and reached 2,500,000 hectares—around 8.5 percent of the Vietnamese territory.

The official aim was, on the one hand, a lasting destruction of the vegetal covering of those regions so that the Vietnamese forces and population could no longer be shielded by the vegetation, and on the other hand, to weaken the Vietnamese army and population through the destruction of crops. The US political and military authorities which took responsibility for these actions did so without any consideration of either their murderous consequences or grave health effects, or of the future of the populations to be contaminated by these products (whether Vietnamese or American). They endorsed these consequences intentionally. That this dispersion took place within the framework of a total war which targeted the entire population appeared to be advantageous.

In the United States, people soon denounced the use of arms which seemed incompatible with the humanitarian rules of armed conflicts. They spoke out through the media and also through the protests of scientists by 1967. But US political and military authorities pursued their actions up to 1971. The question of war reparations was touched on in a somewhat ambiguous way (Article 21) in the course of the negotiations that ended the war through the Paris Agreement of January 27, 1973, without clearly fixing the obligation for reparations on those responsible for the conduct of the war.

Today, the Vietnamese population, which has been lastingly exposed to these noxious products, is victim to grave pathologies whose linkage to this dispersal is beyond doubt. Three generations are now concerned by malformations, as experts try to scientifically establish the role of the high level of toxicity of these products in their development. In the face of such sufferings and damage, one cannot avoid considering the legal routes that might allow prosecution of the crimes committed and reparation for the victims.

This path is full of pitfalls for the reasons we will now examine. In actuality, the Vietnamese government was not in a position either to demand or obtain war reparations. Avenues for inter-governmental legal recourse through an international procedure were closed to it. The issue has recently been revived due, on the one hand, to the pressure of victims and of Vietnamese politicians, physicians, and foreign NGOs, who could attest to the extent of consequences, and on the other to the actions of US veterans who also suffered from the same illnesses or malformations of their descendants. The latter were well organized, and succeeded in 1991 in getting an agency created to address compensation for victims, then in 1996, an Executive Order of President Clinton authorizing the indemnification of veterans after the US Academy of Medicine established a list of illnesses and handicaps linked with exposure to Agent Orange. If the causal link were not strictly established, the veterans affected by pathologies that might be linked to Agent Orange were to enjoy the benefit of the doubt. They thus obtained more thorough medical exams and an acknowledgement in principle of the necessity of indemnification by the US administration. On the other hand, a lawsuit against the US government itself had been avoided, and claims were directed to the companies that had produced the herbicides. The companies first accepted to contribute to a special fund for indemnification. But it turned out to be insufficient as new victims were registered, particularly among the descendants of the veterans, and it closed in 1997. Apparently, lawsuits have now been initiated against the companies.

Encouraged by this precedent, the Vietnamese victims took note that no possibility was being offered to their government to start an action in their name before an international civil or criminal jurisdiction. They then decided to initiate a lawsuit before the United States District Court, Eastern District of New York on January 30, 2004, on the basis of a judicial class action: this means that what is obtained for one victim can be equally obtained for any person in the same category. The matter followed its course according to the procedures then in place in an American court, and a first instance judgment was issued on March 10, 2005. It dismissed the Plaintiffs' case on the grounds that there was no basis for such a complaint either in American or international law and the plaintiffs had failed to sufficiently demonstrate a causal link between the chemical products used by the US army and their pathologies. The judge considered that the mechanism that led to indemnities for the veterans was based on exceptional procedures and could not be extended to foreigners. Nevertheless, the long and well-considered judgment included a number of elements which encouraged the counsels of the victims to appeal, in the hope, at this stage, to get a positive decision, particularly if they could rely on improved scientific arguments on the causal link. In fact, new studies had brought encouraging results in that direction.[2] The Court's decision will be delivered in the course of 2008.

It is of course very frustrating to see that the condition of persons that have been so cruelly affected by intentional and voluntarily aggressive actions of representatives of a foreign country should depend on a judge of the very country that is responsible for these actions. And one cannot avoid questioning why it is so difficult to prosecute such a massive and evident violation of humanitarian law to obtain reparations, even as one notes the obvious insufficiencies of international law.

2. The self-proclaiming and ineffective character of International Humanitarian Law

Humanitarian law, long considered to be applicable only in armed conflicts, is today understood in a broader manner, and concerns the set of judicial rules for the protection of human beings in times of crisis. This distinction is not useful in our example. The spreading of dioxin in Vietnam took place in the course of what is characterized as an armed conflict. Those very rules of humanitarian law applicable in the case of war should have been and must still be applied here. Hence the questions are simple: were these actions authorized by the rules applicable in armed conflicts? If not, what mechanisms can be used to condemn them and allow reparations for the victims? Is it possible to act at the criminal level (condemnation of an action considered as criminal) and at the civil level (obligation to indemnify the victims)?

The corpus of humanitarian law includes a number of Conventions, some general on the duties and obligations of the various parties in times of war, others specific to particular weapons. On the basis of these texts, the use of a certain procedure of war or weapon can be categorized. Humanitarian law also includes means of sentencing for its violations. While these were weak in the 1949 Geneva Conventions and their additional 1977 Protocols, the means of criminal repression have been reinforced since the '90s with the creation of international criminal tribunals and of the International Criminal Court. However, the conditions of accession to these jurisdictions are such that there is a priori no possibility for Vietnam along these lines.

2.1 Is the spreading of chemical products permissible or is it a prohibited action, possibly a crime and of what nature? This is the central question that we have to clarify according to humanitarian law.

First, such a spreading is prohibited on the basis of general texts that prohibit methods of war that might blindly strike at civilians without any discrimination. In this connection, the first important document is the The Hague Convention of July 20, 1899, followed by that of October 18, 1907. The United States has been party to those Conventions from the outset.[3] At a time when war itself was not prohibited by international law, they state that the various belligerent parties do not have an unlimited right of methods of injuring the enemy and prohibit the use of arms, projectiles, or material of a nature to cause superfluous injury. With the Geneva Conventions of 1949, the protection of populations is at the very heart of the concern, and indiscriminate attacks against civilian populations are prohibited (Article 51.1.4 of the Additional Protocol I adopted on June 8, 1977).

More specifically, the Geneva Protocol of June 17, 1925, prohibits the use of asphyxiating, poisonous or similar products. The United States had signed it on the very first day but ratified it only in 1975. Moreover, during the first years of the Vietnam War, it supported the idea that herbicides were not included in the Protocol. The General Assembly of the United Nations clarified that point in its resolution 2603A of December 16, 1969, declaring that all chemical products that might have toxic consequences on human beings, animals or plants were included in that prohibition. After the Vietnam War, and not without link with it, a Convention prohibiting the military or any hostile use of environmental modification techniques was adopted on December 10, 1976 and entered into force in 1978. Its adoption resulted from an initiative by US senators who were worried about the use of chemical arms as had been practiced in Vietnam. The United States signed and then ratified the Convention—but this was due to the fact that the terms of the Convention represented a compromise made with the Soviet Union and were sufficiently vague to imply no judicial consequences for States.

Let us finally note that war crimes represent a much more precise category in the Statutes of the two international criminal tribunals (for ex-Yugoslavia and Rwanda) and of the Rome Statute of the International Criminal Court. At last, a very important convention was adopted on the prohibition of chemical weapons and was even completed with effective mechanisms of control. But herbicides are not included in the prohibition: this is a retreat with respect to the 1969 resolution of the UNO General Assembly.

We now have to explain the humanitarian situation in Vietnam with respect to this corpus of law. The spreading of Agent Orange did not aim at any specific military objective. It was the peasants and their lands that were blindly attacked. This is well within the framework of a flagrant and massive breach of the rules of war. Even though most of the texts mentioned above have entered into force only after the acts that caused the deaths or damages, even though the State concerned (the United States) has ratified them only after these acts, these rules of international law should be applied here for two reasons. The first one is that general prohibitions can be considered as embodying rules of customary international law. As such they are also binding on States which are not formally (or not yet) parties to them. The second reason permitting legal texts which were enacted subsequent to the dispersal to be retroactively applied is that, while the events occurred at a specific time in the past, they have led to consequences lasting until the present day, so that one is concerned here with ongoing acts which belong as a whole to a category little by little being defined by law. From the viewpoint of temporal judicial argumentation, the acts cannot be conditioned only by the rules in force at the moment the original acts were committed, but by the full law developed during the period wherein they produced their effects. The US judge did not accept this argumentation. Instead, he considered that, at the time acts were committed, there was no prohibition of the use of herbicides according to international law then in force. He also accepted the doubt of defenders concerning the possibility, even today, of considering herbicides as among prohibited chemical weapons. This is what the victims will contest in their appeal.

The developments above concern the category of war crimes. But one must also raise the question of the possible application to this situation of the categories of crimes against humanity or crimes of genocide. This cannot be done lightly. Nevertheless, it can be said that the large scale targeting of the Vietnamese population, the actual intent to strike at its vital conditions, permit one to raise that question. All these categories of international crimes cannot be prescribed. Lawsuits aiming to address such crimes thus cannot be extinguished by time. This enduring character follows from precise conventions,[4] but also from a customary recognition confirmed in the statutes of international criminal tribunals and of the International

Criminal Court.

2.2 However, it's one thing to label certain behaviors in time of war—and it is easy to assert that the use of herbicides containing dioxin is prohibited by the rules of the laws of war—and another thing to ask oneself what procedures are opened by these laws to put an end to these crimes and punish those who breach them. An effective right is one that facilitates one's claims for justice.

All procedures presuppose that parties having an interest in pursuing justice be determined and also those that have to be prosecuted.

The notion of victims must therefore be clarified. On the one hand, there are all those who have been contaminated because they were present in the zones where the chemical dispersal took place. These zones are known and military archives allow one today to know exactly what the plans of the Pentagon were in that respect and the routes followed by the aircrafts during their operations. If one was to include all those who lived in contaminated zones, almost all the population of South Vietnam would be concerned (this would not be void of justification: there has been an important risk for all and effects might still appear today after a long time). Fortunately, the entire population that was in contact with these products did not (and will not automatically) suffer from the pathologies they might generate. Therefore one has to combine the criterium of presence on the ground with the occurrence of one of the illnesses that can be attributed to effects of Agent Orange. This is the viewpoint proposed by the Vietnamese government, in particular through the studies published by the Vietnamese Red Cross.[5] It is possible to make things even more precise by using an index of exposure to chemical weapons: direct exposure for persons present in the zones where the spreading took place at the time it occurred, indirect exposure for persons that arrived later on in these zones. However, it is not yet possible to know with precision the number of persons affected with congenital malformations or grave illnesses in relation to the introduction of these products into the environment. Estimates of the number of victims vary greatly, from several tens of thousands to four million.

If people are victimized at the individual level through the consequences on their lives and their health, the Vietnamese State, as a collective entity, is also a victim. The war was directed against it. By choosing these particular very dangerous weapons, the enemy targeted the entire national community and its territory. And the Vietnamese State is the one that is confronted today with the sufferings of a part of its population which it must relieve and with the state of the lands and waters which have to be decontaminated.

It is also necessary to determine which persons should be prosecuted. There are clearly physical persons, those who took the direct responsibility of participating in these criminal actions, but the main actor responsible for these crimes is a State, the United States, which made the decision to carry out the dissemination. The present judicial complaints (only at the civil level) are directed against the companies that produced the products. This is certainly justified since they had the duty to check the international rules concerning the products they produced. But the US government cannot be exempt from its responsibility on that basis.

The case of Vietnam confirms that, in spite of recent progress, the criminal part of international humanitarian law—that which allows the punishment of individual authors of international crimes by international judges without the shelter of immunities due to their official functions—remains in an embryonic and deficient state. The International Criminal Court was established in 2000 as the result of an agreement between States. But its jurisdiction is not retroactive. It thus cannot initiate investigations into acts that took place before 2000. As we discussed above, it is nevertheless true that there is a continuity of the effects of the criminal actions up to the present day.[6] But even so, there is a second obstacle. Vietnam did not ratify the Statute of the Court, and the United States did not do it either and is in fact hostile to it. Assuming Vietnam ratifies the Statute of the Court, it could only bring a suit against people present on its territory: the US military or political persons responsible for the decision to use these chemical weapons would therefore avoid prosecution by the Court.

One possibility remains open: the universal jurisdiction of national tribunals. Some of the gravest international breaches are within the jurisdiction of tribunals of all countries, independently of the place where the breaches took place and of the residence of the criminals or of the victims. This idea was expressly stated in the Geneva Conventions relative to armed conflicts (Article 146 of Convention IV). However, it was not followed by practical application. It is also at the origin of the procedure carried out against Pinochet. Under the pressure of public opinion, some national jurisdictions became more audacious and accepted the idea that, if some crimes have an international character, then all national jurisdictions should be qualified to judge them. In the present case, one would have to identify those persons, among the US political or military authorities, responsible for decisions on the use of Agent Orange. Then victims should lodge a complaint in those countries where judges would be willing to open an investigation and take the benefit of any opportunity for prosecution when the persons responsible would be present in the country.

Vietnamese tribunals are, of course, particularly competent since the victims are Vietnamese and since the facts took place on the territory of

Vietnam. Its tribunals could therefore either judge those persons responsible who are not present on its territory (though the judgment would then have no actual effect), or make use of the presence on its territory of a visiting US veteran in order to prosecute and judge him. This would have the advantage of alerting the international community but would considerably worsen the relations of Vietnam with the United States.

As we see, criminal procedure is thus hazardous. Nevertheless, it is of major importance that authors of crimes be prosecuted and sentenced with respect to the values of society and to the feeling of justice that must prevail. It is therefore important to rally the interest of public opinion on these matters and on the unacceptable deficiencies of international law.

3. Blockages due to structural weakness of international law

Exposing deficiencies is not sufficient; their causes must be analysed. The ineffectiveness of humanitarian law is linked to the general crisis of international law. An effective functioning of the principle of responsibility must ensure that damages caused to individual or collective persons by other persons be repaired by those responsible for the damages.

The Commission of International Law in charge of codifying this right affirms the principle of international responsibility of the State for internationally illicit acts. This principle thus today enjoys a customary basis. To know what an internationally illicit act is, one must refer to conventions or customs which are the source of international law. But responsibility (whether criminal for punishing the guilty or civil for achieving reparation for damages) makes sense only if there are jurisdictions to make this happen. Why is it that the Vietnamese government cannot bring the question of damages caused to its population through prohibited methods of war to international justice? As a matter of fact, the International Court of Justice does exist in The Hague. But the only conflicts within its jurisdiction are those which occur between States and only if the latter accept it. The victims as private persons have no access to it. The Vietnamese government should act on their behalf and in its own name, as is a priori possible. But, just as in the case of the more recent International Criminal Court, neither the government of Vietnam nor that of the United States have accepted the jurisdiction of the Court. Vietnam might do it in order to open the procedure for reparations as discussed here. But it would be confronted by the fact that the United States, which had in the past accepted the jurisdiction of the Court, no longer accepts it since being sentenced to reparations in a question initiated against it by Nicaragua in 1986.

One possibility remains, but it is also obstructed by the reluctance of States to really accept international justice. Some treaties include a clause according to which all signatory States accept the jurisdiction of the Court for all conflicts involving the application or interpretation of the treaty. This is the case with the Convention on the Prevention and Punishment of the Crime of Genocide of December 9, 1948. As discussed above, the systematic spreading of Agent Orange might, under some conditions to be checked, be considered as belonging to this category. The Court would have the responsibility to confirm or deny this opinion. If it confirmed it, the question of reparations would be within its jurisdiction. Unfortunately, this possibility is excluded in the present situation because the United States, when ratifying the Convention, made reservations which prevent it, as did Vietnam. Both have declared that any request related to the Convention would be possibly within the jurisdiction of the Court only with the express acceptance of the states involved.

As we see, the judicial issues are filled with obstacles. But a right that cannot be used has no concrete existence. There will be no progress without deeper thought on the general structure of international law. The latter, based since its origin (15th century) on the central principle of the sovereignty of States, requires the acceptance of States to advance. And a rule can be opposed only by States which have formally accepted it. And a State, as we have just seen, is free to adhere or not to a treaty which is essential for the international community. Even if it adheres to it, it may make reservations which make some of its clauses ineffective. As a result, the international community is not based on common values that would make it a society with actual solidarity.

Humanity is therefore at an essential turning point in its history. States remain necessary to represent the various peoples. But it is this precise attribute of sovereignty that has to be overcome. It is this very concept and the use made of it that prevent common values from being imposed on States from which they cannot withdraw. The basic challenge in the battle for humanitarian law, as also more generally for human rights, is the need for a judicial system permitting that states or their representatives be judged, without any obligation to request their permission. This is the basic reform we need, which was not part of the laughable program of reform of the United Nations and for which a well-targeted mobilization of peoples is still missing. Without it, that reform will not succeed…and the only thing left to us will be to do, time and again, what we are doing here: meeting together to lament on impunity.

Bibliography on the "chemical war" in Vietnam

Agent Orange in the Vietnam war. History and consequences. Profesor Le Cao Dai. Vietnam Red Cross Society. 2000.
Long-term consequences of the Vietnam war. Ethics. Law. Policy. Report to the environmental conference on Cambodia, Laos, Vietnam. Stockholm.

2003.

The extent and patterns of usage of Agent Orange and other herbicides in Vietnam. JM Stellman, SD Stellman, R Christian, T Weber and C Tomasallo. Nature. 17 April 2003. Page 681 ff.

Environnement et santé au Vietnam. 30 ans après l'opération Ranch Hand. Hoang Dinh Cau. Maison d'édition Nghean. Institut de recherche et d'universalisation des connaissances. Hanoi. 2003.

ENDNOTES

1   See *Nature*, 17 April 2003.

2   Collaborative USA-Vietnam Agent Orange Research from 1968 to 2002. Arnold Schecter and others.

    Also see *"Federal Benefits for Veterans and Dependents"*. Department of Veterans Affairs. 1999 Edition. Office of Public Affairs (80D) 810 Vermont Ave. N.W. Washington, DC 20420.

3   See the various texts in Schindler et Toman. *"Droit des conflits armés"*. Comité International de la Croix-Rouge et Institut Henri Dunant. Geneva. 1996.

4   Already in the Judgment of the Nuremberg Tribunal, the judges had mentioned the customary nature of the prohibitions with the consequence that acts committed by the Nazis were considered as crimes, and had made it the basis for their sentences. One may also mention the basic contribution represented by the opinion expressed by the International Court of Justice on July 9, 2004, on the problem of the wall constructed by Israel in Palestine. The Court confirmed the applicability in that case of the whole of humanitarian law, in particular The Hague Convention, to which Israel did not adhere : the Court based its application in Palestine on the customary value accorded to this text.

5   In particular the Convention on lthe Non-Applicability of Statutory Limitations of War Crimes and Crimes against Humanity, November 26, 1968.

LES ROBERTS

MORTALITY AFTER THE 2003 INVASION OF IRAQ

The text of Les Roberts which follows consists first of a brief analysis of the study on mortality in Iraq due to the war, undertaken in September 2004 by a group of researchers from the United States and Iraq under his direction. The result was a prudent estimate, probably under-estimated, according to the authors, of at least 100,000 unnecessary deaths due to the war, the greater part of which were violent deaths, attributed principally by the families to attacks by the coalition led by the United States. The major portion of his article is then devoted to an analysis of the reception of the study (largely negative) at the time by the media and political spokespeople, as well as the reactions of the public. He asks, in conclusion, whether the results could be confirmed or denied by inquests of greater depth which could, and in fact should, be taken by the United Nations.

If, this article concludes, that which happens in Darfur or in Iraq is permitted to continue throughout the years without an establishment of the facts and without governments having to render an accounting, then one must ask oneself: what purpose does the United Nations serve ? Since, a new study bringing the situation up to date, also published in the British review, The Lancet, *was done by the same group of researchers in 2006. The analysis was again based on a series of interviews of families on the deaths having taken place since the invasion, and on their causes. Some fifty zones in different regions were randomly chosen for this new study, and in each, some 40 families or households were interviewed from May to July 2006, covering some 12,000 persons in total.*

We summarize below the aspects which seem to us to be the most interesting, with the agreement of the authors of the study, and based upon figures and analyses that they have communicated. We take full responsibility, however, for the presentation and part of the commentaries thereon.

The population of Iraq is around 26 million. The rate of morality in the period preceding the invasion was 5.5 per thousand per year, of which a part is very weak (0.1) due to the violence. After the study, the rate mounted in average to more than 13 for the period which followed the invasion. It has regularly mounted with a peak at close to 20 during the year following the invasion. This, calculated in relation to the population of Iraq, corresponds to an excess mortality due to the war of around 650,000, being around 2.5 percent of the population, of which around 600,000 were violent deaths. The new study confirms the figure of a little more than 100,000 excess deaths for the period covered by the study of September 2004. The results confirm a regular augmentation of deaths due to the Coalition led by the United States with, however, some differences in relation to the preceding study. The violent deaths due to the Coalition are on average still in the majority, but a little fewer among those whose death has been clearly attributed by the families. Notably, around half of the violent deaths were attributed to unknown causes when there was any doubt. Certain aspects of this analysis differ from that of the preceding analysis, for example the number of violent deaths of women is on the whole low. Among the non-violent excess deaths, we note the increase in heart attacks. Habitual causes of non-violent excess deaths (problems tied to deterioration of health services, availability of drinkable water, cuts in electricity, displacement of populations...) remained, but appeared here very much less important than in other conflicts. The authors discussed different aspects of the results and advanced, insofar as it was possible, some hypotheses permitting an understanding, but still without a clear explanation on certain points.

The authors recall estimates of the number of victims of other conflicts due to wars, including in the variable proportions of deaths by violence and those due to humanitarian catastrophies resulting from conflicts. According to them, among the most murderous in the past, 3 million for the Vietnam war, from 3 to 4 million in the Congo, 200,000 out of a population of 800,000 in East Timor, and for the recent period, around 200,000 in Darfur (the estimate, which they do not provide, of deaths during the Khmer Rouge period in Cambodia would be around a million or more, according to some sources, out of a population which then numbered around 7 million). The estimate for the previous period of the Lon Nol government established by the United States would be around half a million, due in particular to the US bombings).

For the case of Iraq, they compare their estimate to those coming from other sources of evaluation of the number of violent deaths. Iraq Body Count gives an estimate a little less than 50,000 (being ten times less than those of the authors). Different figures higher than the Iraq Body Count come from other sources. The authors note that there is still, in different conflicts, a very great difference between the figures deriving from the results of "passive surveillance" of the type undertaken by Iraq Body Count, and more realistic estimates, the first not exceeding in general more than twenty percent of the second. Qualitative data flowing from "passive surveillance" are, however, in general close to those issuing from more realistic estimates—

for example, for Iraq, the evolution of the number of victims since 2003, and the part due to the Coalition or to other causes...

The authors recognize the difficulties and the potential sources of error in their analysis, even if the estimates given seem approximately correct to them. They reiterate that an independent international organism endowed with adequate means must intervene to verify their results—a call which they had already made following the preceding study, which has not met with success to this day. They consider that it is essential to have trustworthy data, which in their view would be in accord with the Geneva Conventions and the humanitarian law of conflicts, and would permit all those who speak for civilians taken in conflicts to contribute to shrinking the tragic cost of wars to come.

—Editors' Note

It has been almost a year since we released a report with the results of a nationwide survey documenting deaths in Iraq. Because the results have been presented in the initial *Lancet* article, I would like to skim over the study itself and focus on the media attention to the study and the lack of appropriate response.

Our survey was typical in size and design among efforts to document mortality in countries where surveillance and death registries do not function. The study consisted of visiting 33 randomly picked neighborhoods, and in each of those locations, picking a random point and interviewing the 30 closest households. Note that virtually every household in Iraq had an equal chance we would visit their home without any preferences regarding security or ethnicity or political leanings. Each house was asked who had lived there on Jan.1st, 2002, who lived there now, and if anyone had been born or died in the interim 32 months.

All of the randomly selected areas were successfully interviewed. The 988 households interviewed had experienced 46 deaths in the 14.6 months before the invasion and 142 deaths in the 17.8 months since the invasion. This implies more than a doubling of mortality. Realize that in this analysis, the household mortality experiences are being compared to themselves. Thus, if by random chance the sample over-represented wealthy people or rural people or some other subset of Iraqis, this increase we measured cannot be explained by sampling error.

Except in the Kurdish north, mortality was elevated in almost all the neighborhoods visited and most neighborhoods had experienced violent deaths.

The range of post-invasion death rates in the neighborhoods visited followed something like a "normal" distribution, with more than half of the clusters falling between 5 and 10 deaths per 1000 per year, except for one neighborhood, the cluster of Falluja. While in most neighborhoods between 1 and 2% of the population had died since the invasion, in Falluja, about a quarter of the members of the remaining households had died. As a statistical practice, when one of many measures does not fit in with the other community of results, the measure is referred to as an outlier, and is often set aside to prevent one measure from overwhelming the overall conclusions. For anyone who had been watching the news in 2004, it was very plausible that a quarter of the Falluja residents had been killed. It was not set aside because it was believed to be invalid, it was set aside because its presence complicated and blurred the task of statistically summarizing deaths in Iraq.

In the 97% of Iraq represented by the first 32 neighborhoods, our best estimate was that 98,000 people had died in excess of the rate seen before the invasion. Most of this increase was associated with a dramatic increase in the rate of violent deaths. In the logic of sampling, each cluster including the cluster in Falluja represented 739,000 people (or 1/33rd of the Iraqi population). Thus the Falluja outlier cluster indicated there were perhaps 200,000 additional deaths associated with the invasion. Because Falluja was by random chance the only cluster picked in Anbar Province, and because it was by chance the only randomly picked city that had experienced a severe siege, it may have represented the experience of hundreds of thousands of Iraqis. Likewise, it may have been by chance one of the worst neighborhoods in the most devastated city in Iraq and therefore represented few Iraqis. Because of the great uncertainty about the significance of this cluster, the finding was simply used to qualify the results found elsewhere. Without the Falluja information, we would have said that there was a 50/50 chance the death toll was above 100,000 and a 90% chance it was above 44,000; with Falluja taken into consideration there was a far more likely chance that the death toll was above 100,000. When we published this, I was naively expecting to get criticized primarily by the anti-war crowd. We had done a survey, our point estimate was that about 285,000 people had died, and we reported it as probably exceeding 100,000. We thought that by being so conservative in our estimate, that the report would be largely unassailable.

The findings were published in the *Lancet* almost a month after they were submitted and a week before the US Presidential election. The main findings laid-out in the *Lancet* article were that:

• If the death toll of this war is not in the neighborhood of 100,000, it is far higher.

• Violence is now the most common cause of death, up 58 fold.

• Families attributed "strikes" by coalition forces as the main cause of violent deaths.

We concluded that:

• If the USG is not collecting "body counts," it cannot claim to be careful protectors.

• If the USG is not collecting mortality information, there cannot be any complete analysis of the costs vs. benefits of going to war.

These findings need to be confirmed or refuted! It seemed to us beyond unacceptable that the best record of what had happened in Iraq would be the effort of a couple of academics with tolerant wives and $ 40000 with which to run a survey on a shoestring.

The press coverage of this report in Europe and the US could not have been more disparate. In Europe, most major newspapers ran the story on the front page. There were several in-depth critiques, such as in the *Economist*, relying on expert interpretation and attempting to interpret the considerable imprecision of the report. Tony Blair was forced to address the *Lancet* article at least three times in the week to follow and British Foreign Secretary Jack Straw wrote a five-page response to the article. In the US, the coverage of the article was very limited. Of the two major newspapers, *The New York Times* ran a wire service story on page A-8 which painted the report as controversial. The *Washington Post* interviewed the authors and wrote their own story. They spoke to a respected weapons analyst at Human Rights Watch named Mark Garlasco who said that he had not seen the report but that the death estimate sounded too high. The *Post* quoted him as saying the estimate seemed too high. Because of his being the first credible authority to discredit the report, he was interviewed on the domestic CNN and one of the major networks regarding the report while none of the authors were interviewed by US media outlets with one-tenth the coverage. What was most effective at limiting the coverage of the *Lancet* report was probably two spin pieces that came out the day after.

One was written by a former Assistant Secretary of Defense and the other was written by a reporter named Fred Kaplan from *Slate Online Magazine*. Both were respectful and focused on the difficult conditions. Both focused on the range in the first 32 neighborhoods without considering Falluja. Both concluded that this report was so vague as to add little new information. Kaplan concluded that this was not a result; it was a "dartboard." This message went out through informal networks, mostly internet based, with lightning speed. The *Lancet* article came out on a Thursday. Two people told me that the following Sunday, their ministers from the pulpit had said how the 100,000 death report had been discredited. On the Monday before the Presidential election, a reporter from Chicago called me and said that he had just called a right-to-life group (meaning want to outlaw abortions) and asked them, if you value life so much, how do you feel about 100,000 dead Iraqis? The interviewee said that she had heard that it might only be 8,000 deaths. The day of the Presidential election, five days after the *Lancet* article had appeared, my next door neighbor told me that she was listening to conservative talk radio that day and heard that the *Lancet* study reporting 8,000 dead in Iraq was flawed and wrong. I suspect to this day, not one in ten Americans have heard that perhaps 100,000 Iraqis have died due to the invasion and occupation.

I am surprised and delighted to say that almost a year after the *Lancet* study was published, certain forces still feel the need to discredit the *Lancet* report. Here is an example from a columnist for US *News and World Report* from a column entitled "Fun with Numbers" published in August, 2005.

He quotes the report as saying, "We estimate there were 98,000 extra deaths (95% CI 8,000-194,000) during the postwar period." Note that his quote begins with a capital letter and ends with a period. In fact, the only similar sentence in the report reads, "We estimate that there were 98,000 extra deaths (95% CI 8,000-194,000) during the post-war period in the 97% of Iraq represented in all the clusters except Falluja." While the adding of the period is a minor issue from a typesetting perspective, it dramatically changed the meaning of the sentence. I pointed out this misquote and another factual error to US *News and World Report* and John Leo, neither of whom responded. Given the reluctance of the mainstream press to grapple with this issue, it is not surprising that President Bush has not been asked about the report and aside from the US Centers for Disease Control steering reporters to the American Enterprise Institute (a conservative think tank in Washington) for epidemiological comment, the US Government has not officially responded to the *Lancet* report.

I realize that there is a lot of speculation as to why the US was so keen to invade Iraq. I am sorry that I have no insight into that topic. But I can say that the attribution of nefarious or capricious intent combined with the lack of verifiable death data has contributed to the gulf in world perspectives regarding the conflict.

There has been a two-and-a-half fold increase in the number of bodies collected at the largest morgue in Baghdad in the couple of months before and the 18 months after the 2003 invasion, with almost all of that increase associated with violence.

If this increase were truly representative of all of Iraq, this would correspond to about 500 violent deaths a day. I am confident this is not representative. I strongly suspect that violent deaths disproportionately appear in morgues and we know that in the best of times over the past decade, more than half of all deaths were never recorded in the hospital- and morgue-based state data collection system. Thus, the dramatic increase above is an artifact of increased violence and an incomplete data source. Nonetheless, verbal and graphical reports such as this are widely cited in the press of countries where anti-coalition feelings run high.

On the other hand, there are people who simply cannot hear information critical of the coalition actions. I accept that.

But there are now at least 8 sources widely cited in the press regarding the number of deaths or rate of violent deaths in Iraq. The three lowest estimates are surveillance-based. Surveillance is never complete in times of war. The highest 4 are survey based. A widely cited estimate of 128,000 deaths that appeared last June is not included because only press accounts have been found. The lowest of the surveys, done by the Iraqi Government and supported by the Norwegian group FAFO, is believed to be an underestimate by the report's author. For the *Lancet* report, this figure just represents the two thirds of excess deaths attributed to violence. Note that the *Lancet* estimate is not the highest. Yet, in the US press, the Iraq Body Count figure, now around 26,000 deaths, is the most widely cited value. Thus, having death rate estimates that differ by a factor of 5 or 10 allows different peoples to have their press paint different images of Iraq. In doing so, the press that should ideally bring views closer together through the establishment of common given facts, is in fact driving the world further apart.

Of note is the fact that four of the death estimate sources attributed the violent deaths to one group or another, and all are in agreement that during 2003 and 2004, the Coalition forces killed far more people than did the criminal elements or the so-called insurgents.

We have a problem in the world: no one is responsible for documenting wars. If we look at Mark White's online encyclopedia of wars and disasters, there have been 14 wars since Vietnam that have death tolls estimated to be well over 100,000.

Among these, only four have death tolls established during the conflict by any epidemiological methods. In all the other circumstances the death tolls were either guessed at or estimated years later by some demographic technique. Thus, the press in the West does not have the chance to report war tallies often and issues of representativeness and precision are not likely to be discussed with any depth or insight. The press just does not get the practice.

Patrick Ball at the University of California at Berkeley has had a lot of experience estimating deaths by comparing lists of people believed killed or disappeared. He has worked for the Truth and Reconciliation Commission in South Africa, estimated the deaths in Kosovo, and done work for the

Government of Guatemala. He has shown that in Guatemala, in the years when there were few political murders, most of them were reported in the press. In those years when there was the highest level of violence, the early 1980's and mid-1990's, the Guatemalan press did not report even 5% of political killings. This phenomenon, the press being averse to being killed and thus avoiding the most violent settings, has been seen elsewhere such as Burundi and the Democratic Republic of Congo. We cannot expect to monitor the horrors of war through the press. Likewise, and perhaps a topic for another day, it would be foolhardy to think that the UN Agencies such as WHO, who have to deal with country officials daily and whose regional directors are elected by the countries they oversee, will ever document that a country has been committing crimes against humanity. For example, WHO has recently done two rounds of mortality surveys in Darfur and the Sudanese government has forbid them to use recall periods more than 3 and 5 months. It takes almost no more effort to ask about deaths in a family over the past two years as it does over the past three months. There is no information regarding the last three months lost if recording deaths over the past two years. And because WHO has done these mortality surveys, a standard activity during emergencies, there is little imperative for someone else to be allowed by the government to make a record of what has occurred over the past three years. Thus, if genocide has occurred in Darfur, WHO has been an active participant in the cover-up.

Our main recommendation in the *Lancet* report was that our findings needed to be confirmed or refuted by a more comprehensive investigation. Years on, I believe that this has not happened. When I was a small child, there used to be ads on the television for the UN saying we have one mission, "world peace." Given the interwoven nature of peace and justice, if Darfur and Iraq can go on for years undocumented and without any governments held accountable, I wonder why we have a UN?

GENEVIÈVE SEVRIN

GUANTANAMO
A MODEL OF ILLEGALITY

Imagine the following scenario: hundreds of nationals of the United States are arrested throughout the entire world by a foreign government which carries on a "war for national security". This government reacts to elements of proofs according to which a recent bomb attack on its territory, which caused several thousand civilian victims, was due to a network with vague contours based in the United States. The persons under arrest are considered as being associated in some way or another with this network, in view of proofs which it declares to hold in its possession but which it refuses to reveal. The prisoners, some of whom are minors, find themselves tied up, hobbled, blindfolded, in transport planes. When arriving on an island, they are detained secretly in tiny rooms, they are not allowed to have any contact with their family or tribunals, and they are submitted to repeated interrogations as well as to a regime of punishment intended to force their cooperation.

Would the United States tolerate such a treatment of its citizens by another government? Would the international community accept such a threat to the state of law and human rights? This is certainly not so. However, the United States perpetrated such violations at Guantanamo Bay. With over one thousand days of detention at the hands of the executive power, it has become a symbol of the attempt by one government to place itself above the law. The example thus given is that of a world in which basic human rights are negotiable rather than universal. The more powerful the state, the more they are negotiable.

Before developing this question, let me first come back to the sequence of facts in view of a better understanding of the situation.

1. January 2001-Middle of 2003:
The Denunciation of the Legal Emptiness of the Situation of Detainees

The Guantanamo camp opened in January 2002 to receive mainly prisoners arrested in Afghanistan since December 2001 in the framework of the international conflict started by the United States after 11 September 2001. The estimates of numbers of prisoners were soon over 600. They were nationals of over 40 countries. These persons are under the "Military Order on the Detention, Treatment and Trial of Certain Non-Citizens in the War Against Terrorism", a military order signed by President Bush on November 13, 2001. One thus deals here with a detention of indefinite length, without indictment or judgment, with no access to a defense lawyer or a tribunal, or to family. The only prospective of a trial is that of a military one.

From the start, conditions of detention were particularly rough: the X-Ray Camp with its cages, then in April the Delta Camp with tiny cells, quasi non-stop confinement and almost no exercise, and Camp IV where conditions would be somewhat less strict for prisoners considered as less dangerous. Interrogations were rough. Before arriving in Guantanamo, there was often an intermediate stop in a base in Afghanistan, in particular at Bagram, which is a camp of extreme roughness where torture is routine practice (there were "officially" two dead persons in Bagram in 2002).

In March 2002, a project of military commissions and exception tribunals for foreign prisoners was written up. It was in fact admitted that no such military tribunal may exist for US citizens.

Confronted with this situation, Amnesty International attacked the legal emptiness, the non-respect of the Geneva Conventions, the absence of precise indications on the number and identity of prisoners, as well as the fact that military commissions are a second order of justice, remote from a fair trial. The US government was requested to allow free access to detainees, to indict detainees and carry out fair trials, or alternatively to liberate them quickly.

On March 11, 2002, the Court of Appeals of the District of Columbia ruled that detainees cannot be presented to a federal US tribunal to contest their detention because Cuba has sovereignty over Guantanamo; hence prisoners are not protected by the Constitution of the United States.

In May 2003, soon after the beginning of the war against Iraq (March 20), the world discovered that, among detainees, there were at least three minors, 13 to 15 years old. Up to that time, only one case of a minor, a 16-year-old national of Canada transferred from Afghanistan in 2002, had been known. Following a mobilization of public opinion, it is believed that all minors were liberated in January 2004.

2. Summer 2003-May 2004: A Bad Example for the World

New elements were revealed in the summer of 2003. In July, President Bush pointed out six foreign detainees as the first " enemy combatants" to be referred to military commissions—pseudo-tribunals totally dependent on the US administration, with no possibility of appeal and possible death penalty, denunciations, arbitrary arrests, secret detention in unknown places, totally illegal interrogations, whose purpose seems to be to gather confessions rather than to search for a fair trial. At the same time, further facts were also denounced, such as transfers of prisoners illegally transmitted to American authorities, for instance from Malawi or Bosnia, as well as transfers in the opposite direction, towards countries where torture is a usual practice. One was then confronted with a total drift of the executive power, which was deciding exceptional measures in the framework of a "war against terror", an expression whose extensive definition allows one to turn legal systems around, either with the methods of detention or the establishment of a parallel justice.

Through documents made available to the public, it became known that the US administration had refused to apply the Geneva Conventions in order to give full freedom to US investigators and to make prosecution for war crimes even less probable. And there was no indication that the administration would be willing to modify this attitude. On the contrary, one of the counselors of the White House, Albert Gonzales, was appointed Attorney-General by President Bush. This was a bad example for the world, which might ruin international law and whose consequences may be, moreover, less security for the world.

In December 2003, two US federal courts denounced the arbitrariness of the detentions. On the following month, Amnesty spoke of "human rights taken hostage", in spite of a few liberations, and this marked the starting point of a long term action in favor of nominative detainees of various countries.

The revelation of the Abu Ghraib scandal in May 2004 was an important new step. Amnesty International spoke of war crimes and emphasized the necessity of putting an independent commission in charge of investigating the conditions of detention in the framework of the "war against terrorism". On June 28, the Supreme Court of the United States gave detainees the right to access US justice concerning the legality of their conditions of detention. It ruled that federal courts may make decisions on appeals of Guantanamo detainees. Some liberations were announced, even though the US administration tried to empty this decision from any practical content and to keep any revision of detentions as much as possible outside legal possibilities.

3. Summer 2004–summer 2005:
Guantanamo and Beyond; Against Torture

On July 7, 2004, the Pentagon interpreted the decision of the Supreme Court in its own way and delegated to Combatant Status Review Tribunals the responsibility of making decisions on individual cases. These tribunals were not courts of justice, nor any competent tribunal according to the third Geneva Convention. They would start to operate in August, almost at the same time as the preliminary audience concerning the first four people indicted, to be possibly presented to military commissions. The prisoner had to prove he was not an "enemy combatant" in the absence of any access to a defense lawyer or to the secret file... Many detainees boycotted this procedure.

In November, a federal judge interrupted the preliminary steps preceding the functioning of these military commissions. Whereas the trials were to start in January 2005, Judge Robertson ruled that prisoners captured in Afghanistan had to be considered as war prisoners and to benefit from corresponding protections. Judgment by military commissions was thus not possible. There was an immediate appeal of this decision by the US government. The appeal was addressed to a higher court on the basis that the decision of the judge constituted an extraordinary intrusion in the executive power in the conduct of military operations.

In October, during the campaign for presidential elections in the United States, Amnesty International asked the candidates to take a clear stand against torture. At this time, the report "Human Dignity Violated" was published. This report denounced the bad treatment inflicted on detainees at the hands of US forces in Guantanamo, Iraq and Afghanistan. The aim was also to oblige the authorities concerned to account for the flagrant violations of human rights. A series of recommendations were then addressed to the US government. They were based on a "Program of twelve points" for the prevention of acts of torture committed by state officers: official sentences; no secret detention or detention in secret places; regular inspection of the places of detention; informing prisoners of their rights; investigations if there are complaints about torture; training on practices excluding torture and possibly the refusal to practice torture; no use of confessions obtained by torture as proofs; no transfer to places where torture might be practiced. This was the starting point of a continued action aiming to confront the US administration with its responsibilities. The first step of this action went from January 20 to the end of April 2005. It was also a call on the US government to address a strong message to other governments that torture is totally unacceptable, and in particular a message to governments who, in the context of fighting terrorism, are tempted to nuance this principle.

In May 2005, convergent declarations of former detainees about torture inflicted on them were revealed in particular by *Time*, as well as by the Red Cross, whose confidential report had already criticized the practices of US authorities in 2004. This situation was the direct consequence of the position adopted by the government according to which some persons have no "legal right" to a human treatment. This was an implicit statement of President Bush in a memorandum (which remained secret over a long period) on the detention policy in the "war against terrorism". According to him, human rights are a privilege to be granted, and hence possibly withdrawn, by the State.

In its annual report in May, Amnesty International compared this situation with the Soviet Gulag, even though the length and extent of the practices concerned were very different. In both cases though, they are out-of-law detention places where the detention is undefined, without indictment or judgment, without access to a lawyer, to a court or to relatives, and where the practice of torture and secrecy is widespread. In fact, the Pentagon still refuses to give precise figures on the number of detainees in Guantanamo. This allows secret transfers of detainees. In view of the revelations concerning the so-called "ghost detainees" in the hands of US authorities in Iraq, and of continued allegations on secret transfers between the United States and countries where torture is a current practice, there were serious reasons to be worried. Many people in the United States then demanded the closure of Guantanamo.

In August 2005, the report "Torture and Secret Detention" gave more precise information on what was until then somewhat vague. There do exist a number of secret places, an "Archipelago of Gulags" managed by US authorities, in which "missing persons" are or have been detained. These places are in countries where torture is practiced. Missing persons are transferred and detained in such countries upon order of the United States, in these same countries or others. The testimonies by missing persons who could be located show that treatment comparable to, or worse than, those inflicted to prisoners in Guantanamo were a reality, made easier by the secret character of these places and by the total isolation of detainees. Jordan, Syria and Yemen are among a number of countries associated with the "war against terrorism". The example of Mamdouh Habib illustrates this situation: in October 2001, the US forces, in cooperation with the governments of Pakistan and Egypt, sent him to Egypt in the knowledge he would be tortured, and with that intention. He stayed six months in Egypt, was submitted to inexpressible brutalities (torture with electricity, water, physical aggressions, suspension by hooks, threats from dogs…). US officers were present during the interrogations in Pakistan following his arrest, and during his transfer to Egypt. Recently, his defense lawyer learnt in the newspapers that the US government was negotiating with Egypt in order to send him back to that country where he would again be tortured.

The symbol of the Gulag is also pertinent in view of the fact that Guantanamo is thus just one among a chain of ghost detention camps, including secret ones. Each one has its own stories of abuses, tortures and criminal homicides. And one does not deal here with isolated facts. They are part of a global, closely linked system of detention, which is unaccountable to any law.

3.1 Guantanamo

At September 2005, there were still over 500 detainees of 35 nationalities, and at least 5 minors (possibly 9). Since it had opened, this center had "received" over 750 persons of 40 nationalities, with transfer or liberation for around 234, including 167 liberated in their country and 67 detained in their country (at least 30 still in detention at that time). These figures are not certain.

Testimonies of detainees in Camp 5, open in the spring of 2004, show that the model was that of the very rough ones among high security camps in US prisons: tiny cells, light without interruption, almost total absence of physical exercise... Among prisoners thus detained, there was at least one minor, Mohammed C., whereas it was believed all minors had been liberated (Amnesty had strongly pressed for such a liberation). Maybe there were still between four and nine.

A hunger strike started in the beginning of the summer 2005. It ended on July 28: detainees stopped it after the US government had accepted, according to what they said, to apply Geneva Conventions in the camp within 10 days. They had been told this decision had been approved by Secretary of Defense Donald Rumsfeld. The hunger strike resumed on August 12, officially by 120 detainees, after the US forces did not respect their promises on several occasions. It was still impossible for the detainees to appeal against their detention, and they were still victims of brutal treatment in the camp. It is to be noted that US authorities published this information, even though they probably lowered the number of detainees participating in the strike. This seemed to be the result of a complex situation, from which the US government had difficulties in withdrawing. Around 15 persons were forced to undergo perfusion.

The US government implicitly said it was willing to reduce the number of prisoners in a non-negligible way. According to various quotes, over 100 Afghans were supposed to be progressively transferred to Afghanistan. The Uighurs of China were apparently certain not to be transferred to their country (where the worst could be expected). For others, there were "diplomatic assurances", which are a rather low guarantee, indicating they would not suffer from bad treatment. Amnesty strongly protested against such merely verbal assurances as a guarantee of the physical and psychological integrity of persons.

3.2 Legal and Judicial Problems

The Combatant Status Review Tribunals examined 558 cases between July 2004 and March 2005; only 38 detainees were not confirmed as "enemy combatants", almost all of them after a federal judge, on 31 January, 2005, declared the revision process illegal (a decision followed by an appeal by the government).

Then, the Commissions for the revision of administrative decisions, composed of military officers, had to determine, every year, if the detention had to be maintained or not. There has been no information on the results. Hearings started in December 2004. Over 150 hearings took place up to June 2005. The government explained once more its view: a regular process cannot be applied to foreigners, arrested in a foreign country and detained on a territory (Guantanamo) where the United States was not sovereign. Another argument is the following: the executive power is the only one competent to determine if a detainee is an enemy combatant, the executive power does not have to account for decisions of a military character, which are at the very heart of powers relative to war.

Sixty-one requests based on *habeas corpus* concerning 169 detainees had been introduced by the end of April 2005 before federal courts (intended to allow an immediate appearance of a detainee before a judicial authority, in order to contest the legality of the detention and possibly to lead to his liberation).

There was an improvement with respect to Amnesty's Program of 12 Points: on May 6, 2005, the government transmitted its periodic report to the Committee on Torture of the United Nations. On the other hand, the secret note of August 2002 giving a restrictive definition of torture was replaced.

In July 2005, the federal Court of Appeals ruled in favor of the government, so that military commissions were in principle in a position to start to operate quickly. The two first trials were planned to be those of the Yemeni Salim Ahmed Hamdam and the Australian David Hicks by the end of September.

Military commissions: late last August 2005, General Thomas Hemingway, legal expert of the Pentagon, announced some changes in this respect. In our opinion, these are only "cosmetic" changes aimed at giving the commissions an apparence of "respectability", not to provide the guarantees of a fair trial. "The principle underneath these changes is that the officer chairing (the tribunal) acts more like a judge whereas the other members of the panel act more as a jury", the Pentagon explains in a release.

The officer chairing the special tribunal, which is made up of a panel of three to seven militaries, will be "in charge" of deciding on most legal issues, while the other members of the panel will have the authority to make the conclusions and to decide the sentence", clarifies the US Defense Department.

Before, all the members of the panel would decide collectively on conclusions and sentence, and on most of the legal issues.

The Pentagon has also decided to clarify the conditions for the presence of the defendant at the trial and his access to classified documents.

From now on, if the defendant is not authorized to have access to information, then the chairing officer "must exclude the relevant evidence if this would compromise the fairness of the trial for the defendant", explained General Hemingway at a press conference.

The fact that the Pentagon held a press conference to announce such changes is a sign of its unease. If the United States really wanted to set up state-of-the-art and fair trials, the detained would be brought before established legal systems, i.e. US federal courts.

Estimates in April 2005

Estimates on numbers of detainees in Iraq are over 10,000, with 3.500 at Abu Ghraib and in Afghanistan, over 450 at Bagram and 70 at Kandahar. It is plausible that there were 40 detainees in secret places in the hands of the CIA, that at least 100 detainees had been transferred to other countries secretly, and that several thousands could be detained in various countries upon order of the United States.

December 30, 2005

President Bush promulgates the 2005 Law relative to the treatment of detainees. It prohibits any cruel, inhuman or degrading treatment (in the sense of the US legislation, rather than that of international law), but strongly restricts the right of Guantanamo detainees to contest the legality of their detention or its conditions.

June 29, 2006

In the case *Hamdan vs Rumsfeld,* the Supreme Court of the United States judges that military commissions established on the basis of the 2001 military decree are violations of the US and international legislation. The Court also says that Article 3 (of the 1949 Geneva Conventions) should be applied, in opposition to the 2002 presidential opinion. On the other hand, it also considers that the 2005 Law relative to the treatment of detainees does not prevent federal courts examining requests in *habeas corpus* that were under consideration at the time the law was promulgated.

September 6, 2006

President Bush announces the transfer to Guantanamo of 14 detainees present in CIA secret prisons, some of them for four years and a half.

October 17, 2006

The president promulgates the Law relative to military commissions according to which the examination of requests in *habeas corpus* by foreign *"enemy combatants"* detained by the United States all over the world are no longer within the jurisdiction of US tribunals. It authorizes the president to establish a new system of military commissions to judge these detainees and restricts the scope of the Law relative to war crimes: in fact, it does not explicitly prohibit unfair trials, in contrast to Article 3, nor *"outrages upon personal dignity, in particular humiliating and degrading treatment"*. According to President Bush, this law will allow the CIA to go on with its policy of secret detentions.

December 13, 2006
A federal judge rejects the request in *habeas corpus* of Salim Ahmed Hamdan, on the basis of the fact that the Law relative to military commissions does not allow federal courts to examine this type of recourse.

February 20, 2007
In the case *Boumediene vs Bush,* the Appeal Court considers that, in view of the Law on military commissions, requests in *habeas corpus* on behalf of persons detained in Guantanamo are not within the jurisdiction of federal courts.

March 30, 2007
David Hicks, an Australian national, is the first Guantanamo detainee condemned by a military commission. In view of a preliminary agreement, he pleads guilty of "*material support to terrorism*" and is condemned to nine months imprisonment, which he will serve in Australia (he was freed at the end of December 2007).

June 4, 2007
In the course of a procedure before a military commission, charges against two Guantanamo detainees, the Canadian Omar Khadr and the Yemeni Salim Ahmed Hamdan, are abandoned. They had been qualified "*enemy combatants*" and not "*illegal enemy combatants*" as demanded by the law on military commissions. After an appeal by the government against this decision, the procedures are resumed in November and December.

June 7, 2007
Amnesty International and five other human rights organizations publish a list of 39 persons probably arrested in the framework of the CIA program of secret detentions, whose present situation remains unknown.

June 11, 2007
A group of three judges of the Court of Appeal of the fourth district decides that the military detention of Ali Saleh Kablah al Marri must cease because "*the president does not have the power to order the US army to capture and detain him for an undetermined period*". The Court concludes that Ali Al Marri, who was a legal resident in the United States, benefits from some constitutional freedoms, notably the right not to be deprived of freedom if legal procedures are not respected. Later on, the full Court accepted to re-examine this case, the hearings started on October 31 and Ali Al Marri remains a military detainee for an unlimited period.

July 20, 2007

President Bush signs a decree authorizing and supporting secret detentions. This decree indicates that Article 3 of the Geneva Conventions applies to the CIA program of secret detentions and that this program will be in accord with the international commitments of the United States to the extent that *"the detention conditions and the methods of questioning"* remain within the limitations mentioned in this article.

August 9, 2007

The Pentagon announces that the tribunals in charge of examining the status of combatants have concluded that 14 detainees transferred to Guantanamo satisfied the criteria of *"enemy combatants"*.

October 16, 2007

The Pentagon announces it authorizes a lawyer to visit Majid Khan, one of the 14 persons transferred to Guantanamo from the CIA secret detention centres in September 2006.

Facts and figures about Guantanamo

- Over 800 persons have been detained in Guantanamo since the opening of the camp on 11 January, 2002.

- At the end of 2007, fewer than 300 persons, nationals of around 30 countries, were still detained without charges or judgment. Over one hundred among them were Yemeni.

- US authorities consider that around a quarter of the detainees might be freed or transferred.

- In November 2007, and since 2002, around 470 detainees have been transferred from Guantanamo to other countries (Albania, Afghanistan, Saudi Arabia, Australia, Bahraïn, Bangladesh, Belgium, Denmark, Egypt, Spain, France, Iran, Iraq, Jordan, Kuwaït, Libya, the Maldives, Mauritania, Morocco, Pakistan, Russia, Sudan, Sweden, Tadjikistan, Turkey, Uganda, the United Kingdom and Yemen, among others).

- According to standard estimates, 80 percent of the detainees were isolated in Camp 5, 6 or Echo Camp.

- Camp 6, initially established for 178 detainees, is the hardest one. Detainees are maintained for at least 22 hours a day in individual steel cells without any window opening towards the outside.

- Four Guantanamo detainees, or more, were less than 18 years old when they were arrested.

- At least four detainees committed suicide in Guantanamo in 2006 and 2007. Furthermore, there have been indications of dozens of suicide attempts.

- Some persons were placed in detention in over 10 countries before being transferred to Guantanamo, without any juridical procedure.

- According to an analysis on around 500 detainees, only 5 percent were captured by US forces; 86 percent were arrested by Pakistan forces or by forces of the Northern Alliance in Afghanistan, then delivered to US authorities, often for several thousand dollars.

4. Conclusion

The United States claim that a world respecting norms in matters of human dignity is "the best antidote to the extension of terrorism", and that this is the world to be built. But, as a matter of fact, they have built a camp of prisoners which has become a challenge to human rights and to the state of law.

President Bush should quickly request the closure of the camp and bring to light the obscure network of detention centers of the United States all over our planet. An independent investigation should be initiated on the US policy and practices on the matter of detention and techniques of interrogation, including those that are similar to acts of torture.

The Guantanamo camp has become a symbol of violence, illegality and impunity; it represents a prison system which betrays values dear to the American people and violates international norms on human rights. It is time to close Guantanamo, to shed full light on the network around it, and to cancel the executive order that created the military commissions.

It is our work as activists and world citizens to rise up to this challenge, and it is what we expect from a great democracy: that a strong signal be sent to all governments to show its attachment to the values of human rights, to reaffirm that human rights cannot be dissolved in the war against terrorism, so that barbarism and impunity can be answered by law.

WILLIAM BLUM

FREEING THE WORLD TO DEATH
HOW THE UNITED STATES GETS AWAY WITH IT

This conference is about impunity, which is the exemption from punishment or penalty. The impunity of powerful states—the case of the United States.

It's not just those of us on the left who are concerned about impunity and it's not just the impunity of powerful states. Here is the American Secretary of War, Donald Rumsfeld, in 2002, about six months before the US invasion of Iraq. He was speaking about the American and British flights over Iraq, which had been going on for 11 years, often dropping bombs, often killing Iraqi citizens. Iraq had been firing at these planes for a long time without getting close, but lately they had been getting closer. And Mr. Rumsfeld was very upset. He declared: "It bothers the hell out of me that American and British air crews are getting fired at day after day after day with impunity."

Most Americans would see nothing wrong with that statement. They would not see the irony or the hypocrisy. Most of them would not even have known that the United States had been invading Iraqi airspace and bombing the country since 1991. And most of those who did know about this were convinced that it was all being done at the request of the UN Security Council, when in fact it was just something thought up by Washington and London with no international approval.

This is the main reason that the United States can get away with what it does all over the world—the lack of awareness of the American people about US foreign policy. These Americans are not necessarily stupid, but there are all kinds of intelligence in this world: there's musical intelligence, scientific, mathematical, artistic, academic, literary, and so on. Then there's political intelligence, which might be defined as the ability to see through the bullshit which every society, past, present and future, feeds its citizens from birth on to assure the continuance of the prevailing ruling class and its ideology.

Months after the invasion of Iraq, polls showed that significant portions of Americans believed that Iraq had a direct involvement in what had happened on 11 September 2001, most of them being certain that Iraqis were among the 19 hijackers; most believed that Saddam Hussein had close ties to al Qaeda; more than 40 percent were convinced that weapons of mass destruction had recently been found in Iraq or they were not sure if such weapons had been found; one fourth believed that Iraq had used chemical or biological weapons against American forces in the war; many others were not sure if Iraq had used such weapons.

The public was asked: "If Iraq had no significant weapons of mass destruction and no close link to Al Qaeda, do you think we were misled by the government?" Only half said yes.

Many Americans, whether consciously or unconsciously, actually pride themselves on their ignorance. It reflects their break with the overly complicated intellectual culture of "old Europe". I might also point out that it's a source of satisfaction for them that they have a president who's no smarter than they are.

This, then, is a significant segment of the audience the American anti-war and progressive movements have to reach.

Friedrich Schiller wrote: "Mit der Dummheit kämpfen Götter selbst vergebens." "With stupidity even the gods struggle in vain."

I believe that the main cause of this ignorance about foreign policy among Americans has to do with the deeply-held belief that no matter what the US does abroad, no matter how bad it may look, no matter what horror may result, the United States means well. American leaders may make mistakes, they may blunder, they may even on the odd occasion cause more harm than good, but they do mean well. Their intentions are always noble. Of that Americans are certain. They genuinely wonder why the rest of the world can't see how kind and generous and self-sacrificing America has been. Even many people who take part in the anti-war movement have a hard time shaking off some of this idée fixe; they think that the government just needs to be given a push to return it to its normal benevolent self.

Here is George W. Bush, speaking a month after the attacks of 11 September: "How do I respond when I see that in some Islamic countries there is vitriolic hatred for America? I'll tell you how I respond: I'm amazed. I'm amazed that there's such misunderstanding of what our country is about that people would hate us. Like most Americans, I just can't believe it because I know how good we are."

When I speak before American university students I say this to them: If I were to write a book called *The American Empire for Dummies*, page one would say: Don't ever look for the moral factor. US foreign policy has no moral factor built into its DNA. Clear your mind of that baggage which only gets in the way of seeing beyond the clichés and the platitudes they feed us.

It's not easy for most Americans to take what I say at face value. It's not easy for them to swallow my message. They see their leaders on TV and their photos in the press, they see them smiling or laughing, telling jokes; they see them with their families, they hear them speak of God and love, of peace and law, of democracy and freedom, of human rights and justice and even baseball ... How can such people be moral monsters?

They have names like George and Dick and Donald, not a single Mohammed or Abdullah in the bunch. And they all speak English. Well, George almost does. People named Mohammed or Abdullah sometimes cut off an arm or a leg as punishment for theft. We know that that's horrible. Americans are too civilized for that. But people named George and Dick and Donald go around the world dropping cluster bombs on cities and villages, and the many unexploded ones become land mines, and before very long a child comes by, picks one up or steps on one of them, and loses an arm or a leg, or both arms or both legs, and sometimes his eyesight.

What makes this low level of awareness about foreign policy even worse is that there's no real opposition party in the United States. There are some small differences between the Republicans and the Democrats on domestic issues, but when it comes to foreign policy the two parties are absolutely indistinguishable. They both strongly support American imperialism, at least in practice and are proud of their country's immense military power.

And this is the way it was during the Cold War as well. So you should not make the mistake of thinking that George Bush and his neo-conservatives are unique in the manner in which they relate to the world. Don't think for a moment that no previous American government has ever exhibited such arrogance and deceit, such murderous devastation, violation of international law, and disregard of world opinion.

No, we've seen all this wickedness before, many times. If not packed quite as densely in one regime as it is under Bush, then certainly abundant enough to earn the animosity of millions at home and abroad. A short sample would include Truman's atom bomb and manipulation of the UN that led to bloody American warfare in Korea; Eisenhower's overthrow of democratically elected governments in Iran, Guatemala and the Congo and his unprincipled policies which led to the disaster known as Vietnam; Kennedy's attempts to crush the Cuban revolution and his abandonment of democracy in the Dominican Republic; Ford's giving the okay to Indonesia's genocide against East Timor and his instigation of the horrific Angolan civil war; Reagan's tragic Afghanistan venture and unprovoked invasion of Grenada; Clinton's war crimes in Yugoslavia and vicious assault upon the people of Somalia.

When the United Nations overwhelmingly voted its disapproval of the Grenada invasion, President Reagan responded: "One hundred nations in the UN have not agreed with us on just about everything that's come before them where we're involved, and it didn't upset my breakfast at all." George W. could not have said it better.

For those who think the United States has been shockingly brutal to detainees in Iraq, here's how the US handled them in Vietnam. This is from the New York *Herald Tribune*: "Two Vietcong prisoners were interrogated on an airplane flying toward Saigon. The first refused to answer questions and was thrown out of the airplane at 3,000 feet. The second immediately answered all the questions. But he, too, was thrown out."

It would be difficult to find a remark made today by an American official about Iraq, no matter how illogical, arrogant, lying, or Orwellian, which doesn't have any number of precedents during the Vietnam War period, that constantly had those opposed to that war shaking their heads or rolling their eyes, as we all do now with Bush.

Here is President Lyndon Johnson in 1966: "The exercise of power in this century has meant for all of us in the United States not arrogance but agony. We have used our power not willingly and recklessly ever, but always reluctantly and with restraint."

And here is Vice President Hubert Humphrey in 1967: "I believe that Vietnam will be marked as the place where the family of man has gained the time it needed to finally break through to a new era of hope and human development and justice. This is the chance we have. This is our great adventure—and a wonderful one it is."

Former US Senator William Fulbright, a critic of the Vietnam War, later observed:

> The causes of the malady are not entirely clear but its recurrence is one of the uniformities of history: power tends to confuse itself with virtue and a great nation is peculiarly susceptible to the idea that its power is a sign of God's favor, conferring upon it a special responsibility for other nations—to make them richer and happier and wiser, to remake them, that is, in its own shining image.

Fulbright wrote those words about the Johnson regime in the 1960s, not the Bush regime in the 21st century.

Does anything done by Bush and his neo-conservatives compare to Operation Gladio? From 1947 until 1990, when it was publicly exposed, Gladio was essentially a CIA/NATO/MI6 operation in conjunction with other intelligence agencies and an assortment of the vilest of right-wing thugs and terrorists. It ran wild in virtually every country of Western Europe, kidnapping and/or assassinating political leaders, exploding bombs in trains and public squares with many hundreds of dead and wounded, shooting up supermarkets with many casualties, trying to overthrow governments ... all with impunity, protected by the most powerful military and political forces in the world. Even today, the beast may still be breathing somewhere in Europe. Since the inception of the Freedom of Information Act in the United States in the 1970s, the CIA has repeatedly refused requests for information concerning Gladio, refusing not only individual researchers, but some of the governments involved, including Italy and Austria. Gladio is one of the CIA's family jewels, to be guarded fervently.

The rationale behind it was your standard cold-war paranoia and propaganda: There was a good chance the Russians would launch an unprovoked invasion of Western Europe. And if they defeated the Western armies and forced them to flee, certain people had to remain behind to harass the Russians with guerrilla warfare and sabotage, and act as liaisons with those abroad. The "stay-behinds", as they were called, would be provided with funds, weapons, communication equipment and training exercises.

As matters turned out, in the complete absence of any Russian invasion (surprise, surprise), the operation was used almost exclusively to inflict political and lethal damage upon the European Left, be it individuals, movements or governments, and heighten the public's fear of "communism". To that end, violent actions like those I just mentioned were made to appear to be the work of the Left.

It may be that President Bush is held in such low esteem as much for his character defects as for his policies, for the man comes off as woefully crass, uninformed, insufferably religious, dishonest, and remarkably insensitive.

Bill Clinton, by contrast, could be rather charming and very articulate. This may have helped him get away with bombing the people of Yugoslavia for 78 consecutive days and nights without mercy, that is still regarded by most people, including many on the left, as an act of humanitarianism. And the United States was able to set up the International Criminal Tribunal for the Former Yugoslavia in The Hague. All participants in the war were supposedly subject to this court, but only former Yugoslavians, mainly Serbs, have been indicted.

A group of international law professionals from Canada, the United Kingdom, Greece, and the United States filed complaints with the Hague Court, charging leaders of NATO countries and officials of NATO itself with crimes similar to those for which the court had issued indictments against Serbian leaders. These lawsuits named 68 leaders, including Clinton, Madeleine Albright, William Cohen, and Tony Blair.

Their complaints were ignored for a long time, but they kept the pressure up on the chief prosecutor of the court, Carla Del Ponte. Eventually, in an interview with *The Observer* of London, Del Ponte was asked if she was prepared to press charges against NATO personnel. She replied: "If I am not willing to do that, I am not in the right place. I must give up my mission."

The court then announced that it had completed a study of possible NATO crimes as a response to public concerns about NATO's tactics. The court declared: "It is very important for this tribunal to assert its authority over any and all authorities to the armed conflict within the former Yugoslavia."

This was in late December 1999, and one could wonder if this was a sign from heaven that the new millennium was going to be one of more equal justice. Could this really be?

No, it couldn't. From official quarters, military and civilian, of the United States and Canada, came disbelief, shock, anger, denials ... "appalling", they said ... "unjustified". Carla Del Ponte got the message. Four days after her *Observer* interview appeared, her office issued a statement: "NATO is not under investigation by the Office of the Prosecutor of the International Criminal Tribunal for the former Yugoslavia. There is no formal inquiry into the actions of NATO during the conflict in Kosovo." And there wouldn't be, it was unnecessary to add.

I think what has distinguished the Bush foreign policy from that of its predecessors has been its unabashed and conspicuously overt expressions of its imperial ambitions. They flaunt it, publicly and proudly declaring their intention—nay, their God-inspired *right and obligation*—to remake the world and dominate outer space as well; "full-spectrum dominance", a term coined by the military, well captures the Bush neo-conservatives style and ambition. And they have not hesitated to put their dominance master plans into print on a regular basis, beginning with their now-famous 1992 Defense Planning Guidance, which stated: "We must maintain the mechanisms for deterring potential competitors from even *aspiring* to a larger regional or global role," and in the White House National Security plan of 2002 which read: "To forestall or prevent ... hostile acts by our adversaries, the United States will, if necessary, act preemptively."

"Preemptive" military action is an example of what the post-World War II International Military Tribunal at Nuremberg called "a war of aggression"; the invasion of Poland was a case in point. US Supreme Court Justice Robert Jackson, the Chief US Prosecutor at the Tribunal, said:

> We must make clear to the Germans that the wrong for which their fallen leaders are on trial is not that they lost the war, but that they started it. And we must not allow ourselves to be drawn into a trial of the causes of the war, for our position is that no grievances or policies will justify resort to aggressive war. It is utterly renounced and condemned as an implement of policy.

The Tribunal's final judgment stated: "To initiate a war of aggression, therefore, is not only an international crime, it is the supreme international crime, differing only from other war crimes in that it contains within itself the accumulated evil of the whole."

The bombing and invasion of Afghanistan and Iraq by the US government are wars of aggression and international crimes, but legally and morally no worse than many other US bombings and invasions, such as against Vietnam, Laos, Cambodia, Cuba, Grenada, Panama, and Yugoslavia. Nobody has ever suggested that Serbia was preparing to attack a member of NATO, and that is the only event which justifies a reaction under the NATO constitution.

In recent years, one of the most stunning examples of the United States acting with impunity is the CIA and other American agents carrying out what they call "rendition". These agents have given themselves the right to go anywhere in the world, kidnap anyone they want, while the person is walking to work or on his way home; it could be anywhere, any time, anyone; all laws, domestic or international, be damned. They grab the man, throw him into a car, tie him up, blindfold him, and drive right to an airport to fly him to a country where he will be tortured. And no one dares to stop them. They've done this more than a hundred times, in dozens of countries, and so far the only country to complain angrily about it is Italy, which in June issued arrest warrants against 13 American agents involved in a rendition and asked Washington for "judicial assistance".

One of the most remarkable examples of rendition occurred in Bosnia. In 2001, the United States informed the Bosnian government of an alleged plot by a group of five Algerians and a Yemeni living in Bosnia to blow up the American and British embassies in Sarajevo. The Bosnians held the men for three months, during which time an investigation failed to substantiate any criminal charges against them. In January 2002, the Bosnian Supreme Court ruled that they should be released. As the men left prison, they were grabbed and thrown into waiting unmarked cars by masked men. They wound up at the US prison in Guantánamo Bay, Cuba.

Guantánamo is where one of the American military judges said: "I don't care about international law. I don't want to hear the words 'international law' again. We are not concerned with international law."

Robert Baer, a former CIA officer who was active in the war on terror, has described the renditions as such: "They are picking up people really with nothing against them, hoping to catch someone because they have no information about these terrorist networks."

It's very good news that Italy is complaining about the rendition in their country, but this is a rare exception to the norm. Apart from China, North Korea, Cuba and Venezuela, and to a much lesser extent, Russia, who dares to challenge American imperialism? Who dares to call it by its right name? Who else loudly and strongly and undiplomatically condemns the empire's flagrant abuses of human rights and international law and its plan for world domination? Most Americans are convinced that France is an implacable enemy of US foreign policy. I'm sure you've heard about "french fries" being changed to "freedom fries". But in actuality, in recent years, the French government has given in to Washington on crucial issues more often than not, for example agreeing to compromises in the language of Security Council resolutions which have enabled the United States to pretend that it's gotten approval for its military adventures. In France, Germany and Canada, government officials who said something insulting about George Bush have all been forced to resign. It's hard to imagine an American official being fired because of saying something insulting about Jacques Chirac.

Do you know that the White House arranged for several Republican Party loyalists who are enthusiastic supporters of US foreign policy to be officials at the United Nations? And they have been promoting Bush's political agenda at the UN. Here is one of them speaking to the *Washington Post*: "I came here at the request of the White House. It's my duty to make the UN more effective. My primary loyalty is to the United States of America." He said this despite having taken an oath of loyalty to the United Nations. And of course, making the UN "more effective" means simply making it cooperate more with the aims of US foreign policy.

Has France or any other country complained about this subversion of the UN? Did France or any other country vehemently condemn the US and the UK for 12 years of flying over and bombing Iraq? The United States can act with impunity because the opposition from other governments and from the UN is as weak as from the Democratic Party in the US. And I would urge all of you who live here in France to put more pressure on your government to take a strong moral stand against Washington's continuing crimes against humanity. Such statements by foreign governments are actually reported in the American media, and when that happens even arrogant neo-conservative government leaders can be put on the defensive.

Although in general, the American media is not much help in challenging their government's impunity.

For example, I do not think there was a single American daily newspaper that unequivocally opposed the US bombing of Iraq in 1991.

Nor a single American daily newspaper that unequivocally opposed the US bombing of Yugoslavia in 1999.

Nor a single American daily newspaper that unequivocally opposed the US bombing of Afghanistan in 2001.

Nor a single American daily newspaper that unequivocally opposed the US bombing of Iraq in 2003.

In a supposedly free society, with a supposedly free press, with about 1500 daily newspapers, it should be very unlikely that this is the case. But that's the way it is.

Much of what I've discussed here this evening is the result of the so-called War on Terrorism. I say "so-called" because the War on Terrorism is primarily a means for expanding the American empire.

If I were the president, I could stop terrorist attacks against American targets in a few days. Permanently. I would first apologize—very publicly and very sincerely—to all the widows and the orphans, the impoverished and the tortured, and all the many millions of other victims of American imperialism. Then I would announce that America's global interventions—including the awful bombings—have come to an end. And I would inform Israel that it is no longer the 51st state of the union but—oddly enough—a foreign country. I would then reduce the military budget by at least 90% and use the savings to pay reparations to the victims and repair the damage from the many American bombings and invasions. There would be more than enough money. Do you know what one year of the US military budget is equal to? One year. It's equal to more than $20,000 per hour for every hour since Jesus Christ was born.

That's what I'd do on my first three days in the White House. On the fourth day, I'd be assassinated.

PASCAL BONIFACE

THE STRATEGY OF THE "CLASH OF CIVILIZATIONS"

I will comment on the strategy of the clash of civilizations within which all events presented so far take place, including Guantanamo and the war in Iraq. This strategy leads us to a dead end and accounts for the dead end in which we are today in terms of international security.

Going somewhat backward in time, let me start with a joke made by one of the advisers of Gorbachev, Serguei Arbatov, in 1987 at a time where an East-West cleavage still existed and when the world still turned around the axis which separated Moscow and Washington. Arbatov had told a close adviser of Reagan: "We are going to give you the worst of services, we are going to deprive you of an enemy". He developed the view that empires exist only through opposition to each other and that if the United States no longer had enemies, it would be obliged to completely redefine its alliances, its strategies, its foreign policies and that it would have huge difficulties. Arbatov had just underestimated two or three things, and notably, the future of the Soviet Union. For him, the fact that the United States would no longer have enemies meant that the Soviet Union was going to adopt a cordial and peaceful position with regard to the United States and that their relations would be transformed from détente to entente. Détente was still the opposition of two systems. Entente would have meant that, in the name of common interests going from the preservation of the environment to the battle against nuclear over-armament, which were credos of Gorbachev, Moscow and Washington would establish pacified relations of cooperation. In that spirit, depriving the United States of an enemy meant the adoption of a policy of cooperation, and certainly not the end of the Soviet Union. The latter was a huge surprise for all strategists, including me, and all political actors: the idea was still that the Soviet Union was an impassable horizon and that the internal contradictions of the system were not sufficient to provoke its end.

As a consequence, a reconstruction of the strategic landscape took place. We were accustomed to a bipolar world. Of course, some actors had tried to get out of this bipolar framework, France and others in the world, but it was nevertheless with respect to this East-West structure that everyone determined their policies. And the question which thus arose at the time of the end of the Soviet Union was whether one would go from a bipolar world to a multi-polar world or to a world with only one pole, and also if we would finally enter into a world without war. To the extent that the Cold War, the East-West opposition, was the main threat to international security, would the end of one of the actors in this confrontation allow one to envisage the end of major conflicts and hence pacified relations? One has to remember that in these already old times, in 1991, a president of the United States was celebrating a new order in the world within which problems of international security would be managed by the United Nations Organization, an organization, he said, relieved from the Cold War constraints, which would finally be able to act in the way its founders had hoped. This president was George Bush, but not William. He was Bush Senior, and he indeed made references to the major role of the United Nations in problems of collective security, and therefore to a new order in the world in which law would replace the use of force. This is rather ironic when one sees what the son has later done.

The debate on a multi-polar world or not is not quite part of this talk. But let me just say one word about it. At that time, one rather believed in a multi-polar world: Russia, without the constraints of communism, would certainly be efficient economically, would put its economic and human capacities and its natural resources to the benefit of a sound management, and development should follow. The converse occurred under the non-linear conduct (in all meanings) of Boris Yeltsin. One also believed Japan would continue along the same lines as before: on the contrary, Japan entered into what has been called the lost decade. While at the end of the '80s, one used to say about Japan what is now said about China, with books titled "The coming war with Japan" similar to the books titled "The coming war with China" more recently, Japan entered into a period of hibernation. What about Europe? One then believed it was going to launch a great redefinition, but there were all the European contradictions of which we are all aware in the '90s.

Let me consider the question of the enemy. Arbatov was even more right than he believed in his prediction and the United States has been quite embarrassed by the absence of an enemy at the end of the '80s. Of course, there has been Iraq. There were debates on that question but I was personally in favor of the resolution of the United Nations requesting Iraq to withdraw from Kuwait. The use of force is questionable, but Iraq had committed a major violation of the Charter of the United Nations by annexing Kuwait. Of course we all know that the actual reason for the intervention was not the defense of the Kuwaiti democracy, that the major threat attributed to Iraq, presented as the fourth military force in the world, was pure manipulation of information intended to make more necessary a total solidarity around the US alliance to combat this huge Iraqi threat: there is no glory to vanquish without danger.

With this background of the Gulf War, the theme of the "South threat" appeared, a threat which is a kind of strategic draft of the clash of civilizations. During that period of the years '90, '91, '92, and its immediate continuations, there was much talk about this threat. This had several advantages. The first one was that there was no need to change the strategic and tactic schemes. What was khaki is now painted in the color of sand, what was oriented towards the East, the turrets of the tanks, is reoriented towards the South. In that way, a South threat replacing the threat coming from the East, is presented. And if there is a South threat as important as was the East threat, the same military budgets must be conserved, the same strategic alliances, and one must conserve a protector which will come to the rescue of countries in the North of the Mediterranean Sea which are not able to defend themselves against that threat.

Among the intellectual swindles at a strategic level, the South threat was a huge one. It was so huge that it finally only lasted a few years, whereas the clash of civilizations, which is also a big swindle, has lasted for a longer time. The South Threat, what was it? Nobody, even the most rightwing people among the rightwing politicians, ever envisaged a total union of all countries of the third world, from Tunisia to Indonesia, from Haiti to Senegal, ready to swoop down on the rich countries of the North. Nobody, even among those most inclined to war, has ever presented such an apocalyptic and really delirious tableau. Well, of course, when one said "South", what did one mean? This was a politically correct and strategically incorrect way to disguise what one believed was the true threat: that coming from the countries south of the Mediterranean Sea. And when people were speaking about the South threat, this is what they had in mind at that time.

Then, it was noticed that the Muslim world was not as united as that, and the war in Iraq, supposed to support the thesis of the South threat, was by itself an illustration that it did not work that way, since that war was an inter-Arab war at the beginning: indeed, an Arab country, Iraq, attacked another Arab country. This was not the war of Arab countries which would together attack Lampedusa, Marseille or Barcelona. Hence, the totally illusory character of all that appeared clearly. But I believe we must now remember that this went to the point that a General Secretary of NATO, Mr Willy Claes (who was obliged to resign but for other reasons, for having accepted money he should not have accepted when he was Minister of Defense) declared that NATO should have new functions and should take care of the *outside zone*. What was called the outside zone meant outside the European zone, outside the NATO countries. At that time, this led to strong protests inside the latter. In fact, NATO said: "No, NATO is only defensive, it is only the defense of European countries and of the United States. The soldiers of NATO do not have to go outside". Today, we see that Willy Claes, strongly condemned at that time, was in actual fact a precursor and his wishes have been fulfilled in Iraq and Afghanistan. There are soldiers of NATO, as such, in these countries, and nobody protests against it, in the name, of course, of the war against terror, in places where, hardly twelve years ago, it would have been totally unimaginable and inconceivable to send them. Hence, we see that the scenarios which are totally refused at a given time nevertheless take place in the long run, that there is a logic to all that, that finally the South threat, even though it was so much contested intellectually, nevertheless remains a little in the facts and that Willy Kresse had made the mistake of claiming loudly what some of the planners of NATO already had in their minds, but it was then too early to say it publicly.

It is precisely at this stage that the famous article by Huntington on the clash of civilizations comes. This article would have a tremendous effect. It gave rise to a book which would become a best seller, even more after September 11. Huntington is a realistic republican and not at all a neo-conservative. He is rather in the line of traditional and rather internationalist US rightwing politicians. What does he say? He says that the paradigm of wars has changed. With the French Revolution, national wars succeeded the wars between princes or kings of the 17th and 18th centuries that were rather limited in terms of numbers of deaths (when Louis the 14th made war, only some thousands of soldiers were involved). This was not really a progress since the notions of an armed nation and conscription are such that entire nations are put on the battlefield and the number of deaths increases exponentially. Then, in the 20th century, it is the turn of ideological wars, communism against capitalism, Nazism and Fascism against both of them, together. And after 1947, it is the time of the Cold War, East against West. The disappearance of the East and the changes at the global level now yield, he says, a new type of conflict, conflicts between civilizations.

He defines seven or eight: the occidental civilization, the Slavic orthodox one, the Muslim one, the Confucian one in China, the Japanese, African, Latino-American (he cites Africa among civilizations but does not care much about it). And he says that the horizon changes: ideology can be changed but civilization is what we are, one does not change it. The question is not: which side do we choose, but who we are. In that way, the conflict becomes an essential one and one cannot change his side in the course of the party.

Why is it that this article received such a tremendous echo? It corresponded to a strong social need, which was to find a way, which had been lost, to "read" the conflicts. Previously everything was simple, even though there were national determiners: from the guerrilla in Nicaragua to wars in Angola, everything was viewed as an East-West problem. This was both true and largely exaggerated, but there was a way of reading at the disposal of people. Che Guevara was speaking of one, two, three...one hundred Vietnams. There was a common way of reading conflicts that took place in any part of our planet. Each one of course had its own special national roots, but there was always a thread which, directly or indirectly, took us back to Moscow or Washington. With the end of the Cold War, this general reading, which was so convenient to explain all conflicts, was lost. Then Huntington came and gave us an alternative recipe: you have lost your universal way of reading, I give you another one. And this came at the right moment since, from the war in Iraq to the Balkan wars, it allowed one again to explain everything: we have a war in Iraq because the Muslim world contests occidental supremacy and the occidental world must protect itself against this challenge to its supremacy. And, when Europe is surprised to see that a real, atrocious war is taking place again on its own ground, whereas there had been no such war from 1947 to 1991, and whereas the Cold War was over, Huntington explained wars in Yugoslavia according to his way of reading: the war is between Slavic Orthodox, Catholic and Muslim people who battle against each other. In the end, this is always the division between the Occidental and Oriental Roman empires, with the further involvement of Muslims. And everybody will start to analyze this thesis.

The paradox with Huntington's thesis is that it is certainly the most contested among theses, but also the most present: there is not a single conference today on strategic questions without discussions on the clash of civilizations, even when it is to express disagreement. Seldom has so contested a thesis been so much developed. Hence, whether one likes it or not, the strategic agenda is fixed by Huntington, the intellectual debate has been around his thesis for now around twelve years, even when it is to refute it.

Then, what should we think about this thesis? On the one hand, it does not correspond to actual conflicts: if one considers all of them, one sees that nine out of ten (at least) of real and not imagined conflicts take place within given civilizations and not between civilizations. This is also true for conflicts that have developed after Huntington's theory. Concerning African conflicts, this is true from the Rwandan genocide to the Africa of the lakes, and the same is true for the Latino-American conflicts. Similarly, the two hot problems of our planet, China-Taiwan and the two Koreas, take place inside the same civilization. Of course, there is the first Gulf War, but here also one sees that it pits Iraq against Kuwait and, against Iraq, there is, of course, the United States but also Saudi Arabia, Egypt and Syria. Hence this is really a political conflict and not one civilization against another. Conflicts of that period therefore do not correspond to that scheme which actually appears as pure imagination outside the strategic reality. It does not correspond either in intellectual terms to what can be reasonably conceived.

The big flaw in Huntington's thesis is to present a deterministic reading of history, to think that there should necessarily be a conflict between the Muslim world and the occidental world because the Muslim world contests occidental supremacy. I believe we will all agree that history is not written in advance by an invisible hand. History is above all what human beings, peoples, leaders, do: one cannot say there will be no conflicts but one cannot say either that there will be conflicts. Therefore, in the end, there are these two major mistakes in Huntington's thesis. For some people, this is great, we have a way of reading, an explanation for the contemporary international relations, hence we have to be prepared for a conflict with the Muslim civilization, and in such a situation, it's best to make the first strike since war is unavoidable. It's best is to strike when they are still weak and cannot protect themselves too much, before they become stronger. And the consequences are clearly seen even though, curiously (and this deserved to be noticed), Huntington himself condemned the war in Iraq and publicly regreted his vote for Bush in 2000. In contrast to others, he actually voted differently and condemned the war in Iraq, saying that it would only stir up the hatred of the Muslim world against the occidental one. But in spite of that, one clearly sees where the intellectual scheme he proposed is leading.

But there is also another mistake made more and more frequently, and I would say that it is embodied in some way by George Bush or Berlusconi (it is a little different for Tony Blair): this is to say, no, there is no war of civilizations, we refute this thesis, civilizations are here to understand each other, but then to follow a policy which in practice leads to it. And this is exactly what the present Bush administration is doing. On the one hand, it says: we are friends of the Muslim world, the United States respects all religions and civilizations, and it presents a discourse hostile to the clash of civilizations. But in practice what do we see? Huntington himself says it: a political imperial practice which directly leads to this clash of civilizations by various means, such as the war in Iraq or Guantanamo. It amounts to spreading oil on the fire, and it increases the clash of civilizations. And the new concept of war against terror, the third stage of the rocket in my view, still worsens the situation.

The South threat was so ridiculous that it did not last long in intellectual circles. In France, only the Front National bought this type of discourse. It was so stupid intellectually that nobody believed it. For the clash of civilizations, it is somewhat different. One might say that, if the South threat was the type of speech that might be heard in a pub, the clash of civilizations belongs to the tearoom: it is much more elegant, it is intellectual, it is a conversation in a salon, it does not have the crude character of the South threat. It amounts roughly to the same thing and is in the direct line of the South threat but, since it is intellectual, it has nevertheless been discussed for over twelve years. But now, it appears to be a little worn.

And the war against terror comes to replace it. In this new scheme, the war is against terror and it allows one to claim that it is not against Muslims, that it is not directed against the Arab, or Muslim, civilization but against the Arab or Muslim terrorists whose first victims would be the Arab or Muslim people. The new slogan is to speak of green fascism. With this false distinction, people come and say, with their hand on their heart, that they make a separation between the wheat and the chaff, between the good Muslims who support the war against terror, and the bad terrorists. Because things are necessarily binary: those who are not with us are against us. This is the new trap and this trap is linked, or at least has an intellectual relation to the clash of civilizations. One will say: who is in favor of terror? Nobody, of course. Hence, if you are against terrorism, you are for the war against terror.

The trap of a policy which leads to what we see today is clear: it is an endless war. The war against terror is just like the quest for the horizon: the closer you come towards it, the farther away it is. This applies at least to the way the war against terror is carried out by George Bush. The advantage of such an endless war is that it reinforces the power of the neo-conservatives both internally and internationally. On the internal level, what was the best argument of George Bush in 2004 for getting really elected that time? He was the president of a nation involved in a war and one does not change the team when there is such a war. And his challenger was embarrassed because he had approved the war in Iraq and had difficulties in presenting an alternative program. In contrast to others who claim to be experts on the United States, I am personally convinced that Dean had better chances against Bush because at least he represented a true alternative. At the international level, if there is this war against terror, a Fourth World War according to another formula, which succeeds World War II and to the third one represented by the East-West conflict, then one has to be patient: defeats today announce the victories of tomorrow. As a parenthesis, if there is a larger and larger gap between the Muslim world and the United States, and as a matter of fact also between the European people and the United States, it may be useful to question our so-called common values. For me, Guantanamo or Abu Ghraib are not common values. They are not values at all and we do not share them, without speaking of the many other exactions.

To go on with my analysis, if we are now involved in a fourth world war, one might consider that it is not tragic: there was Pearl Harbor but at the end, the war was won, and even if there is a defeat in Iraq, the war will be won at the end. Mainly, if there is this war against terror, or this fourth world war, we must unite behind the chief since the United States is the only one able to conduct it. Hence minor differences that we might have with the US hyper-power are less important than the survival of occidental society and the preservation of public freedoms. Therefore, we should not think too much, but rather blindly follow those who conduct the war and express our solidarity with them.

Where this type of discourse leads us is clear: not only into a trap (it is always possible to get out of a trap), but rather into an abyss. The way to conduct this war against terror amounts to nourishing it endlessly and this is an endless motion. Look at what is said about Al Qaeda: every day an important leader is eliminated. It looks like a Mexican army: every day there is an arrest or elimination of a leader and Al Qaeda apparently still exists. Because the way this war is conducted leads to new terrorist vocations each day. Because when you do what has been done in Fallujah or elsewhere, look: the British officials do not say so, but the authors of the bomb attacks in London claimed they acted in that way after seeing cassettes of what takes place in Iraq. It might be said they were or were not well integrated but they obeyed their visions of these events. At the same time, this also serves the interest of those who conduct this war against terror because, since it has no end, it reinforces solidarity with them.

As a conclusion, we are not in a trap but in a hole that has been dug. Some people in favor of force always refer to Churchill and claim that those opposed to this "war against terror" are neo-Vichysts, unable to resist. Churchill did appeal to combat but he also had a formula that neo-conservatives should meditate: "When one is at the bottom of the hole, it is preferable to stop digging".

—

MICHAEL PARENTI

RULERS OF THE PLANET
THE REAL REASONS FOR
THE US INVASION OF IRAQ

It is not enough to condemn US policy in Iraq and elsewhere, we must also try to understand it. Having demonstrated that the official explanations are false—Iraq had no weapons of mass destruction, Saddam had no links to al Qaeda, he was not building nuclear weapons—do we conclude that the U.S. policy of invasion and occupation is simply "misled," "mistaken," "based on faulty intelligence"? I am not one of those who thinks that U.S. foreign policy is stupid and riddled with folly and ignorance. I believe it is brilliantly ruthless and frequently triumphant. More often than not, it succeeds in its goal which is to keep the world safe for the giant investor cartels. I shall explain this as we go on.

To understand US global policy, we should devote some attention to the massive contradictions between what US leaders say and what they actually do. They long have professed a dedication to democracy, yet over the last half century or so they have devoted themselves to overthrowing democratic governments in Guatemala, Guyana, the Dominican Republic, Brazil, Chile, Uruguay, Syria, Indonesia (under Sukarno), Greece (twice), Argentina (twice), Haiti (twice), Bolivia, Jamaica, Yugoslavia, and other countries. These governments were all guilty of pursuing policies that occasionally favored the poorer elements and infringed upon the more affluent. In most instances, the US-sponsored coups were accompanied by widespread killings of democratic activists.

US leaders have supported covert actions, sanctions, or proxy mercenary wars against revolutionary governments in Cuba, Angola, Mozambique, Ethiopia, Iraq (with the CIA ushering in Saddam Hussein's reign of repression), Portugal, South Yemen, Nicaragua, Cambodia, East Timor, Western Sahara, and elsewhere.

US interventions and destabilization campaigns have been directed against other populist nationalist governments, including Egypt, Lebanon, Peru, Iran, Syria, Zaire, Venezuela, the Fiji Islands, and Afghanistan (*before* the Soviets ever went into the country).

And since World War II, direct US military invasions or aerial attacks

118

or both have been perpetrated against Vietnam, Laos, Cambodia, Cuba, the Dominican Republic, North Korea, Yugoslavia, Lebanon, Grenada, Panama, Libya, Somalia, and Iraq (twice).

There is no "rogue state," "axis of evil," or communist country that has a comparable record of such criminal aggression against other nations.

Be it a social democratic coalition government as with Allende in Chile or Arbenz in Guatemala; or a populist nationalist one like Iran under Mossadegh; or a Marxist-Leninist government as in Cuba and Vietnam; or even a right-wing nationalist government as Iraq under Saddam Hussein—all had one thing in common, a desire to reclaim some portion of the land, natural resources, capital, labor, and markets that have been preempted by local plutocrats and giant foreign corporations.[1]

In contrast, US leaders have been markedly supportive of dictatorial capitalist client-states like Chile (under Pinochet), the Philippines (under Marcos), Iran (under the Shah), Zaire (under Mobutu), Peru (under Fujimoro), apartheid South Africa, autocratic Turkey, feudal Saudi Arabia and feudal Kuwait, and other autocracies like Turkey, Pakistan and Nigeria. In short, Washington policymakers are less critical of democracy's mortal enemies than of capitalism's democratic opponents.

*****

US intervention in Africa is a story in itself. Through the World Bank, and the IMF, US leaders have demolished African economies, including their public health and education sectors. Most African nations have sunk into a debt structure that leaves them in peonage to Western investors. US leaders also have fueled eleven wars on the continent, resulting in the death of some seven million people, with millions more facing malnutrition, starvation, and a deepening poverty. Washington has given arms and military training to 50 African countries (out of a total of 53), helping Africa to become the most war-torn region in the world. During the 1990s alone, 32 African countries experienced violent conflict.[2]

The more war ravaged and poverty stricken are the African nations, the more ready they are to sell their labor and natural resources at rockbottom prices to U.S. investors and other western interests. Asad Ismi reminds us that almost 80 percent of the strategic minerals that the USA requires are extracted from Africa, including cobalt, platinum, gold, chromium, manganese, and uranium, ingredients needed to make jet engines, automotive vehicles, missiles, electronic components, iron, and steel.[3]

Africa also accounts for 18 percent of US oil imports (as compared to 25 percent from the Middle East), with new reserves yet to be tapped. The African continent in toto has been designated a vital interest area to the United States. Plans are in progress to build new US naval and military bases on the continent. And according to the African Oil Policy Initiative Group (composed of representatives from the Bush Administration, the oil industry, Congress, and some foreign consultants), Washington intends to establish a regional military command structure in Africa "which could produce significant dividends in the protection of US investments."[4]

Across the entire world, US policymakers have fueled the military capacities of cooperative capitalist nations. In 2004, worldwide arms sales by the United States to other countries was about $40 billion, much of it going to nations like Saudi Arabia that do not even remotely maintain a democratic facade. Since World War II the US government has given over $240 billion in military aid to arm, train, and support some 2.3 million troops and internal-security forces in more than eighty countries, not to defend these nations from outside invasion—since relatively few have ever been threatened by attack from neighboring countries—but to protect ruling oligarchs and multinational corporate investors from the dangers of domestic insurgency.

How can we determine the purpose of this military aid? By observing that:

• US-supported military and security forces and death squads in these various countries have been used repeatedly to destroy popular reformist movements and insurgencies within their own borders that advocate some kind of egalitarian redistributive politics.

• US sponsored forces have never been used to assist a popular reformist, let alone revolutionary, movement in any of these nations.

• The regimes most likely to win US favor are those that are integrated into the global system of neoliberal corporate domination, that leave their economies open to foreign penetration on terms that are singularly favorable to transnational investors.

• The regimes that are targeted as anti-West or anti-American are most likely to be committing the sin of egalitarian reform and national self-definition. And when there are no longer any leftist reformist governments to compete against, US globalists begin competing against other capitalist powers.

*****

US leaders have long struck a defensive pose: America is besieged by menacing opponents; we have no choice but to maintain this enormous military apparatus. In reality, far from having their backs to the wall, US policymakers have been pursuing total world domination.

This policy has been explicitly enunciated by a right-wing think tank called Project for the New American Century (PNAC). A lengthy report of September 2000 entitled *Rebuilding America's Defenses* lays out PNAC's vision for US global control, including a huge boost in military spending, an unwillingness to be bound by the restraints of previous treaties or any international law, and a dramatic expansion of a US military presence and use of force around the world.[5]

Not only did the PNAC report serve as a blueprint for the Bush Administration, but many of PNAC's members became White House policymakers, including Vice President Dick Cheney, Secretary of Defense Donald Rumsfeld, Deputy Secretary of Defense Paul Wolfowitz (now head of the World Bank), and Undersecretary of State John Bolton (now US ambassador to the United Nations). Numerous other PNAC members came to occupy important posts in the Bush Administration, mostly in the Defense and State Departments.[6]

The goal of the PNAC plan is to take full advantage of America's unparalleled ability to maintain the United States "as the world's preeminent power." The intent is anything but defensive. Every means of coercion and domination is to be assiduously pursued. *Rebuilding America's Defenses* even hints that the United States might develop biological weapons "thát can target specific genotypes" in order to "transform biological warfare from the realm of terror to a politically useful tool."

The PNAC report bemoaned the fact that US public opinion might not go along with a totalistic global policy unless it felt under attack from "some catastrophic and catalyzing event—like a new Pearl Harbor." In another of those seemingly fortuitous happenings that work so well for the plutocracy, the 11 September 2001 attacks on the World Trade Center and the Pentagon served as just such a catastrophic catalyst.

The role played by the Bush Administration before and during 9/11 is still a subject of some controversy. The White House ignored repeated warnings proffered by the intelligence agencies of eleven other nations regarding an impending attack. A month before the attacks, one FBI agent wrote about a plan afoot to crash into the Twin Towers; that report was ignored.[7]

In the year before 9/11—as legally required—the US military launched fighter planes on at least 67 occasions to chase suspicious aircraft or airliners that had moved significantly off their flight plan. But on 11 September itself, in the almost two hours during which the four airliners were hijacked and the attacks occurred, not a single US fighter plane was scrambled.

President Bush's own behavior suggests cover-up.

• He unsuccessfully opposed the formation of an independent bipartisan commission (set up by Congress) to investigate the events around 9/11.

• He then tried to appoint former US Secretary of State Henry Kissinger to head the investigation, a man whose entire career had been devoted to dissembling and misleading the public.

• Bush then refused to hand over numerous documents requested by the commission. Meanwhile US National Security Adviser Condeleeza Rice refused to testify and Bush did not order her to cooperate with the commission.

• Finally, he and Vice-President Cheney refused to appear before the full commission, agreeing only to a one-hour secret meeting with the two commission heads, and refusing to testify under oath.

What did they have to hide?

*****

After 9/11, and in keeping with the PNAC plan, Bush took a number of momentous steps:

First, he announced a "war on terrorism," inviting all the nations and organizations of the world to get in lockstep behind his administration, declaring: "Either you are with us or you are with the terrorists." Heretofore all other countries were to be categorized as either *cooperative* (accepting US hegemony) or *adversarial* (not letting US leaders have their way in all things). Any recalcitrant nation ran the risk of being targeted for US attack.

Second, the White House declared that it would not be bound by any previous treaties or accords. International law was now nothing but an irksome restraint that the world's only superpower would brush aside whenever it wanted.

Third, Bush announced the US withdrawal from the Anti-Ballistic Missile Treaty. The nuclear arms race was to resume, and the USA would win it handily by establishing total domination of land, air, sea, and outer space.

Fourth, Bush removed the United States's signature from the treaty establishing the International Criminal Court. The court was a wonderful step taken by many nations to prosecute leaders and operatives of any nation who violated the human rights of others. Instead US leaders pressured various countries to grant immunity from prosecution for all US governmental and military personal.

Fifth, the White House announced its right to wage preemptive war against any nation it disliked. Various countries were fingered as being on Uncle Sam's hit list—some of the same ones as listed in the PNAC plan: Iraq, Iran, North Korea, and Syria for starters.

Sixth, war was pursued in Afghanistan, and major military bases were established in several other Central Asian states.

Seventh, a war of conquest was launched against Iraq. The PNAC plan, published a full year before the September 2001 attacks, shows that the Bush Administration had intended to take military control of the Gulf region whether or not Saddam Hussein was still in power. Since then the

Downing Street paper reveals that Bush and Blair both intended to hit Iraq, regardless of the case that was confected against Saddam Hussein.

Eighth, the White House embarked upon a massive escalation in military spending, including almost $200 billion spent on the Iraq venture. Given the enormous deficit that resulted from this kind of spending and tax breaks, Republicans called for cuts in the domestic budget, specifically such frivolous luxuries as health care for the elderly, disability assistance, environmental regulations and protections, old-age pensions, and public education. So the Empire feeds off the Republic.

The PNAC plan envisions a strategic confrontation with China, and a still greater permanent military presence in every corner of the world. And today television reports and articles are appearing in the mainstream U.S. media talking about how China is emerging as a serious competitor to the United States and might pose a menace to us.

Seen in this larger context, the war in Iraq is not a failure. True, an insurgency has arisen that was not anticipated. Things may be going poorly for the US soldiers in that country and for the US taxpayers who must pay more and more on the war.

But Iraq is not a disaster for the US plutocracy: they now have their hands on the largest oil reserve in the world (except for Saudi Arabia), 113 billion barrels of fine crude, $5 trillion dollars worth, the biggest oil grab in history. All competing contracts held by Russia, France, and other countries have been canceled.

The Iraq economy has been privatized, deregulated, and impoverished. Its statist development no longer looms as a bad example to other countries in the region who must learn to tread the free-market path, as Iraq is learning.

And there are about 70 US corporations contracted by the US government to do business in Iraq, all of them pulling in fat profits. Even the Pentagon admits that it cannot account for as much as a third of the money that has been spent in Iraq. So Iraq is not such a disaster if you are pocketing huge sums of money off the bloody venture.

*****

The objective of US global policy is not just power for its own sake but

• power to control the world's natural resources and markets,

• power to privatize and deregulate the economies of every nation in the world,

• power to prevent alternative self-defining, self-developing economic models from arising,

• and power to hoist upon the backs of peoples everywhere—including Europe and North America—the blessings of an untrammeled global "free market," The end goal is to insure not merely the supremacy of global capitalism, but the supremacy of an *American* global capitalism. And this is to be achieved by preventing the emergence of any other potentially competing superpower or, for that matter, any potential regional power such as Iraq.

The US "war on terrorism" would be better recognized by its real name: *imperialism*, a U.S. dominated free-market imperialism.

ENDNOTES

[1] For evidence of these various cases, see these several books of mine: *Against Empire* (City Lights,1995); *To Kill a* Nation (Verso,2000) *The Terrorism Trap* (City Lights 2002) and the writings of James Petras, Gregory Elich, William Blum, and Chalmers Johnson.

[2] Asad Ismi, "Ravaging Africa," *Briarpatch*, February 2003.

[3] Ismi, "Ravaging Africa."

[4] Dena Montague, "Africa: The New Oil and Military Frontier," *Peacework*, October 2002; also Ismi, "Ravaging Africa."

[5] Gregory Elich, "Imperial Enterprise: War Mongers Run Amuck," *Swans*, March 17, 2003, www.swans.com.

[6] Other PNAC members in top positions in the Bush Administration: Richard Perle, Eliot Cohen, Devon Cross, Stephen Cambone, Richard Armitage, Lewis Libby, Don Zakheim, and William Kristol.

[7] Michael Meacher in *Guardian* (UK), 6 September 2003; also *Daily Telegraph* (UK), 16 September 2001; and *Newsweek*, 20 May 2002.

PART II

HUMANITARIAN LAW: LEGAL AND MORAL VALUES TO DEFEND

DANIEL IAGOLNITZER

INTERNATIONAL LAW RELATIVE TO WAR AND THE UNITED STATES
A GENERAL SURVEY

Introduction

This article aims to present a survey of international law and justice relative to war, and of the way they are applied. The international law under consideration here includes the general principles of the United Nations and its role to maintain or restore peace, and a major part, called International Humanitarian Law, which fixes rules to be respected regardless of the legality or legitimacy of the cause defended: it aims to protect persons who do not, or no longer, participate in the combat, prohibits or limits some methods of war and some weapons, and establishes means to judge persons responsible for war crimes (as well as crimes against humanity and genocide), universal jurisdiction of national courts and international tribunals.

Rules of international law are outlined in each section, with mention of the record of the United States and other aspects of direct relevance to its case. More details, deeper analyses and various viewpoints will be found in other contributions to this book.

Humanitarian law in armed conflicts has preceded the prohibition of wars of aggression. Though the existence of laws or customs of war is older, it has been mainly developed in various treaties since the middle of the 19th century. Section 1 outlines its evolution up to World War II with, in particular, the 1863 *Lieber Code* promulgated by President Lincoln in the United States and the 1899 and 1907 Conventions of The Hague which e.g. prohibit "the attacks or bombardments of towns, villages, habitations or buildings which are not defended" and the use of arms causing unnecessary suffering.

After World War II, new developments took place under the aegis of the ICRC, International Red Cross Committee and in the context of the United Nations. The 1949 Geneva Conventions and their 1977 additional Protocols, under the aegis of the ICRC, are presented in Section 2. They introduced in particular "grave breaches" or war crimes to which universal jurisdiction must apply, such as torture, inhuman treatment and unlawful confinement (1949 Conventions), and attacks and bombardments that target civilians or may cause grave civilian losses in the 1977 Protocol I. The latter, not ratified by the United States, is a major advance for the protection of civilian populations, as well as for the recognition of organizations resisting occupation or of national liberation organizations.

Universal jurisdiction corresponds to the idea that grave breaches concern the whole humanity: each State party to the Conventions or the Protocol "shall be under the obligation to search for persons alleged to have committed or to have ordered to be committed grave breaches, and to bring them, *regardless of their nationality,* before its own courts. It may also hand them over for trial to another Party provided the latter has made out a prima facie case". The way it is or is not applied will be discussed, in relation in particular to the United States.

Section 3 describes the system of the United Nations, its organization and general principles. Wars of aggression are prohibited in its 1945 Charter and are the first of the "international crimes" of the Nuremberg Principles recognized by the UN General Assembly, with war crimes and crimes against humanity. The 1948 Convention on Genocide and 1968 Convention stating that no statutory limitations will apply to these crimes are also mentioned.

The Charter delegates the main responsibility for maintaining or restoring peace and security, possibly through military force, to the Security Council. Wars issued from or linked with its resolutions are outlined and discussed in Section 4, where recent evolutions such as possible interventions in internal conflicts, in opposition to the principle of sovereignty of States, and the "international responsibility to protect populations" are also discussed.

International tribunals are presented in Section 5 and their actions are discussed. The Security Council has established tribunals for ex-Yugoslavia and Rwanda in the 90s. Other recent tribunals with international character, e.g. for crimes committed in Sierra Leone or by the Khmer Rouge regime in Cambodia, but not for the crimes committed by the United States in its Indochina wars, will also be mentioned.

The International Criminal Court (ICC), presented in Section 6, is a permanent court competent so far to judge the most serious war crimes, crimes of genocide and against humanity. Established by the 1998 Rome Treaty between States, it is nevertheless linked to the United Nations and may initiate investigations upon request of the Security Council, whether States concerned have ratified its Statute or not. It has initiated actions to date in several African countries. Its Statute, ratified so far by 105 countries, reinforces the provisions of previous treaties in various respects, but has weakened others, such as those concerning attacks causing grave civilian losses, in favour of powerful countries. To date, the United States has not ratified it.

Finally, specific conventions and treaties on weapons are outlined in Section 7. They prohibit biological (1972), chemical (1993) and a few conventional weapons (such as mines, 1980-97), and fix the (theoretical) goal of nuclear disarmament (Non-Proliferation Treaty, 1968). The present situation, in relation in particular to the United States, will be discussed.

All texts mentioned can be found on the sites www.icrc.org of the ICRC and www.un.org of the United Nations. The present article is a condensed version of (part of) the book *International Law and War* by this author.

1. Humanitarian Law: from the middle of the 19th century to World War II

War has long been considered as a regrettable but "natural" way of solving conflicts that could find no other resolution. A basic idea of the second part of the 19th century is that, in the period of civilization supposedly reached by humanity, suffering should be avoided as much as possible and one should not inflict it for pleasure or revenge, but only if there is "military necessity". A first approach has concerned the protection of wounded soldiers on the battlefield, with a first Geneva Convention in 1864, and later the protection of prisoners and of civilians in the hands of a party to the conflict. It will be developed after World War II in the 1949 Geneva Conventions. A second one, outlined below, has aimed to prohibit methods and arms which inflict superfluous injury, and to protect populations against the hostilities. It will be developed in the 1977 Geneva Protocols.

The *Lieber Code* (1863), promulgated in the United States by President Lincoln during the civil war, is the first attempt to codify laws of war. If there is "military necessity", it considers it lawful to bombard towns, with or possibly without previous warning, or to starve populations "in order to get a speedier subjection of the enemy". Such practices will be largely prohibited later by humanitarian law, but are still used to some extent by the United States.

However, the Code also introduces important prohibitions, including torture:

> Military necessity does not admit of the infliction of suffering
> for the sake of suffering or revenge, nor of wounding except
> in fight, nor of torture to extort confessions. It does not admit
> of the use of poison in any way or of the wanton devastation
> of a district... (Art. 16).

The record of the United States in that respect since 1945 is well known: for torture, one may look to Iraq or Guantanamo, for poison to its "chemical war" in Vietnam from 1961 to 1971 (large-scale use of weed-killers containing dioxin, a poison with consequences still present today), and there have been many murders, as well as the devastation of districts in its wars. Revenge for Pearl Harbor and the Japanese treatment of US prisoners was one of the arguments President Truman used to justify atomic bombings of civilian populations in 1945.

The Code gives some protection to prisoners (but not to deserters), and considers it unlawful "to give no quarter" during the fight ("except when the situation makes it impossible to cumber oneself with prisoners"). The private unarmed citizen "is to be spared in person, property, and honor...as much as the exigencies of war will admit".

The 1868 *Declaration of Saint-Petersburg*, ratified by 20 (mainly European) countries, is the first international agreement prohibiting the use of some weapons, in the present case some types of bullets. It also opens the way to further advances:

> the progress of civilization should have the effect of alleviating the calamities of war, the only legitimate object States should endeavor is to weaken the military forces of the enemy; it would be exceeded by the employment of arms which uselessly aggravate the sufferings of disabled men, or render their death inevitable...

The 1899 and 1907 *International Peace Conferences of The Hague* have led to a new codification of the laws of war with a number of conventions or declarations ratified by 20 to 50 countries each. A third Peace Conference had been planned for around 1914-1915... Besides prohibitions that had become traditional, such as killing or wounding an enemy who has surrendered, or "to declare that no quarter will be given", we note the following:

> The attack or bombardment of towns, villages, habitations or buildings which are not defended is prohibited" (Article 25 of Conventions II or IV, of 1899 or 1907)

Massive bombings of towns, which caused tens or hundreds of thousands of civilian victims each, were carried on by countries which had ratified this text, in particular by the United States in 1945. Can one argue that these towns were defended? The bombings reached essentially habitations which were not. Any ambiguity, if there was one, would be removed in the 1977 Geneva Protocol I, not ratified by the United States.

It is especially forbidden to employ arms, projectiles, or material of a nature to cause unnecessary suffering (Article 23 of Convention II of 1899).

Specific weapons are explicitly prohibited: "poison or poisoned arms" (also prohibited in the *Lieber Code*; poison is an old taboo in the history of humanity); "projectiles, the sole object of which is the diffusion of asphyxiating or deleterious gases" (hence asphyxiating gases were already prohibited with, however, a technical restriction); and "bullets which expand or flatten easily in the human body, such as bullets with a hard envelope which does not entirely cover the core or is pierced with incisions" (also called "dum-dum" bullets from the name of the locality in India where the British army produced them).

In spite of the limited number of States parties and of a clause according to which the provisions cease to be binding if a non-contracting State joins one of the belligerents, the Peace Conferences of The Hague are an important development of humanitarian law. Today their general provisions are largely considered to have become part of the customary law of war and thus that all states are bound by them.

The emotion caused by the use of asphyxiating gases in World War I led to the 1925 Geneva *Protocol for the prohibition of the use of Asphyxiating, Poisonous or Other Gases, and of Bacteriological Methods of Warfare*, which extends the provisions of The Hague mentioned above and has been ratified by 134 countries. It would be completed by further conventions after World War II on biological and chemical weapons (see Section 7)

2. Geneva Conventions (1949), additional Protocols (1977) and universal jurisdiction

The Geneva Conventions I to III improve previous ones on the protection of wounded or sick combatants, on earth or at sea, and of prisoners. Convention IV, new in 1949, concerns the protection of civilians in the hands of a party to the conflict or of an occupying power (a first project in that direction had been established in 1934 under the aegis of the ICRC and should have been examined by an international conference planned for 1940...) The Conventions apply mainly to international conflicts. They introduce, in particular, so-called "grave breaches":

wilful killing, torture or inhuman treatment, including biological experiments, wilfully causing great suffering or serious injury to body or health, unlawful deportation or transfer or unlawful confinement of a protected person, compelling a protected person to serve in the forces of a hostile Power, or wilfully depriving a protected person of the rights of fair and regular trial, taking of hostages and extensive destruction and appropriation of property, not justified by military necessity and carried out unlawfully and wantonly.

These grave breaches are submitted to the universal jurisdiction of national courts to be discussed in more detail later in this section. The common Article 3 of the conventions also states rules for internal conflicts that are similar to those above, but are more restrictive and without the notions of grave breaches and universal jurisdiction.

The additional Protocols I and II of 1977 apply respectively to international and internal conflicts. Protocol II is again more restrictive. Protocol I specifies that "armed conflicts which peoples are fighting against colonial domination and alien occupation, and against racist regimes in the exercise of their right of self-determination" are included among the international conflicts it applies to. It has been ratified so far by 167 countries with the exception of the United States (as well as India, Pakistan or Israel). The primary European countries (France, Germany, Italy, Spain and United Kingdom) ratified it with non negligible reservations, in particular on nuclear weapons or on attacks inflicting grave civilian losses. Grave breaches of the Protocol, also described as war crimes, to which universal jurisdiction is extended, include in particular:

i) making the civilian population or individual civilians the object of attack.

The presence of isolated non civilians "does not deprive the population of its civilian character".

ii) launching an indiscriminate attack affecting the civilian population or civilian objects in the knowledge that such attack will cause loss of life, injury to civilians or damage to civilian objects...excessive in relation to the direct and concrete military advantage anticipated.

The Protocol includes also a number of other prohibitions (which are not included among grave breaches), among which are indiscriminate attacks in general (attacks that are not or cannot be directed towards a specific military objective and might also reach civilian targets).

Guerrilla warfare
Organizations which fight against colonial domination or alien

occupation are recognized by Protocol I. While only States can become actual Parties to the Protocol, they can, if they wish (Art. 96), officially declare acceptance of its provisions to its depository. (Since there is not much interest in practice in so doing, no one has done it so far. Palestine had asked to become an actual Party to the Protocol, but was not accepted as such.)

Prohibitions of the Protocol (which are not grave breaches) include "the use of the presence or movements of the civilian population to render certain points or areas immune from military operations". The presence of guerrilla fighters or weapons within the population is sometimes considered as an infraction of this prohibition. However, the Protocol adds that any violation "shall not release other Parties to the conflict from their legal obligations with respect to the civilian population and civilians".

The Protocol also prohibits killing, injuring or capturing an adversary "by resort to perfidy", namely "acts inviting the confidence of an adversary to lead him to believe that he is entitled to, or is obliged to accord, protection under the rules of international law in armed conflict, with intent to betray that confidence". Moreover, the use to that purpose "of the distinctive emblem of the red cross, red crescent or red lion and sun or of other protective signs recognized by the Conventions or this Protocol" is listed as one of the grave breaches.

Among other instances of perfidy, which are not grave breaches, the Protocol cites: "the feigning of civilian, non-combatant status". According to some interpretations, a suicide attack carried out e.g. in a civilian car against a military vehicle of the enemy would therefore be an act of perfidy If the attacker has not clearly indicated in advance that he was a combatant... This interpretation does not seem in accord with the general definition of perfidy.

The Protocol insists on respect for the distinction between civilians and combatants ("In order to promote the protection of the civilian population, combatants are obliged to distinguish themselves from the civilian population while they are engaged... in a military operation... "). However, taking into account guerrilla warfare, it adds:

> Recognizing, however, that there are situations in armed conflicts where, owing to the nature of the hostilities, an armed combatant cannot so distinguish himself, he shall retain his status as a combatant, provided that, in such situations, he carries his arms openly... A combatant who falls into the power of an adverse Party while failing to meet the requirements set forth shall forfeit his right to be a prisoner of war, but he shall, nevertheless, be given protections equivalent in all respects to those accorded to prisoners of war...

According to the reporter of this text, the purpose is to "conform to the reality (of guerrilla warfare), while at the same time giving the guerrilla fighter an incentive to distinguish himself from the civilian population where he reasonably could be expected to do so".

If attacks against civilian persons or populations, as such, are always war crimes, according to the Protocol, in the course of an armed conflict, attacks against military targets are not, except if they are carried in the knowledge they may cause excessive civilian losses or are carried by perfidy through the use of well defined protective signs (Red Cross...). They are also prohibited, without being war crimes, in some further situations. In all cases, including attacks against civilians, persons responsible for such acts may be judged for their acts, but must benefit from the general protections granted by the Conventions and Protocol.

The Case of the United States

On torture and inhuman treatment, the United States claims either that the "terrorists" are not covered by the 1949 Geneva Conventions or that the US authorities are not responsible: when contraventions occur, a few subordinates are prosecuted by the US justice under pressure of public opinion when the facts are too blatant. On attacks inflicting civilian losses, the present official policy is to reject attacks against civilians or civilian populations "as such" but permit bombardments when the presence of the enemy is suspected within the population, and massive destruction of civilian infrastructures inflicting civilian losses which are most often excessive in relation to the *direct and concrete* military advantage that can be anticipated. They are thus war crimes according to the 1977 Protocol I. In view of the systematic nature of such methods, persons responsible are the top leaders of the United States.

There are also a number of direct murders of civilians in all recent US wars, from Indochina to Latin America, Iraq and Afghanistan. In a few cases, persons responsible are judged before US military tribunals. One subaltern was judged and condemned to prison for the My Lai murder of hundreds of civilians in Vietnam (one of the many murders of this type)... and he was quickly released. In Iraq, some soldiers responsible for the murder of around 20 civilians (as a revenge for the death of one of them in an ambush) are presently being tried (US authorities had at first, as usual, claimed that the civilians killed were "terrorists").

Universal jurisdiction

Universal jurisdiction is addressed in the common Articles 49, 50, 128, 146 of the 1949 Conventions I to IV respectively, cited in our Introduction. It is extended to the new grave breaches of the 1977 Protocol I in its Article 85.

In its large (*a priori* natural) sense, it should be applied by national courts of State parties independently of the place where the crime was committed and of the nationality and residence of the suspects or of the victims. It is also found, with some variations, in other treaties such as the 1984 UN Convention prohibiting torture (which requests the presence of the suspect in the country). It is also largely considered that it should also apply to crimes against humanity in times of peace or war.

States most often do not apply it. One argument against doing so is the diplomatic immunity of heads of states or other officials, often considered as a customary law which prevails. This view is partly confirmed in a 2002 judgment of the International Court of Justice (ICJ) of the United Nations (see Section 3), in a case opposing Belgium and Congo (a Belgian tribunal had emitted a warrant for arrest against a Congolese Minister of Foreign Affairs, for official acts in Congo). According to that judgment, heads of states or of governments and ministers of foreign affairs must freely represent their country and hence must benefit from such an immunity in other countries for all their official acts, even after they have left office. This is *a priori* contradictory to the Nuremberg Principles and to those of other international tribunals (see Sections 3, 5 and 6), but the ICJ judgment adds these officials might be prosecuted in their own country or precisely before international tribunals.

In spite of this judgment, it is largely considered that universal jurisdiction should apply, at least after persons concerned have left office, both for heads of states or of governments and ministers of foreign affairs and *a fortiori* to other officials.

On the other hand, States often consider they cannot apply their international commitments without prior adaptation of their national law. Often, many did not do it. It is also often considered that universal jurisdiction can be applied only in a restrictive sense: if the suspect is present in the country, or if the victims are nationals of the country. Finally, States rightly consider that it is primarily the role of the national justice system of the suspect to prosecute him. However, this is not realistic when the main persons responsible are top officials. Sentences against a few subordinates are then abusively used to justify inaction against their superiors.

There are various possibilities for applying universal jurisdiction in some countries, and there have been a few applications meeting with limited success. We mention below the case of three European countries (there are also possibilities e.g. in Canada or Spain)

Belgium had adopted in 1993 a law on universal jurisdiction in its large sense, for grave infractions of the Geneva Conventions and Protocol I. It was extended in 1999 to crimes against humanity. However, Belgium totally changed its law in 2003 after a complaint was lodged against the US General Franks for crimes in Iraq, and the resultant pressure from the United States. It is now restricted to cases in which e.g. suspects live in Belgium.

Germany has adopted universal jurisdiction in its 2002 Code for crimes close to those defined in the Statute of the International Criminal Court (see Section 5). A complaint was lodged in 2004 against Donald Rumsfeld, then US Secretary of Defence, and other US officials for crimes committed in Iraq. However, it was rejected: the German judge considered that US justice was taking care of these problems...A new complaint was then lodged at the end of 2006, after Donald Rumsfeld left the US government. It has again been rejected...

Universal jurisdiction can be applied in France for the crimes defined in the UN 1984 Convention on torture and in a few other cases, if the suspect is present in France. A Mauritanian officer was arrested, released for diplomatic reasons, but judged and sentenced in his absence in 2004, for acts of torture in Mauritania. A complaint has also been lodged in 2001 against the Head of State and other officials of Congo-Brazzaville, after many people, coming back to this country in 1999 after a civil war, disappeared. Congo-Brazzaville asked the ICJ to order the cessation of the procedure in view of diplomatic immunity, the French government answered that the immunity of the Head of State was guaranteed by French law, and the procedure is still going on after various episodes.

More recently, in October 2007, a complaint was also lodged in France against Donald Rumsfeld, present at that time in Paris. In contrast to the case mentioned above (but the United States is not a weak African country), it was rejected after the French Ministry of Foreign Affairs wrote that Donald Rumsfeld should benefit, "by extension", from the immunity recognized by the ICJ for heads of states or of governments and ministers of foreign affairs.

Independently of the obstructions by States for diplomatic and political reasons, a number of general questions can be raised about universal jurisdiction, mainly if is applied only by a small number of countries. It might be used abusively (e.g. for political reasons) or might appear inappropriate (e.g. if complaints are lodged against some suspects in the former colonizing country). International tribunals might appear a better solution. However, in view of the present limitations of the latter (see Sections 5 and 6), universal jurisdiction remains very valuable: complaints lodged in various countries against US officials, at least after they left office, would not allow them to travel to these countries. This would already be a strong signal against impunity.

3. The United Nations: Charter, organization and general principles

The Charter of the United Nations (1945) starts with the famous formula: "We, the peoples of the United Nations, determined to save succeeding generations from the scourge of war..., to reaffirm our faith...in the equal rights of men and women *and nations large or small*..." It confirms the equality and sovereignty of nations and excludes any threat or use of force of one country against another one: "All Members shall refrain from the threat or use of force against the territorial integrity or political independence of any State". The Nuremberg principles confirmed by the General Assembly (see below) will introduce aggression as the foremost of international crimes.

The Charter indicates that "Nothing shall authorize the United Nations to intervene in matters which are essentially within the domestic jurisdiction of any State". However, it adds: "but this principle shall not prejudice the application of enforcement measures under Chapter VII", entitled "Action with respect to Threats to the Peace, Breaches of the Peace and Acts of Aggression". Enforcement measures of Chapter VII may include military force. It *a priori* refers to threats or breaches of peace between States. However, the notion of "threat against the peace" might also apply to internal conflicts within a State, according in particular to recent evolutions, if they are considered to be a threat to international peace and security, in opposition to sovereignty. This is e.g. the justification given in resolution 1203, mentioned in Section 4, of the Security Council with respect to the problem of Kosovo, which was *a priori* an internal problem of Serbia as recognized by the Council itself. This large interpretation is in particular promoted by the United States when it finds it useful for its own interests.

The "international responsibility to protect populations" in cases of genocide, crimes against humanity and other crimes has also been recently reaffirmed in particular in two resolutions of the Security Council in 2006. These questions are discussed in Section 4.

The *General Assembly* may discuss any questions or any matters and "may make *recommendations* to the Members or to the Security Council or to both" (our italics). It may establish various commissions (Disarmament Commission, International Law Commission, Peace-building Commission, Human Rights Council,...) Through its resolutions, it is at the origin of various recommendations to the Security Council, which the latter does not always follow, and of conventions submitted for the ratification of States, which are sometimes ratified only by a small number of States even when they had been adopted by the General Assembly.

The *International Court of Justice* (ICJ) makes decisions in any conflict submitted by States, if they accept its jurisdiction: the United States does not. Each Member of the United Nations "undertakes to comply with decisions of the Court in any case to which it is a party". Another role of the Court is to give an advisory opinion on any legal question upon request of the General Assembly or of the Security Council. We will come back to this on several occasions.

The *Security Council* is the main organ concerning international security and peace. In fact:

> In order to ensure prompt and effective action, the Members
> confer on the Security Council primary responsibility for the

maintenance of international peace and security. They agree that in carrying out its duties under this responsibility the Security Council acts on their behalf.

The Council is presently composed of 15 members, including 5 permanent ones (United States, United Kingdom, France, Russia and China) and 10 others elected every two years by the General Assembly. Its decisions "shall be made by an affirmative vote of nine members including the concurring votes of the permanent members", more precisely "of *all* permanent members" in the French, equally official, text: a *positive* vote of all permanent members is thus *a priori* needed. However, in practice, a resolution is rejected only by a negative vote, and not by abstention, of a permanent member (see the Korea War in Section 4 in that respect).

Under Chapter VII, the Council may decide any measures it will judge appropriate to "maintain or restore international peace and security", including military operations. To that purpose, "all Members undertake to make available armed forces, assistance, and facilities". Plans for the use of armed force have to be made by a Military Committee established by the Security Council and "responsible under this Council for the strategic direction of any armed forces at the disposal of the Council". We will see how this has been applied in Section 4.

Nuremberg Principles and other texts

In 1946, the General Assembly of the United Nations affirmed the validity of the *Principles of International Law recognized by the Charter of the Nuremberg Tribunal* (the military tribunal which judged the primary Nazi criminals). These principles, reformulated in 1950 by the International Law Commission, define international crimes whose authors must be punished: crimes against peace, war crimes and crimes against humanity. Crimes against peace are: "Planning, preparation, initiation or waging of a war of aggression or a war in violation of international treaties, agreements or assurances" and complicity in the latter. War crimes are close to the "grave breaches" of the 1949 Geneva Conventions. Crimes against humanity include "Murder, extermination, enslavement, deportation and other inhuman acts done against any civilian population, or persecutions on political, racial or religious grounds, when such acts are done or persecutions carried on in execution of or in connexion with any crime against peace or any war crime". Complicity is also a crime under international law.

The fact that a person acted "as Head of State or responsible Government official" or "pursuant to order of his government or of a superior" "does not relieve him from responsibility" (provided, in the second case, "a moral choice was possible to him").

The *Convention for the Prevention and Punishment of the Crime of Genocide*, adopted by the General Assembly in 1948, has been ratified by

140 States, with non-negligible reservations in particular by the United States. Genocide refers to acts committed with intent to destroy, in whole or part, a national, ethnical, racial or religious group as such. Conspiracy, incitement or attempt to commit it, as well as complicity, should also be punished.

The 1968 *Convention on Non-Applicability of Statutory Limitations to War Crimes and Crimes against Humanity* has been ratified only by 51 States but not by any permanent member of the Security Council apart from Russia. It states that "no statutory limitation shall apply to the following crimes, irrespective of the date of their commission": war crimes and crimes against humanity in time of war or of peace, as defined in the Nuremberg Principles (particularly the grave breaches of the 1949 Geneva Convention), as well as genocide and "eviction by armed attack or occupation and inhuman acts resulting from the policy of apartheid".

4. Wars issued from, or linked with resolutions of the Security Council and "humanitarian" military interventions

Besides sending forces to various countries to maintain peace, or interposition forces, with the agreement of governments concerned, the Security Council has adopted resolutions which have directly or partly led to a number of wars against some countries. We mention some of those which have been particularly intense and involved the United States, and discuss their character with respect to the Charter, regardless of any judgment of the political regimes of the countries involved and on the problems at stake.

The war against North Korea and the 1991 war against Iraq were justified by acts of aggression by those states, or were presented as such, and followed precise resolutions of the Council. The NATO 1999 war against Serbia and the recent US war in Iraq were also linked with resolutions by the Council, but in a more indirect way: resolutions by the Council under Chapter VII had addressed demands to Serbia and Iraq respectively, with the implicit (Serbia) or explicit (Iraq) statement that grave consequences would follow if these demands were not satisfied. There was no further resolution deciding the use of military force. The US war against Afghanistan was initially launched on the basis of "self-defense". It was later authorized in a resolution of the Council.

The UN war against North Korea (1950-53) was decided by the Security Council after a war, whose primary responsibility is attributed to the North by Western sources, had started between North Korea and South Korea. The legality of this UN war can be questioned on two grounds. First, the Soviet Union, a permanent member, was absent (as a protest against the non recognition of the new communist Chinese government by the United Nations), whereas a positive vote of *all* permanent members was *a priori* requested by the Charter: see Section 3. On the other hand, this action was an intervention in a civil war (the division of Korea, linked to the surrender of the Japanese army to US and Soviet troops in South and North respectively, was in principle temporary; South and North would separately become UN members only in 1991). A large number of war crimes were committed on each side, in particular by US troops. The United States conducted the military operations by decision of the Council.

The 1991 UN war against Iraq followed Iraq's invasion of Kuwait, which had been a British protectorate up to 1961 and (after its independence) had been admitted as a UN Member in 1963, though it was claimed by Iraq as one of its districts. A large number of war crimes were committed, in particular by US troops, including intense bombardments of civilian targets during the first weeks of the war, as well as against people running away to escape the advance of US troops at the end of the conflict.

The 1999 war against Serbia, in relation with Kosovo, was not conducted by the United Nations, but by NATO in opposition to the Charter. The October 1998 resolution 1203 of the Council, under Chapter VII, had requested Serbia to respect various agreements, including air verification missions over Kosovo by NATO. The Kosovo conflict was an internal one in Serbia, but the Council had decided it was a threat to international peace and security. There was no subsequent resolution authorizing the military operations conducted by NATO against Serbia in 1999 outside the United Nations framework, so this war was largely illegal. There was no condemnation; instead, a further resolution of the Council in May 1999 ratified the consequences of the war and the presence of NATO troops in Kosovo "to guarantee its autonomy and the rights of its population". In order to give some satisfaction to Russia, a permanent member, it also reaffirmed that Kosovo was part of Serbia, a part of the resolution which does not seem to be respected in view of recent events.

In the course of the 1999 bombings, Serbia had requested the UN International Court of Justice to order the cessation of the attack and the condemnation of NATO countries, with indemnities for losses. A judgment took place only in 2004. Concerning the United States, there was no possible examination: it does not accept the jurisdiction of the Court. Concerning other NATO countries, it was decided that Serbia was not clearly a UN Member after the end of the ex-Yugoslavia (there were arguments either way), so that the complaint by Serbia could not be accepted...

The US war against Iraq in 2003 is also linked to the previous resolution 1441 (in 2002) of the Council, under Chapter VII of the Charter, demanding the destruction of its supposed weapons of massive destruction. One could not be sure of the exact situation at that time, but it was obvious that Iraq did not represent a threat against peace after having undergone years of inspections, bombings and embargo. As is well known, the United States did not submit a new resolution on the use of force in view of the opposition of several members of the Council, including France, a permanent member.

Instead, it decided that the previous resolution was sufficient. The illegality of the war is again confirmed by the fact that it was not conducted within the UN framework, but in opposition to the rules of the Charter.

Once more, the United Nations did not condemn that war. On the contrary, the UN force of interposition at the border between Iraq and Kuwait was removed, and the US occupation of Iraq was officially ratified by the Security Council in a further resolution. Intense war crimes, torture, inhuman treatments, bombings causing grave civilian damages,..., were committed by US forces and their allies, without any condemnation.

The present war in Afghanistan followed the events of 11 September 2001. The United States launched that war with their allies on the basis of Article 51 of the Charter authorizing self-defense. Later, a resolution of the Council authorized Western troops, now under NATO command, to pursue their military operations in Afghanistan "in order to ensure the security of the country". The legality of that war is questionable both because it is not conducted within the UN framework and because it has aimed not only to seek the persons responsible for the September 11 events, but also to establish a new government in Afghanistan.

"Humanitarian" military interventions

Military interventions so far for claimed humanitarian purposes lead to some perplexity. In Rwanda in 1994, the United Nations military force present to protect the population (following previous events) remained passive during the genocide. Later on, when the government of Rwanda responsible for the genocide was defeated in the war against the "Rwandan Patriotic Front", France (which had given direct military support to the Rwandan government before and even during the genocide: see Section 5) carried out the military "Operation Turquoise" with the accord of the Security Council: its claimed goal was humanitarian but it had also other purposes and served to protect persons responsible for the genocide.

More generally, the selective character of these interventions gives rise to consternation. The humanitarian problem of Kosovo did exist in 1999, but did not have the acute character of many other crises in the world, internal conflicts in which a minority requests its rights or its independence such as the Kurds in Turkey, a country allied to the United States, or the occupation of a country (Palestine), etc. The war against Serbia had other reasons and better results might have been achieved in other ways.

After having given other pretexts, the United States presented the 2003 war against Iraq as humanitarian—to liberate the Iraqi people from dictatorship and "establish democracy", or to contribute to the "war against terror" and hence to the freedom of humanity as a whole. Similar arguments are given to justify the war in Afghanistan, whereas democracy should follow from internal evolutions since foreign interventions only reinforce the very extremist groups they supposedly combat.

An example of an intervention totally outside the UN framework, thus illegal but on the legitimacy of which there are various opinions, is the invasion of Cambodia by Vietnam in 1979, which overthrew the Khmer Rouge regime. On the one hand, it also had nonhumanitarian purposes; on the other hand, the Khmer Rouge regime had been responsible for large scale murders and other actions which had led to an acute humanitarian crisis and one to two million victims, according to sources. There was no intervention in any form by the United Nations (just as is the case with US wars). Non-military interventions by the United Nations or by some countries before 1979 might have been useful.

Such non-military interventions were made in September and October 2007 in the case of Myanmar, where peaceful protests against the military government had been brutally repressed. Though these internal events did not have the gravity of those in Cambodia mentioned above, the UN Secretary General decided on non-military actions to remedy the situation and requested (non-military) interventions by several countries from the region. The United States had expressed a desire for stronger actions, including military ones, even though these events were not a threat to international peace and security.

Recently, a military intervention had been envisaged against Sudan in relation with the Darfur crisis. This was in particular the idea of Bernard Kouchner, French Minister of Foreign Affairs (since June 2007), who had previously supported the 2003 US war against Iraq and the 1999 NATO war against Serbia. This idea has been abandoned to the benefit of a new UN military interposition force for the protection of populations, accepted by the Sudanese government at the end of 2007. Several NGOs had emphasized the complexity of the problems, expressed strong doubts about a war, and had insisted on the need to separate military and humanitarian actions.

To conclude, international law allows military interventions, even in the absence of the accord of the governments involved, but only by the United Nations and in the case of grave internal events that represent an imminent danger for the populations and a threat to international peace and security. Military interventions outside the UN framework are prohibited. The fact that permanent members of the Security Council, like the United States, are themselves responsible for some of the gravest wars of aggression and war crimes leads to some consternation regarding its possible decisions which have so far been selective in favor of their own interests.

5. Special international tribunals

The Security Council has established two ad hoc special tribunals:

i) the International Tribunal for the Prosecution of Persons Responsible for Serious Violations of International Humanitarian Law Committed in the Territory of the Former Yugoslavia since 1991, established in 1993; and

ii) the International Criminal Tribunal for the Prosecution of Persons Responsible for Genocide and Other Serious Violations of International Humanitarian Law Committed in the territory of Rwanda and Rwandan citizens responsible for genocide and other such violations committed in the territory of neighboring States, between 1 January 1994 and 31 December 1994, established on November 8, 1994.

The Council declared in both cases that " the situation continues to constitute a threat to international peace and security", and that it is therefore "determined to put an end to such crimes and to take effective measures to bring to justice the persons who are responsible for them", and "is convinced that in the particular circumstances, the prosecution of persons responsible for serious violations of international humanitarian law would enable this aim to be achieved and would contribute to the process of national reconciliation and to the restoration and maintenance of peace".

The crimes within the jurisdiction of the Tribunal for ex-Yugoslavia include the grave breaches of the 1949 Geneva Conventions and other "violations of the laws and customs of war", as well as crimes of genocide and against humanity. The list of war crimes does not include all grave breaches of the 1977 Protocol I, but includes e.g. the prohibitions of The Hague of "attacks and bombardments of towns, villages, habitations or buildings which are not defended". Nevertheless, its Prosecutor, after probable pressures from the United States, refused to investigate the bombardments committed by the US army against undefended civilian targets during the 1999 NATO war against Serbia. On the other hand, doubts are expressed about the impartiality of the tribunal which mainly prosecuted Serbs, even though it also prosecuted other persons from Croatia or Bosnia. The prosecutions were often largely justified, for instance those against Serbs responsible for the murders in Srebenica. There are various opinions on the degree of responsibility of the former Serbian government and of its president Milosevic (who died in prison) for the crimes committed by the Serbs of Bosnia. Responsibility is linked to the military support of Serbia. The International Court of Justice judged in 2007 that Serbia was not responsible for genocide in relation to Srebenica.

The crimes within the jurisdiction of the Tribunal for Rwanda include crimes of genocide and against humanity, and those of the 1977 Protocol II; 27 persons were sentenced between 1994 and 2006 (including the first sentence of an international tribunal for genocide). The question of the implication of France, which had given military support to the government of

Rwanda before and during the genocide, is raised by some NGOs. Others regret the absence of any action against officials (now governing the country) of the Rwandan Patriotic Front, also suspected of war crimes (different, however, from genocide). The tribunal should stop its work soon, so that some suspects should be judged before some European courts or sent back for judgment to Rwanda as proposed at the end of 2007. Several NGOs have expressed their opposition, considering that the rights of defense would not be guaranteed there.

Other special tribunals with international character

The *Special Court for Sierra Leone* was established in 2002 by an Agreement between the United Nations and the government of Sierra Leone to judge "persons who bear the greatest responsibility for serious violations of international humanitarian law and Sierra Leonean law committed in the territory of Sierra Leone since 30 November 1996." A terrible civil war had started in 1991. In 1996, an Agreement for Peace was signed between the government and its opponents, but the latter resumed hostilities and took soldiers of the United Nations force present to maintain peace as hostages. The tribunal was created after the capture of their leader. Crimes within its jurisdiction include crimes against humanity, those of the 1977 Protocol II, attacks against civilian persons or populations as such, or against humanitarian assistance or peacekeeping missions, conscripting or enlisting children under the age of 15 years, and crimes under Sierra Leonean law, such as abusing small girls.

The former president of neighboring Liberia, Charles Taylor, was arrested in 2006 in Nigeria where he had been a refugee since 2003. He is suspected of a primary responsibility for the crimes committed in Sierra Leone in view of his support to its opponents. His judgment started in 2007 and continues in 2008 after an interruption requested by the defence. According to some sources, the United States have some responsibility in the wars in Sierra Leone and Liberia. It has traditional economic interests in these countries and its companies benefited in various ways from the war.

Among other recent tribunals, one may cite the tribunal created in Cambodia to judge the leaders of the former Khmer Rouge government (responsible, as already mentioned in Section 4, of one to two million victims, according to sources). This tribunal, established by a 2004 Cambodian law, includes both national and international judges. It started its work in 2006 and the primary Khmer Rouge leaders still living were arrested at the end of 2007. No official tribunal has so far been envisaged to judge the crimes of the United States in Vietnam, or in Cambodia and Laos, which probably caused an even much larger number of victims (several millions in Vietnam, 300,000 to 700,000 in Cambodia itself, according to sources, due to US bombings during the period of the Lon Nol government established by the United States, which was defeated by the Khmer Rouge organization.

6. The International Criminal Court

The ICC Statute, which entered into force in 2002, has been ratified so far by 105 States. The ICC is intended "to exercise its jurisdiction over persons for the most serious crimes of international concern" and to "be complementary to national criminal jurisdictions" which should judge their nationals apart from the gravest cases. Universal jurisdiction is not mentioned: its possible place in the new ideal system of international justice to be established with the ICC is subject to various interpretations. Crimes within the jurisdiction of the Court include war crimes, crimes of genocide and against humanity and might include crimes of aggression "once a provision is adopted defining the crime". The responsibility of officials and of persons acting pursuant to orders of superiors is confirmed and "the crimes within the jurisdiction of the Court shall not be subject to any statute of limitations".

The Court may exercise its jurisdiction for crimes committed after 2002 (or after a State has ratified its Statute). On the other hand, it may exercize it only upon request of the Security Council, or if at least one of the States concerned (the State where the acts have been committed or of which the person accused is a national) has ratified its Statute or declares it accepts its jurisdiction. It may act upon request of a State or the Prosecutor may himself decide to initiate an investigation. The Security Council may stop actions of the Court under some conditions (Article 16). The definitions of crimes of genocide and against humanity within its jurisdiction are close to those of previous conventions (see our Section 3). They are completed to take into account the historical evolution of crimes committed

War crimes include those of the 1949 Geneva Conventions. Those of other treaties such as The Hague Conventions and the 1977 Protocol I are modified in a way presented and discussed in more detail below, in the part of that section on attacks causing civilian losses.

The Court has intervened so far in African countries which ratified its Statute (Congo, Uganda, Central African Republic), and also against Sudanese officials (for crimes committed in Darfur) upon request of the Security Council (Sudan did not ratify the Statute). Requests concerning these officials have not been accepted so far by the Sudanese government.

The ICC cannot exercise its jurisdiction for war crimes such as those committed by the United States in Iraq since the United States and Iraq have not ratified its Statute and have not declared acceptance of its jurisdiction (this is not a surprise in view of US control of the present Iraqi government). The same is true concerning Israel and Lebanon in relation to the 2006 war: the fact that Lebanon did not declare acceptance of the jurisdiction of the

Court may be surprising in view of the violence of the Israeli attack. It is probably due to the influence of the United States on the present Lebanese government, which would also be pleased to get rid of Hezbollah, the official target of Israel. Note, however, that Hezbollah itself did not want any intervention of the ICC, suspecting its partiality (see also remark at the end of this section in this connection). Concerning Chechnya, it is officially part of the Federation of Russia, which has not ratified the Statute of the Court and has not declared acceptance of its jurisdiction.

The Prosecutor might have solemnly asked all governments concerned to accept the jurisdiction of the Court, even with little chance of success. He did not do it. On the other hand, it would also have been possible for him to initiate investigations concerning crimes committed in Afghanistan (which has ratified the Statute) by the US army, or in Iraq by the British army (the United Kingdom has ratified the Statute). He has refused to do it in spite of requests from some NGOs.

Attacks causing civilian losses in the ICC Statute

Intentional attacks against civilian population or persons "as such" is again a war crime in the ICC Statute. However, the precision of the 1977 Protocol I according to which the presence of isolated noncivilians does not deprive the population of its civilian character is not reproduced. On the other hand, the list of war crimes now includes:

- "Attacking or bombarding towns, villages, dwellings or buildings which are undefended *and are not military objectiv*es"

- "Intentionally launching an attack in the knowledge that such attack will cause incidental loss of life or injury to civilians or damage to civilian objects ...which would be *clearly* excessive in relation to the concrete and direct *overall* military advantage anticipated".

Words put in italic by us introduce ambiguities which open a way to theses close to those of the United States mentioned in Section 2. Concerning civilian objects, the ICC Statute also restricts the statement of the Protocol to those *"which are not military objectives"*. These changes, though *a priori* minor, weaken previous formulations (civilian losses have to be *clearly* excessive, as emphasized by the ICC Prosecutor in relation with the crimes committed by the British army in Iraq) and they introduce ambiguities. In a tendentious interpretation, civilian infrastructures might be considered as military objectives, even when their destruction does not give a direct military advantage, because they might be useful to the enemy in the course of the conflict. And, following a reservation of primary European countries when they ratified the 1977 Protocol (the military advantage should, according to them, refer to the advantage "of the overall attack and not of its particular or isolated parts", thus giving to the word attack a meaning different from that of the Protocol), civilian losses would not be *clearly* excessive in relation to the *overall* advantage anticipated.

Prohibited weapons in the ICC Statute include those prohibited in The Hague Conventions (see Section 1 as well as (following a 1980 Convention: see Section 7) "Employing weapons, projectiles and material and methods of warfare which are of a nature to cause superfluous injury or unnecessary suffering or which are inherently indiscriminate...*provided [they] are the subject of a comprehensive prohibition and are included in an annex to this Statute*". Arms usually considered to be prohibited by the first part of the sentence (e.g. cluster bombs) are no longer necessarily covered in view of the second part.

We conclude with the following remark on the war launched against Lebanon in 2006. As already mentioned, Lebanon did not declare acceptance of the jurisdiction of the Court and Hezbollah itself did not want any intervention of the ICC. In fact, the following scenario would not be excluded in spite of the disproportion between the war crimes committed by Israel and Hezbollah, and of the fact that the latter (indiscriminate launching of rockets) were committed to try to stop those of Israel. The Israeli leaders would not be prosecuted: the Court would decide they did not order attacks against civilian populations or infrastructures "as such" (a few subordinates might be prosecuted in particular cases, if it was possible to prove they knew perfectly well the absence of any military presence of Hezbollah when they attacked civilian populations. Concerning the use of cluster bombs in the South of Lebanon at the end of the war, see above). On the other hand, Hezbollah leaders would be prosecuted for having ordered indiscriminate attacks.

7. Recent treaties on methods of war and weapons

Environment

Article 55 of the 1977 Protocol I, on *Protection of the natural environment* prohibits "the use of methods or means of warfare which are intended or may be expected to cause widespread, long-term and severe damage to the natural environment and thereby to prejudice the health or survival of the population*"*. In its recent wars (Serbia, Iraq,...), the United States has nevertheless used arms which, at least according to some sources, inflict significant damage on the environment such as Depleted Uranium Bombs, not to mention the damage caused by its intense conventional bombardments.

The 1977 Protocol has followed the 1976 UN Convention called ENMOD, prohibiting *the military or any hostile use of environmental modification techniques*, ratified by a smaller number of countries (including the United States). Both followed in particular the "chemical war" carried out by the United States in Vietnam from 1961 to 1971 (spreading of weed-killers containing dioxin over large surfaces).

Biological and chemical weapons

The UN 1972 convention on biological weapons demands *the Prohibition of the Development, Production and Stockpiling of Bacteriological (Biological) and Toxin Weapons and their Destruction* (1972). It has been ratified so far by 155 States. The 1993 convention on chemical weapons is similar. It has been ratified by 183 States. Means of control are not specified in the former and the present situation is unclear. Specified means of control do exist in the latter. Both complete the 1925 Geneva Protocol mentioned in Section 1 and moreover demand the destruction of existing stocks. The destruction is only partial so far and dates planned for their destruction are not respected, in particular by Russia and the United States (the reasons given are technical and financial). On the other hand, the United States still uses some chemical or related arms in its recent wars (it claims they do not strictly belong to the category of prohibited arms).

Conventional weapons

A 1980 Convention on *Prohibitions or Restrictions on the Use of Certain Conventional Weapons Which May be Deemed to be Excessively Injurious or to have Indiscriminate Effects* is accompanied by several specific Protocols. The first one on *Non-Detectable Fragments* prohibits the use of any weapon the primary effect of which is to injure by fragments which in the human body escape detection by X-rays. A second one restricts the use of *Mines, Booby-Traps and Other Devices*, a third restricts the use of *Incendiary Weapons* and a fourth, in 1995, prohibits *Blinding Laser Weapons.*

A fifth Protocol on *Explosive Remnants of War* followed in 2003. It aims to reduce the threat posed by unexploded artillery shells, mortar shells, hand grenades, cluster munitions, bombs and similar weapons, after the end of active hostilities. However, it does not prohibit their use. Arms such as cluster or fragmentation bombs and similar weapons are largely considered to be prohibited by the conventions or customary laws prohibiting the use of weapons which may cause superfluous damage, but there is no consensus on this, and they are used by the United States and were also used by Israel during the 2006 war in Lebanon. The Protocol has been ratified only by 33 States, including India and France but not the United States, Russia, Israel or China.

The 1980 Protocol on Mines was completed in 1997 in a *Convention on the Prohibition of the Use, Stockpiling, Production and Transfer of Anti-Personnel Mines and on their Destruction*, also called the Ottawa Convention. It has been ratified so far by 153 States with the exception of the United

States, as well as Russia and China.

Nuclear weapons

There is so far no treaty explicitly prohibiting nuclear weapons. However, it is generally considered that their use is largely prohibited by existing treaties in view of their effects on the environment and populations. This viewpoint is largely confirmed in an advisory opinion expressed on the subject by the UNO International Court of Justice in 1996, where it declares the threat or use of nuclear weapons generally illegal. However, it declared it could not reach a conclusion in an instance "when the very survival of the State would be at stake". On the other hand, the aim of nuclear disarmament is part of the 1968 Non-Proliferation Treaty. This treaty asks non-nuclear nations not to acquire nuclear weapons. As a counterpart, Article 6 asks all Parties to negotiate nuclear disarmament as quickly as possible: "Each of the Parties undertakes to pursue negotiations in good faith on effective measures relating to cessation of the nuclear arms race at an early date and to nuclear disarmament, and on a Treaty on general and complete disarmament under strict and effective international control".

The procedure followed in 1998 can be understood: the priority was to avoid proliferation, and more time was needed for an actual treaty on nuclear disarmament: problems had to be solved for the elimination of stocks and for efficient means of detection of possible nuclear programs (in order to avoid them). But nuclear countries, with the primary responsibility falling on the United States, have to date prevented any important progress in that direction.

Present situation

In spite of the advances mentioned above, today we have a situation in which powerful countries, and more particularly the United States, can maintain their military domination of the world. Their nuclear weapons allow them to threaten other countries and their immense conventional forces can be (and are) used against weaker countries without *a priori* possible military opposition, in particular since the United States did not ratify (or does not respect) international treaties like the 1977 Protocol I which would limit its possible actions. Instead of disarmament, as was hoped for at the end of the Cold War, US policy has pursued the development of its armaments, new military bases around the world, projects of militarization of space, and so forth, leaving no choice to other countries but the development of their own armaments, albeit in a much weaker way.

ROBERT CHARVIN

THE CO-OPTATION OF HUMANITARIANISM AND ITS LEGAL CONSEQUENCES

Humanitarian law has a long history that dates back to Grotius and his attempt to elaborate standards that would protect victims of conflict. A century later, Rousseau contributed an essential element to that search: disarmed soldiers are no longer enemies, "they become ordinary men again, and one no longer has any right over their lives."

Since that time, there has been a jerky path towards the construction of a system of standards defining a specific branch of international law: humanitarian law. This movement was constantly disrupted, even completely stopped (with fascisms, Nazism and colonial wars) by the return of the "absolute enemy" to whom all humanity is denied. The "signs of the victim syndrome" and the scapegoat function, analyzed by R. Girard, in fact transform the adversary, a foreigner to the society at war, into an "enemy" that has to be wiped out by all means.

It should be noted that, if the East-West conflict, with its "hot" wars (like the Korean and Vietnam wars) started on this premise, the politics of peaceful coexistence initiated by the USSR led progressively to the disappearance of the absolute enemy, thus creating conditions for humanitarian law, including a mechanism of effective penalties.

As a matter of fact, it should be noted that it is in the periods directly following conflicts that humanitarian law makes some progress: the case of the 1949 Geneva Conventions is exemplary; so is the 1977 Protocol I, following the experience of the wars of national liberation at the peak of the Non-Aligned Movement.

Conversely, despite the dominant humanitarian discourse and following a phase of quasi absolute hegemony of human rights ideology initiated by the United States (once it was no longer at war in Vietnam) and taken up by European powers (in particular France, which no longer had to turn a blind eye to the spirit of humanity, as it had no more wars of decolonization to fight), we witness a process of humanitarian law deconstruction and, at the same time, a total demolition of generally accepted principles of international law. The "new humanitarian order," supposedly in the process of being developed after the end of the USSR and under American hegemony (Resolution 43/131 of 8 December 1988, voted by the United Nations General Assembly), has been leaning towards the same global fiasco as the previously decided New Economic Order and New Information Order.

This de facto deconstruction of humanitarian law came with a relegation of the ICRC (International Committee of the Red Cross), which had until then been its instrument of choice, to the background, to the benefit of NGOs with deeply different and very widely publicized values and practices. If the primary responsibility for these challenges obviously lies with the United States, European States (including France) are far from being innocent and this is also the case with a number of NGOs whose strategy curiously matches certain diplomacies.

We thus witness a strong co-optation of humanitarianism, resulting in a drifting in humanitarian law and, consequently, a reinforced ineffectiveness, despite the media "display show" put on in the West.

1. The co-optation of humanitarianism

By tradition and caution, legal doctrine often does not try to describe evolutions and merely describes the state of the law at a given time.

The end of world bipolarity (which characterized the era from 1945 to 1990) and the rise of a unipolar international society did not do away with conflicts, but changed their nature. Moreover, this last decade has clearly uncovered the hegemonic will of the United States, freed—temporarily—from any opponent at the same level, and its unilateral practices hostile to the United Nations and its Charter, as well as to any necessarily restrictive international legality.

Proclaiming itself, in a messianic manner, to be a champion of universal values, modernity and progress, the United States could not, without political fallout, free itself of the obligations of international legality and the resulting responsibility, without an effective motive. Human rights and humanitarianism, in general, have thus been effectively co-opted in American opinion and, more generally, in Western opinion.

Humanitarianism has paved the way for the "circumvention" of international political law, moving it in an "expedient" manner into the zone of a "soft law" that cannot fulfill its purpose. This co-optation of humanitarianism can be checked through a number of clues.

• *The first symptom* is the date of the rise of its diplomatic and media priority. The initiative originated from the United States when, freed from all risks of direct lawsuits on humanitarian grounds, it first of all grasped the human rights issue as a tool to put its Soviet adversary on the defensive, due to Soviet democratic deficiencies. It is not an act of sacrilege to wonder about the origin of this encroachment on humanitarianism, under the pretext that humanitarian action is indisputable and "natural"! Who would believe that a "humanitarian conscience" suddenly appeared among the authorities of certain superpowers which maintain an international order that is the source of unbearable inequalities, creating all the conditions for the outbreak of international and internal conflicts, and which at the same time declare forcefully that they want to correct the outcome of their actions?

The "progress—apparent—of the human conscience" cannot be spontaneous, more so because it comes after a period (the 1970s) when the pressing concern was to take action against the causes of extreme poverty that, in M. Bedjaoui's words, was denounced as an "unacceptable" order, and to transform international structures or even to prepare a revolution!

The dominant Western values have remained the same. Admittedly, the Catholic Church officially (and belatedly) decided to support human rights during the 1960s, but the theory of "the intervention of humanity" remained, while its practice re-emerged brutally. The Universal Declaration, which originated essentially in the West, and the Covenants of 1966 had been in force for a long time. It cannot be accidental that a rise in the importance of the role of humanitarianism in general came simultaneously with interference, allowing for the by-pass of the fundamental principle of the United Nations Charter, the sovereign equality of States!

A likely assumption is that, at the instigation of Western States, an actual pedagogy of interference through humanitarianism actually occurred, first of all with United Nations General Assembly Resolution 43/131, in the wake of the earthquake in Soviet Armenia, authorizing NGOs to substitute for a State considered to be ineffective, and sanctioning the principle of free "access to victims." Subsequently, it continued with a series of resolutions linking the humanitarian and the military in an ingenious combination of contradictory words, moving further and further away from the principles of the "Geneva Law" and of the ICRC. Thus, Western States, various media-based NGOs, and the mercenary-doctrine legitimize unjustifiable actions, even as they are proclaiming indisputable values!

• *The second symptom* is the nature of the directors and implementers of the "new humanitarianism."

Admittedly, part of the legal doctrine considers, with absolute sincerity, that, despite "self-serving motives, either through the search for the publicity provided by the media or through the implementation of political projects", "the aid indirectly benefits humanity". However, acknowledging that humanitarian law was established in an era when human rights were not yet recognized within the international order, R.J. Dupuy, Professor at Collège de France, for example, emphasizes that it was at least partially imposed due to the "caution" of the ICRC "that runs its operations away from all political and military interference".

However, the dominant doctrine that emerged with substantial media coverage in favor of another conception of humanitarianism, (the "Bettato-Mitterrando-Kouchnerian" style), was driven by a very "political" opportunism, quite close to the American analysis of international relations.

With this conception, humanitarianism becomes a "political show" of primary importance, within which the ICRC fades, to the benefit of NGOs which have little concern for neutrality, but on the contrary are driven by political choices leading them, in some cases, into partnership with some combatants against others (in Afghanistan, for example). The humanitarian action of "civil society" has not only gone into partnership with a State humanitarianism, obviously becoming part of its diplomatic strategies, but is also moving towards an alliance with the military.

These practices in fact bring us back to the most archaic conceptions, not to say ancient beliefs, of the Christian West, mixing the compassionate, the mystic and the political, with the new priests of this mix being the "French Doctors" and a few NGOs and American sects!

It so happens, in fact, that the implementer of this new "humanitarianism" is essentially the United States, which frequently uses its military force! But for all that, no one will dare to conclude that the United States has a messianic calling to save the world, other than American authorities themselves!

• *American foreign policy*, and sometimes that of some European countries such as France, clearly shows that, in spite of official claims, humanitarianism is at the service of certain strategies. In fact, the sites of "humanitarian interference" correspond precisely to the strategic needs of these powers. On the other hand, places where humanitarianism would be most needed do not benefit from any significant action when the country under consideration does not present any particular interest or when the humanitarians cannot control the use of their aid. Coherence in humanitarian practices has little to do with actual humanitarian needs, primarily when they do not arise from an exceptional crisis but rather from the structure of international economic relations.

The ambiguous character of this "humanitarianism" mixing the actions of States and that of NGOs disappears when it is accompanied by the military, even when the pretext is the safeguarding of human rights. The "helmeted virtue", using Rony Brauman's expression, cannot be neutral! The interference is then always discriminating, in violation of the rules of the Fourth Geneva Convention (article 27).

• *Another symptom* of this ambiguity is the media-based policy of Western superpowers, which very strongly valorize some NGOs that receive significant financial support from State sources, against others (an example being the priority given in France to Doctors Without Borders/Médecins Sans Frontières). While the Third Geneva Convention (art. 126), the Fourth Convention and the additional Protocol I (art. 81) give the ICRC the right to intervene in all places where there are war prisoners or imprisoned civilians, and to speak with them without witnesses with all needed facilities in the accomplishment of their humanitarian actions, this institutional place of the ICRC in the framework of the Geneva Conventions is treated as minor: the attention of public opinion is instead turned to the actions of NGOs which have close links with these states, have a relatively close political orientation and are sometimes even close to their army. Nevertheless, this media-based action succeeds, at least to some extent, in "de-politicizing politics" and rallying a consensus.

This enumeration is not exhaustive. Nevertheless, it seems sufficient to confirm the very strong co-optation of humanitarianism by those States which have the means for it, with the United States in the forefront. We therefore witness a "colonization" of humanitarianism, again according to the expression of Rony Brauman. Decolonization would presuppose the end of the interference between what is political, military and humanitarian, through giving sufficient means to the main United Nations agencies (UNHCR, UNICEF, WFP) and through their emancipation from states.

But such a decolonization also means a renunciation of compromises with the deep sources of the distresses. Humanitarianism does not have the function of soothing the pain; humanitarian activism often allows one to mislead people on the true intentions of the "humanitarian" powers. Humanitarianism as an alibi is the worst of all perversions practiced today. It can be avoided only by a protesting humanitarianism. But the stakes are huge. The question is not merely, as was initially the case, to limit the military carnage between Europeans such as those of Sebastopol or Solferino in the middle of the 19th century, and to "soften the horrors" of wars, as Henry Dunant dreamt, beginning with a commitment based on compassion which led to the creation of the ICRC, which became mandatory on the community of European States. The fracture and hence the clashes between North and South are becoming more and more complex with the arrival on the market of emerging powers, taking on such a scale that humanitarianism has transformed itself into one tool among others of this confrontation.

One of the first consequences of this confrontation is the dismantlement of humanitarian law.

2. Deconstruction of humanitarian law

The United States is the main power responsible for the deconstruction of general international law. The UNO and multilateralism are condemned. The non-acceptance of any constraining legal norm and unilateralism are articles of faith. This behavior, destructive of international legality, is based on religiosity of a fundamentalist character: it marks the return of the motto "the end justifies the means" and of a moral doctrine close to that of the 19th century replacing the gains of the United Nations Charter and of the many Conventions ratified by most states. The US authorities are not alone in this work of demolition; some European states actively participate in it either from subordination to their "Great" ally or for their own purposes.

This practice corresponds to a will to hegemony in the framework of the accelerated process of globalization presently underway. In particular, it permits the reversal of one of the core principles of international law, the principle of the equal sovereignty of states. A de facto sovereignty remains for powerful states: what is defeated for the greater benefit of the most powerful is equal sovereignty. A strong symptom of this dismantling can be seen in the fact that international law—which was always violated by powerful states—is now violated openly, without reference to this law, and even without strong reaction from smaller states (which fear to see the law applied to them in a discriminating way) or from public opinion (which more and more ignores it). What had still, yesterday, to be openly violated to be overcome is today bypassed by establishing a pseudo ethical regulation in the name, for instance, of "just war", an old religious concept which has reappeared these last decades!

Entire zones classically regulated by international law have become no-law zones or zones of "soft law", for the sole benefit of those powers with sufficient means of action. Some lawyers inspired by the United States (e.g. Mario Bettati) transform what is illegal into something which is in the process of becoming legal! So-called humanitarian interference, an obvious violation of the non-interference principle of the UN Charter, thus becomes a "custom in gestation", and Bernard Kouchner goes even further, claiming that "the supreme reference cannot be the law, but moral doctrine and compassion".

Under the pretext of the promotion of humanitarianism, confusion is practiced between various branches of international law. Humanitarian law is included in the law of human rights in times of peace, in the law of refugees, and in the international law in charge of maintaining peace between States.

What makes the connection, in these various branches, is the condemnation of the sovereignty of states, "a major obstacle to the application of human rights". With everything being in everything, and international law being mixed up with internal order, "humanitarian law contributes to peace to the extent it is an obstacle to the recourse to force", "by emphasizing assistance to victims, it gives a larger dimension to the classical notion of human rights": therefore "the new dimension of humanitarian law considered in its largest sense is to take it into account in situations which are not protected by the Geneva Conventions and their additional Protocols". And "it can be seen that the law of refugees is complementary to humanitarian law".[1]

As a matter of fact, the promotion of humanitarian law through confusion is not guaranteed. The converse is true. For instance, there are derogatory clauses in the applicability of the law of human rights; it is not so in the case of the humanitarian law.

With humanitarian interventionism without the consent of the parties involved, humanitarian law, which to that point had been universal, becomes a law of inequality.

The Geneva Conventions emphasize the neutrality of the party which is to apply humanitarian law, whether it is the ICRC itself or the "protecting power". In spite of the extreme difficulty, in any armed conflict, of finding a "protecting power" in charge of safeguarding the interests of all parties involved in the conflict (this was nevertheless possible in cases such as Suez, Goa and Bangladesh), and in spite of the obstacles encountered in its activities, the ICRC has globally succeeded in gaining an authority that permits it to be accepted in the zones of conflicts. In El Salvador, in the 1980s, its delegates were accepted both by the army and by the guerrillas of the Farabundo Marti National Liberation Front; through their contacts on each side, it succeeded in reducing the violent acts of the belligerents.

To achieve this goal, the ICRC has accepted self-limitation, but it also has never accepted to "soften" the prohibitions of the Geneva Conventions and Protocols which, for example in the matter of bombardments, were very unpleasant for the United States and their military practices, such as their bombing of zones with civilian populations. This prohibition, without reserves, as Hans Blix noted in 1986 (Blix demonstrated his own courage in Iraq against US pressure), is "an important humanitarian advance".

The notion of weapons of mass destruction (arms that only certain powers have accorded themselves as having the right to possess), replacing the notion of "arms of a nature to cause superfluous injury" of humanitarian law, is a notion "with varying geometry" aiming to justify the resort to armed force.

The reappearance of the notion of "just war", of combat against "rogue states" or "terrorists" has removed all self-restraints: there we have, face to face, "Good" and the "Evil", which cannot be trusted in any way.

There are "good" victims and the others who do not deserve any consideration. There are the "true" religions and those which only produce fanaticism, whereas classical humanitarian law guarantees respect for the religion of everyone (whether it concerns imprisoned civilians, war prisoners, even according a special protection for ministers of cults).

One is far from the conclusions of the first Conference on Human Rights of the United Nations in Tehran in 1968: "Peace is the first condition for the full respect of human rights. War is the negation of human rights" (Resolution 23 of 12.5.68). On the contrary, Israel and the United States have invented the notion of "legitimate preemptive defense" which makes the resort to force a necessary and vital way to protect human rights: war paradoxically becomes the tool of humanitarianism!

From now on, humanitarianism is armed, whereas in humanitarian law, it was unarmed by its very nature. The notion of a neutral "protecting power" has been depraved de facto in the form of a tutelary power, a de facto reintroduction of the protectorate in international relations (Afghanistan, Iraq,…) and of new forms of neocolonialism in the name of human rights (as, yesterday, in the name of the *mission civilisatrice*).

The rights of prisoners of war, as is attested to by the fate of detainees at Guantanamo, as well as the prohibition against torture, no longer apply, according to the United States, to terrorists or to those suspected of terrorism.

As for the ICRC, which did not welcome the interference of NGOs in favor of the Taliban during the war against the Afghan Communist Party and the Soviet army, and which rejects discriminatory armed intervention, it is no longer, for the United States and other Western countries, the service privileged with applying humanitarian law.

This global challenge to humanitarian law is crowned by obstacles posed by the United States to the United Nations, which had nonetheless in 1991 created the "Department of Humanitarian Affairs" (DHA) and has been at the origin of the International Criminal Court (ICC). The United States has not ratified the ICC Statute (the Rome Statute) despite its participation in its preparatory works and the "cautious" character of this Statute to the sole benefit of the powerful members of the Security Council.

3. Conclusion

The condition of humanitarian law is even worse than that of general international law, which is itself in a quasi coma. Humanitarian action, at the instigation of the United States and some of its allies, has been profoundly transformed, with their new actors, their new justifications, their media, and their armies, outside any rigorous legal regulation.

This mutation follows neither from a progress of human conscience nor from a positive maturation of international society due to the disappearance of the USSR. The very existence of humanitarian law and the development of international opinion's awareness of it are obstacles to the pursuit of Western practices in the framework of globalization. The "new" humanitarianism is on the contrary the alibi justifying the continuation of the model of development which claims to rule the planet in spite of its unjustifiable consequences. The accelerated decline of true humanitarian practices based on classical humanitarian law thus leads to an accelerated questioning of the "model" itself, of the sources of conflicts and not only of their consequences. The crisis of humanitarianism or rather of its paradoxical explosion in the media at the very time of its collapse, is symbolic of an incapacity to master reality even through recourse to armed force, as is obviously illustrated by the case of Iraq.

After a limited period, the pseudo "humanitarianism", as well as "human-rightsism", become less and less fascinating for public opinion. Of course, this is not the end of ecological or economic intervention, but the international order of extreme poverty gives rise to the same adversaries opposing those who benefit from it: the strong demand for a legal regulation guaranteeing a more equitable share can only be repeated. The union of Machiavelli and of Lady Philanthropy cannot last long.

ENDNOTES

[1]   Citations from the anticipating paper by J. Patrnogic, in *International Journal of the Red Cross*, 1988.

BARBARA DELCOURT

THE BUSH DOCTRINE'S IDEOLOGICAL ROOTS:
POSING PROBLEMS FOR HUMANITARIAN LAW

The neoconservative discourse is generally known and even accepted as being in conflict with the discourses that make international law a normative reference and a constraining force for states and international institutions' actions. Although the US neoconservatives do not have a monopoly on criticizing the UN and general international law, their positions are based on a doctrinal foundation which inclines them to take a critical stance towards the current international legal order. In the first part I will briefly review what conditions the neo-conservative discourse with a view to demonstrating the eventual contradictions with international law in general. Thereafter I will analyze in more detail, what aspects could be in conflict with humanitarian law.

However, other elements than those linked to a doctrine need to be taken into consideration in order to understand the current situation. It seems as if the revolution in military affairs, the re-legitimization of imperialist discourses and practices, and the establishment of 'legal black holes' all contribute to create tensions in the heart of the international legal system and more precisely, in the respect for fundamental rights. This evolution is not only attributable to the US administration. In fact, it is the convergence of some tendencies today that are really worrying, and not only the ideological foundations of the leading team's discourses.

1. International Law and the UN as Constraining Forces: The Neo-Conservatives' Credo

At first sight, the neoconservative discourse cannot be considered as inherently hostile towards the universal values that are promoted by general international law. On the contrary, through continuing references to democracy and freedom, it seems as if they want to consolidate and propagate these values. The propaganda for a universal ideal based on the liberal democracy model[1] is certainly part of the political program promoted by Washington's governmental team. This vision is integrated to the point that even the American foreign affairs specialists have not hesitated in linking the Bush discourse to that of his renowned predecessor, Woodrow Wilson (who, moreover has already inspired Ronald Reagan in his crusade against the "Evil Empire").[2]

Indeed, the notion of regime change in Bagdad was rapidly set forth as a justifying discourse for the intervention in Iraq, which from the beginning was mainly concentrating on questions regarding the proliferation of weapons of mass destruction and terrorists' possible use of the latter.[3]

The justifications based on democratic change have thus been integrated into the politicians' discourses which have often even been qualified as "realist".[4] The document on the national security strategy from September 2002 is, moreover, abounding with references concerning the importance of letting values considered as universal dominate.[5] However, it is understood that the democratization process must take into account local cultures, as adviser Richard Haass demonstrated when talking about the "The Goal Becomes Muslim Democracy".[6] Yet President Bush situates his approach in a strict moral framework which does not tolerate drifts from the "relativist and agnostic liberalism": "Some worry that it is somehow undiplomatic or impolite to speak the language of right and wrong. I disagree. Different circumstances require different methods, but not different moralities".[7]

It is in this citation that a problem concerning the neoconservative discourse and the current legal order is visible.

1.1 The Doctrinal Elements which are Posing Problems for International Law

The influence of conservative, anti-liberal and religiously-inspired doctrines seems undeniably crucial to explain the critique against international law and the UN, but also, and in particular, to account for the legitimization of pre-emptive actions. It is therefore not surprising to find some "Christian" testimonials supporting the Bush-Cheney administration, in particular on some of the most self-righteous media web sites. The specialist on questions about a "just war" (Michael Cromartie), invited to TV channel Fox News, reminds us that there are many different doctrines regarding the "just war".[8]

The common components are: the repairing character of the action (to address an evil or a wrong suffered), a just intention, a last resort action and conditions linked to the quality of the authority that declares the war. In this case, it has to be a civil authority (a nation...).[9]

When it comes to the question of whether only the UN can give its accord to lead a "just war", we have to remember, as these commentators tell us, that there is no reference to that in the just war doctrine.[10] In case the global organization has a temporary blackout, it is just normal that President Bush would make arrangements to protect potential victims in tyrannical regimes.[11]

In addition, many observers have underlined the ideological proximity, however contradictory it may seem, giving rise to a connection between the conservative Christians and certain American *Zionist* movements that are at least as hostile towards the UN as the neoconservatives.[12] Searches relating to the preventive war or to "pre-emptive" actions leads to websites expressing opinions which, when favorable to this sort of behavior in international relations, clearly can be linked to a conservative tradition (which is anti-liberal, no matter what Robert Kagan says)[13] and at times even fascist.[14]

However, the influence from the anti-liberal, religious right needs to be put into perspective. Sebastian Fath, a specialist in the sociology of religions at C.N.R.S., does not think that Bush is led by an anti-Muslim Crusader spirit. What sort of "religiosity", then, is driving the American president? Besides interest coming from the environment of industry and oil, there is an increasingly secularized messianic or at least a-Christian message, which is in particular led by people such as Rumsfeld (a person who is not very religious). In this respect a digression through cinema proves to be illustrative:

> When the film Independence Day invaded the screens, four decades after the classic War of the Worlds, one could trace the road it had travelled. The two films basically talk about the same thing: the Earth is invaded by combative extraterrestrials. But their conclusions differ: In 1953 the scientists try to stop the invasion with a sophisticated weapon, but their weapon is destroyed and they fail. The panicked population then turns to God. They pray, and it is only then that deliverance comes: the invaders are overcome by a bacterium that kills them. The conclusion of the film: everything that people tried, failed. Liberation comes from God alone. This is where one finds a messianic message impregnated with Christianity. This is no longer the case in the contemporary adaptation of the scenario. Independence Day shows certainly the same notion of prayers and the same panic. But the salvation this time comes exclusively from the hyper-sophisticated military technology operated against the enemy. It is thanks to the excellence of the distance-scaled bombs that the world has survived. In Gun we trust... The Goddess for whom Bush goes to war today

is first and foremost America. For a majority of Americans, the star-spangled banner and the way of life that it represents, have replaced Jesus Christ as the eschatological figure of a Millennium of happiness. And it is first for this God that they fight".[15]

1.2. Back to the law of nature?

There are however other hypotheses too, among them that developed by Alain Frachon and Daniel Vernet in the newspaper *Le Monde* which mainly contends that American politics draws its sources from Leo Strauss' anti-modern philosophy.

> American neo-conservatism is situated in the junction between two reflections presented by Leo Strauss. The first one is linked to his personal experience. As a young man, he experienced the decay of the Weimar Republic under the converging attacks from the communists and the Nazis. He concluded that democracy was never going to prevail as long as it was that weak and refused to stand up against tyranny, which was by nature expansionist, even if it meant to allow the use of coercive action…[16]

For Simone Goyard-Fabre, this speculative philosophy is incapable of adapting to the present reality; the perspective is a-historical, or trans-historical but also trans-social, trans-moral and trans-religious.[17] This is certainly also part of the *"all azimuths"* seduction that the "Straussian" bible is able to evoke.

Likewise, Daniel Vernet gives us an explication which can help us understand the reasons for the mistrust regarding modern international law:

> The second reflection [by Leo Strauss] is the consequence of his interest in the ancient philosophers. For us, as for them, the fundamental question is that of the political regime which shapes the character of the people. Why did the 20th century give rise to two totalitarian regimes which, returning to terms employed by Aristotle, Strauss prefers to call tyrannical? To this question which torments contemporary intellectuals, Strauss responds: because modernity has provoked a rejection of moral values, of the virtue that needs to be at the base of democracies, and a rejection of European values which are *"reason"* and *"civilization"*. The source of this rejection, according to him, were the philosophers of

the Enlightment, who almost necessarily produced histori-
cism and relativism; that is to say the refusal to admit the
existence of a superior Good. Accordingly, for Leo Strauss
there exist bad and good regimes: political reflection does
not have to deprive itself of having value judgments, and
good regimes have the right—and even the duty—to defend
themselves against the bad [...]. Preaching a return to the
ancient philosophers against the traps of modernity and the
illusions of progress, Strauss nonetheless defends liberal
democracy, the daughter of the Enlightenment—and the
American democracy which seems to be its core. A contradiction? No doubt, but a contradiction that he takes on,
following the example of other liberal thinkers (Montesquieu,
Tocqueville). Because the critique against liberalism—which
is necessary for its survival—runs the risk of losing its value
in relativism; if everything can be said, the search for the
Truth loses its value. For Strauss, the incapacity to react
against tyranny is the consequence of the Good's relativism".[18]

This results in a conviction according to which, the "nature of political
regimes is more important than all the international institutions and
international arrangements for the maintenance of peace in the world".[19]

Besides the iconoclastic notions put forward by Richard Perle in his
article entitled "Thank God for the Death of UN",[20] there is also a more "rational"
argumentation to justify the setting aside of the existing juridical arsenal.
This consists mainly of asserting that because of the norms' outdated
character, new norms should be elaborated—norms which would be better
adapted to the challenges which democracies are or will be confronted with
in the future. In short, the legal rules are no longer adapted to the world we
are living in; they are made for reasonable nation states and were not formed
with a view to addressing the anti-terrorist fight.[21] This will to innovate in legal
matters—which is mainly justified by looking at *new* threats and their
unforeseen character—falls, paradoxically enough, within the framework of
a discourse legitimizing the American strategy that draws its references
from the founding fathers of international law:

Moreover, the recognized right of a state to use force for the
purpose of self-defense traditionally included the pre-emptive
use of force, *i.e.*, the use of force in anticipation of an attack.
Hugo Grotius, the father of international law, stated in the
seventeenth century that '[i]t be lawful to kill him who is
preparing to kill'. Emmerich de Vattel a century later similarly
asserted: 'The safest plan is to prevent the evil where that is

possible. A Nation has the right to resist the injury another seeks to inflict upon it, and to use force...against the aggressor'.[22]

It is notably through natural law's bias for legitimate defense that the justification for "pre-emptive actions" is constructed.[23] The demonstration by Richard G. Maxon in "Nature's Eldest Law: A Survey of a Nation's Right to Act in Self-Defense" is an illustration of this.[24] Once again, it is possible to see in this seduction of a certain model of "natural law" a trace of the seduction of certain political and philosophic doctrines, such as those of Leo Strauss and Edmund Burke.

As Simone Goyard-Fabre reminds us, Leo Strauss has always shown modest enthusiasm for philosophical-political doctrines based on human rights as conceptualized by the Enlightenment's philosophy, and in particular for the principle of equality.[25] He has always pleaded for a return to natural normativity while rejecting the claims of rational normativity that positivism and humanism have established in dogma.[26] "The natural law of the Classics offers political law the ideal of harmony and equilibrium which represent cosmic truth and become, in the City, the benchmark for normativity: [thus] there is a benchmark for just and unjust which is independent of, and superior than, positive law (Natural law and history)".[27]

One could not imagine a conception further away from the contemporary legal order based on states' voluntarism and consent to be tied by certain legal obligations:

[T]he thesis that law and justice are conventional, signifies that their roots are not in the nature, that they are in the last analysis against nature, without any other reason to exist than human communities' arbitrary agreement, explicit or not: they do not have any other foundation than common accord. Although the common accord might be enough to maintain peace, it is unable to give rise to the truth.[28]

In addition it is worrying to note that the main argument addressed to the elected Americans with a view to their authorizing the Executive to use force against Iraq was constructed in reference to UN Security Council resolutions ("we intervene in Iraq in order to make them respect 17 UN resolutions").[29] From that we infer a new form of tension, leading to a new unstable form of discourse as, on one hand, a part of the legitimacy of the international action of the US is based on a virulent critique of the UN and on an observation of the obsolete character of the legal order that it is preserving,[30] and on the other hand, it is established on justifications based on the conformity of the same actions with the UN Charter and international law. Indeed, one has to remember that Operation Iraqi Freedom was presented by the President as the implementation of a law "above humans" and "beyond nations". It was with these words that President Bush ended his speech before the General Assembly in September 2003.[31] In the same speech before the General Assembly, Bush developed an argument, particularly popular with Secretary of State Colin Powell, which asserted that such an action was pre-eminently taken to respect the 17 resolutions concerning Iraq that were voted through by the Security Council.[32] Combined with the reference to natural law, this interpretation seems to rule out all objections based on the non-respect for particular procedures, in this case a positive vote in from Security Council.

It seems hence as neither a traditional positivist conception, nor a classical natural law conception could make the American discourse logical.

1.3. The pragmatic turn?

A third possibility consists of considering that the American leaders are influenced by a more "pragmatic" conception of international law, inspired by authors such as Edmund Burke. In certain texts, one finds indeed a will to interpret the rules of international law more in line with the actual practice of states, at least some of them (the "*leading states*"). Such a tendency is justified by an intuitive distrust of the narrow, French-spirited "legalism".

Simone Goyard-Fabre, reminds us therefore that Burke "considers traditions and precedents as playing the most important roles and, because he values jurisprudence, he estimates that public law as well as private is only efficient through the cautious realism which links them to each people's experience".[33] He is hence extremely critical of modern political law ...

> With a sense of reality grounded in empiricism, he has always considered that specific conditions were more important than the large theoretical principles and speculations of the philosophers, whom he doesn't hesitate to label as 'chatty sophists'. In examining the problems of English politics, he has constantly refused to search for their solution in the French philosophers' rational legalism and secular dogmatism. He states that political law cannot develop from abstract and generalized thought that is lost in utopian universalism. Like Montesquieu, he thinks that the laws which a nation needs have to respond to the spirit of its people, to their morals, their religion, their internal life…, in one word, to a people's real individuality. Like Thomas Paine, he valorizes the traditional order, in which the specific nature

of a people is reflected, and he denounces the artifice of the rational order, the coldness, the impersonality; he lauds the spirit of chivalry which the dryness of reason has made disappear. The heritage received from the ancient Constitution of a people, the customs, the beliefs…are the substance of the practical wisdom of which England, in face of constructivism and icy suppositions from the French ethos, provides, in his eyes, a warm image.[34]

In addition one finds a justification for 'conservatory' or preventive intervention in Burke's texts…

From this follows a theory of political and social security, and the programme of counter-revolutionary intervention for which Burke is best known […] Burke argues, in effect, for a *pre-emptive war against revolutionary* France, to strike down before it engulfs the rest of Europe […] for any international order to maintain peace it needs not only to evolve norms of inter-state behaviour, but to produce a community of states with broadly similar internal constitutions.[35]

On a political and doubtlessly more unrefined level, a more pragmatic conception can be found in the address delivered by Tony Blair in Chicago in April 1999. The Prime Minister suggested five criteria conditioning a military intervention from the British troops which revealed an approach rather distant from moral or strictly legal considerations: "1) Are we sure of what we are going to do? 2) Have we exhausted all available means? 3) Are there military operations that could be implemented in a rationalistic and cautious way? 4) Are we ready for a long lasting operation? 5) Are our national interests at stake?"[36]

*

The doctrinal influences in the neoconservative discourse do not prompt it, despite a seemingly strong attachment to universal values and freedom, to defend the existing legal order and the world organization which it incarnates. The system of collective security developed after the Second World War was justified, on an empirical level, by the fact that the latitude given to each state to do justice in the name of superior principles or by referring to just war doctrines had provoked the worst abuses. From a more theoretical point of view, one notes that the process of legalizing the prohibition of use of force has been produced at the price of disconnecting the norm from moral considerations.[37] It was in effect, hardly conceivable to let each state in a collective security organization, certainly equal but politically and culturally different, use force unilaterally, contingent on their own conceptions of what is "fair" and "unfair". In some ways, the Security Council's powers in terms of the maintenance of peace and international security establish, even if it is not perfect,[38] a form of procedure permitting a pacific coexistence between entities that do not necessarily share the same values or conception of "good" and "fair".[39]

This evolution is interpreted by the neoconservatives as the symptom of modern liberalism's degeneration, which, due to its relativism (everything can be discussed), would have contributed to the exclusion of superior values (European to start, and then Western). In addition, questioning the existence of a "superior good" would limit the capacity to react against tyranny.[40] In their eyes, the nature of political regimes justifies a different legal regime depending on their liberal or anti-liberal character. It is hence inconceivable that abstract considerations linked to multilateralism and the central character of international institutions should impose themselves as determinant criteria and in particular as a constraint for US political action on the international scene.

2. The Specific Obstacles Concerning Humanitarian Law

In fact, one finds few considerations or clear-cut developments on this question in the official discourses. The only relevant indications come from the debates concerning the status of the prisoners in Guantanamo[41] and the people in Iraq who are deprived of their freedom.[42] Following what has been said and supported regarding international law, it is striking to note that in general, the neoconservatives estimate that the legal corpus no longer corresponds to the current context of the war against terrorism. In short, the argumentation goes back to the notion of rules not being adapted to contemporary challenges. Moreover, the report from Amnesty International in June 2005 reminds us that President Bush's assertion that the Guantanmo prisoners are treated according to the Geneva Conventions is contradicted by the presidential decree, of the 7th of February 2002, which recommends a treatment "adapted to the military necessities".[43]

However, as Nico Krisch reminds us in his work on interactions between imperial politics and international law,[44] the partial rejection of international law does not mean a complete rejection of all possible legal regulation. There is, in this type of case, a tendency to "externalize" the rules of internal law, or at least consider the application of some of them outside the national territory. Moreover, it is a mark of imperialism to contemplate some form of "nationalization" through the transposition of internal legal norms intended to regulate activities in a territory under external actors' authority. He explains that the preference for a domestic sort of governance instead of governance based on international law is partly because the latter depends on cooperation and not coercion and in particular because it assumes a relation between equals, which definitely does not rhyme with a scenario marked by imperialism.

In an exceptionally detailed analysis, Fleur Johns has thus underlined the fact that the Guantanamo prisoners' status and their detention conditions have gradually become subject to a legal regulation adapted to the US administration's demands and their strategy for war against terrorism.[45]

2.1 The Reason for the "Legal Black Hole"

The work by Ralph Wilde concerning the conditions of the implementation of the protective conventions of human rights concludes that states are bound to respect human rights in their extraterritorial activities, that is, the activities outside their own territory.

This is most certainly the opposite position to that defended by Alberto Gonzales.

At the time of the Congressional hearings related to his nomination as Attorney-General, he suggested that the prohibition of cruel, inhuman, or degrading treatment was not applicable to American personnel dealing with non-American citizens abroad.

Since September 11, 2001, an aggravation of this type of extraterritorial activities is visible, especially relating to the war against terrorism.[46] This phenomenon has compelled several observers to underline a flaw in the legal framework, a phenomenon often qualified as a "legal black hole". With the recent revelations concerning the bad treatment of detainees in the war against terrorism, Ralph Wilde believes that the delocalization of some activities, such as the interrogation of suspects in states which are not particularly respectful of human rights, is deliberately done to avoid certain rules.

From this point of view the existence of spaces allegedly "anomic" or "lawless" is not an unfortunate consequence of loopholes in the law, it is more of an "excuse" justifying the non-respect for some fundamental rules regarding human rights in armed conflict.

2.2 The Revolution's Impact in Military Affairs?

The impact and definition of the concept "Revolution in Military Affairs" (RMA) rests controversial, in particular its impact on the management of operations.

It was approximately during the first Gulf War that the concept was brought up in American discourse. Since then, the literature has developed around the concept but without a definitive consensus on its definition and impact. For some, the RMA indicates a breaking point regarding military efficiency because of the introduction of electronic equipment in the military (computers, means of command, control, intelligence, etc.). For others it is just a military-technical evolution with only a limited impact. According to some commentators, the war in Iraq constitutes a type of test to evaluate the effectiveness of this "revolution". In short, if the RMA succeeds in becoming a *modus operandi*, future wars will be *high-tech*, computerized, robotized, conducted from a greater firing distance, with more precise targeting, less lethal… and thus, with a greater respect for human rights[47].

For Christophe Wasinski, the RMA fits perfectly into the Western logic of war, which is particularly visible in a code of representation between Self and Other, just as a military syntax is established starting from the position of the military commander of units. It consists of elements placed in a hierarchy (setting the "top" where the ideal vision of an officer is situated, and the "bottom" where those who execute the orders are), and constraining elements (indicating where and what to watch).

However, as an American solider describes the innovation of current technical and ultra advanced equipment in the wake of the Revolution in Military Affairs:

> The technique is not applicable to many political and military situations for basic reasons. The sensors can track activities and physical objects which have electromagnetically formatted or other signatures. But the sensors cannot identify human motivations, measure human emotions, quantify the coherence of human organization or evaluate the importance of the information that they are gathering; they can thus only provide a limited amount of useful information to analyze and the information depends on what they have been programmed to look for.[48]

Which is the basis for Wasinski's argument that: "Where the machine (radar or various sensors connected to a screen) broadcasts a live representation of reality, it is in fact a simulation of reality which tries to grasp reality but at the same time creates a new 'reality'.[49] It seems indisputable that these representations can provoke a dehumanization of individuals.[50] Although suffering is difficult to represent in all discourses seeking a minimum 'objectivity', the elements from the visual code discussed above tend to facilitate the social capacity to inflict suffering to others by transforming them into some sort of object (both the soldiers sent to fight and the other side which must be defeated)." The example of images broadcast on TV channels around the world of American soldiers in Iraq firing in the night on convoys and mobile targets as if they were in a video game, seems to exemplify the risk evoked by this specialist strategy.

2.3 What is the Impact of the "Militarization of the Humanitarian and the Privatization of the Military"?

The work by Sami Makki on this topic brings into focus the fact that the issue also concerns a structural tendency, not specifically linked to the neoconservative ideology, even though the neo-liberal conceptions that it carries can reinforce the effects of these transformations.[51] The scandal arising from the bad treatment and humiliation of detainees in Iraq is, for him, the result of systematic practices similar to torture, where private contractors have played a significant role. As a report from *Human Rights Watch* in April 2004 reminds us: "if the Pentagon plans to use private contractors for military missions, it has to make sure that they are under legal control and restrictions, because the legal gap is an invitation to abuse the lack of regulation."[52] Indeed, it seems apparent that the delegation of certain functions to the private sector makes the upholding of the Geneva Conventions even more problematic.

In this regard, the NGOs are also playing an important role in monitoring and denouncing violations committed by soldiers, above and beyond their traditional role in the aid and care sector. However, the NGOs, especially in the US, are increasingly considered as centerpieces in the management of operations, especially on the level of "reconstruction", and as such, they are integrated into the military strategy. Therefore, Sami Makki stresses that the "War on Terrorism" has contributed to transform the conditions of these civilian-military interventions. Following October 2001, the Secretary of State, Colin Powell, declared that the American NGOs were "force multipliers" and American "combat instruments" against terrorism. And from that, Makki concludes that the Bush team's orientation aggravates the liberal structural tendencies of militarization and commercialization of humanitarian and development aid in favor of American strategic interests. From that perspective, one could interpret it as the military gradually taking over the humanitarian space.

Now, the use of NGOs for political-military objectives entails a modification of the perception that the parties to the conflict might have; non-respect for the neutrality principle risks endangering the humanitarian programs and those who are implementing them in the field. As a consequence, the respect for neutrality signs which is at the heart of civilian protection in war times, is therefore at risk of being seriously affected.

Conclusion

One major problem can be highlighted resulting from this analysis.

It goes back to the general manner of conceiving of international law that the American administration defends. It seems obvious that an anti-liberal (anti-relativist) conception of "good" and "fair" plays a part in the reconsideration of the collective security system established by the UN Charter. The consequence of this conception is to justify the removal of all restrictions, notably legal, that could encumber the US in their fight against terrorism. At the same time, the reference to "law" and to the Security Council's responsibility remains, but primarily when they can be used to justify constraints on a third party.

This results in a rather ambivalent attitude from the political leaders and a discourse marked by a certain confusion, which nevertheless serves as a basis for some ideas—old, but renewed for the current context—like the one which foresees different legal systems depending on the ideological profile and the particular responsibility of political entities in the war against the threats of the moment.

From this perspective, the plea from Robert Cooper, liberal imperialism's herald, could not be clearer:

> The challenge to the post-modern world is to get used to the idea of double standards. Among ourselves, we operate on the basis of laws and open cooperative security. But when dealing with more old-fashioned kind of states outside post-modern continent of Europe, we need to revert to the rougher methods of an earlier era-force, pre-emptive attack, deception, whatever is necessary to deal with those who still live in the nineteenth century world of every state for itself".[53]

Are we seeing a revival of the *"droit des gens européen"* from the model ruling during the 19th century? Probably not, although, in a certain way, it is still about placing the principle of liberty (integral to civilization) above the principle of sovereign equality between nations.[54] We see again the idea that we should finally abandon the principle of reciprocity which is inherent in that related to states' sovereign equality. Richard Haass expressed this very clearly:

> With the 'securitization' of international politics after September 11, we have entered in a world in which emergency regulations are increasingly often replacing normal or regular rules. The pre-emptive doctrine announces the end of reciprocity for the sake of American security and in the name of their *special responsibility concerning world affairs*".[55]

As some observers have underscored, the US' strong belief in messianic messages and their self-proclaimed exceptionality can be traced back to their historical and ideological tradition, a tradition that has been revitalized by the collapse of the Berlin Wall[56]. The accession to power of a team with different doctrinal currents, but sharing similar conceptions of the US special role, and in particular the need to guarantee its supremacy, seems only to have reinforced this tendency. The terrorist threat, presented as an existential threat, gives the opportunity not only to override political criticism but also to open up a register of arguments based on American exceptionalism. In such a context, humanitarian law and its supporters could appear as key allies of terrorism; at least that is the message conveyed to viewers of the popular series "24", (in particular the 4th season) produced by Fox News, and broadcast by Canal + in Europe.

Finally, isn't the most worrying part the fact that there is a sort of trivialization of certain forms of institutionalized violence? On one hand, the neo-conservative rhetoric is strongly criticized and has provoked discourses against it, showing that there is a resistance towards the "Empire's intoxication".[57] On the other hand, the elements introduced in the second part of the article could lead us to the conclusion that this is a more structural than conjunctional tendency that is not limited to the US.

ENDNOTES

[*] Lecturer at Free University Brussels; bdelcou1@ulb.ac.be. Translated by Nina Wilen.[1] Edward RHODES, "Onward Liberal Soldiers? The Crusading Logic of Bush's Grand Strategy and What Is Wrong With It", <http://www.ciaonet.org/special-_section/iraq/analysis>

[2] Pierre Hassner and Justin Vaisse, *Washington et le monde. Dilemmes d'une superpuissance*, Paris, CERI/Autrement, 2003, pp. 23-25.

[3] See Barbara Delcourt, «Les dommages collatéraux de la nouvelle stratégie états-unienne : de la sécurité collective à la sécurité sélective», in Barbara Delcourt, Denis Duez, Eric Remacle (Eds.), *La guerre d'Irak, prélude d'un nouvel ordre international?*, Bruxelles, Bern, Berlin, Frankfurt/M, New York, Oxford, Wien, P.I.E.-Peter Lang, 2004, pp. 21-39.

[4] Bill Sammon, "Cheney makes case for war", *The Washington Times*, 27-8-2002 ; Condoleeza Rice, "A Balance of Power That Favors Freedom", U.S. Foreign Policy Agenda, December 2002/IIP E-Journals.

[5] "People everywhere want to be able to speak freely; choose who will govern them; worship as they please; educate children—male and female; own property; and enjoy the benefits of their labour. These values of freedom are right and true for every person, in every society—and the duty of protecting these values against their enemies is the common calling of freedom-loving people across the globe and across the ages [...] Freedom is the non-negotiable demand for human dignity; the birthright of every person—in every civilization"[5]. [...] America must stand firmly for nonnegotiable demands of human dignity: the rule of law; limits on the absolute power of the state; free speech, freedom of worship; equal justice; respect for women, religious and ethnic tolerance; and respect for private property", Ibid., p. 3.

[6] Richard Haass, "The Goal Becomes Muslim Democracy", *International Herald Tribune*, 11-12-02, op-ed.; James MANN, "The Curious disconnect in US Foreign

Policy", *Financial Times*, 16 April 2006.

[7] President Bush, Discourse at West Point, New York, June 1, 2002.

[8] The objectives also need to be strictly defined and there must be a reasonable chance for the action to succeed (a small country can hence not start a just war against a stronger state). It is also morally justified to act in a preventive manner. In the case of Iraq, the fact that there is no cease-fire and that Iraqis constantly violate the prohibition to fly over part of their territory also seem to constitute a legitimate condition for the American action. To go to war as a last resort should never be an excuse for inaction. From this perspective, the commentator pinpoints that the Pope, Jean-Paul II never said that the war was not fair; he just recalled (just as his messenger) the rule of exhaustion of all other means...

[9] Michael Cromartie, "Hopeless Wars and Hopeless Causes Are Not Morally Justifiable", Fox News, 11 mars, 2003.

[10] Which is why most of the texts on the just war were written before the UN was created.

[11] The Institute on Religion and Democracy, Robert P. George, January 10, 2003, p. 2; see also the position taken by US intellectuals in "Lettre d'Amérique, les raisons d'un combat", *Le Monde*, 14 February 2002.

[12] See Rabbi Mendel Weinbach "Slay their Murder first", on the site Ohr Somayach, September 28, 2002. See also; Abraham H. FOXMAN, "Blame the Terrorists, not Israel", September 21, 2001, Anti-Defamation League website

[13] Robert Kagan, "Puissance américaine, faiblesses européennes", *Le Monde*, 26 July 2002 (site lemonde.fr, p. 3)- Swiss revisionist site (Wilhem Tell Revisionism evokes Hitler's preventive war against the Russian Soviet)- Crapouillot July, 1933 ("Hitler's external politics", the preventive war against bolshevism is legitimized by the necessity to avoid the communist expansion and the proletarian revolution). All of these sites have been visited within the year 2003.

[15] Sébastien Fath, « Comme un vol de faucons hors de la 'cage d'acier'», *Le Monde*, Saturday15 March 2003.

[16] Robert Kagan's widely diffused theories on America's power and Europe's weakness is clearly in line with this sort of reflection.

[17] The reference to Leo Strauss has also been made by a journalist from the *Herald Tribune* who estimates that the attraction for the Bush team's lie, also can be explained through the influence by their mentor "Mentir aux masses? Une nécessité, Le Courrier international, n°656, p. 40.

[18] Alain Frachon et Daniel Vernet, "Le stratège et le philosophe", *Le Monde*, Wednesday 16 April 2003.

[19] See the conversation between Brit Hume and General McInerney on the website Fox News, 6 June 2002; see also the address by the Dutch Defence Minister, International Society for Military Law and the Law of War conference, 14-11-2002, as the critical reflections from John Orme, "The Utility of Force in World of Scarcity", *International Security*, vol. 22, n°3, Winter 1997.

[20] CRS Report for Congress, RS21314, Updated September 23, 2002, p. 2.

[23] The notion of preventive war has been used by the Japanese government to justify the attack on Pearl Harbour. The current Japanese prime minister has clearly rejected this theory and was surprised that the US considered it as legitimate, see his declaration at the Asian-Europe conference at the end of September 2002, <http://news.ninemsn.com.au/World/story_39630.asp>, visited 26 September 2002.

[24] Richard G. Maxon "Nature's Eldest Law: A survey of a Nation's Right to Act in Self-Defence", efreedoms.com, from Parameters, autumn 1985, pp. 55-68.

[25] Simone Goyard-Fabre, Les principes philosophiques du droit politique moderne, Paris, PUF, 1997, p. 304.

[26] Ibid. p. 386.

[27] Ibid. p. 389.

[28] Leo Strauss, Droit naturel et histoire, Flammarion, 1986, p. 22. See also the critical comments by Marshall COHEN, "Moral Scepticism and International Affairs", *Phi-*

losophy and Public Affairs, vol. 13, n°4, autumn 1984, pp. 299-346.

[29] In this kind of justification it is recalled that the Security Council did a declaration in January 1992 qualifying the diffusion of weapons of mass destruction as "threat to peace and international security ", which then could be used for a justification of a military action aimed at neutralising them.

[30] Frederic L. Kirgis, "Pre-emptive Action to Forestall Terrorism", American Society of International Law Insights, June 2002.

[31] "President Bush Addresses United Nations General Assembly",12 September 2003, accessible on <http://www.whitehouse.gov>

[32] "Powell Confident of Strong 'Coalition of the Willing' Against Iraq. Powell Press Conference with U.K. Foreign Secretary Jack Straw', 23 January 2003, accessible on   <http://www.uspolicy.be>

[33] Simone Goyard-Fabre, *Les principes philosophiques du droit politique moderne*, op. cit., p. 303.

[34] Ibid.

[35] Fred Halliday, "International Society as Homogeneity: Burke, Marx, Fukuyama", *Millennium: Journal of International Studies*, 1992, vol. 21, n°3, p. 451 (red. emphasis).

[36] Jolyon Howorth, "L'intégration européenne et la défense : l'ultime défi ?", *Cahiers de Chaillot* 43, November 2002, p. 93, note 170.

[37] Olivier Corten, "Droit, force et légitimité dans une société internationale en mutation", Revue interdisciplinaire d'études juridiques, 1996, n°37, p. 90.

[38] Nicolas ANGELET", "Brouillage institutionnel et légitimation procédurale dans la gestion dela crise du Kosovo", in Olivier Corten et Barbara Delcourt (Eds.), *Droit, légitimation et politique extérieure : l'Europe et la guerre du Kosovo*, Bruxelles, Bruylant, 2001, pp. 207 and ff.

[39] Olivier Corten, "La référence au droit international comme justification du recours à la force : vers une nouvelle doctrine de la guerre juste ?", in A.-M. Dillens (Ed.), *L'Europe et la guerre*, Bruxelles, Facultés Universitaires Saint-Louis, 2001.

[40] That is at least the explanation given by Leo Strauss to explain democracies' complacency towards Nazism, see above cited article by Daniel Vernet and Alain Franchon.

[41] On this question, see Eric David, "Le statut des personnes détenues par les Etats-Unis à la suite du conflit afghan", in Théodore Christakis, Karine Bannelier, Olivier Corten et Barbara Delcourt (eds.), *Le droit international face au terrorisme*, Paris, Pedone, Cahiers internationaux n°7, CEDIN-Paris I, 2002, pp. 321-330.

[42] Laurent Colassis, "Personnes privées de liberté en Irak. La protection du droit international humanitaire", in Barbara Delcourt, Denis Duez et Eric Remacle (eds.), *La guerre d'Irak, prélude d'un nouvel ordre international?*, op. cit., pp. 77-86.

[43] Sami Makki, Militarisation de l'humanitaire, privatisation du militaire, Cahiers d'Etudes stratégiques 36-37, CIRPES, 2004.

[44] Nico Krisch, "Imperial International Law", Global Law Working Paper 01/04, New York University School of Law, pp. 47 and ff.

[45] Fleur Johns, " Guantánamo Bay and the Annihilation of the Exception", *European Journal of International Law*, vol. 16, n°4, 2005, pp. 613-635.

[46] Ralph Wilde recalls also some European proposals regarding asylum (See the proposals aimed at organising camps for asylum–seekers outside of Europe) are adopting a similar strategy, see "De Guantanamo à Abu Graib. L'applicabilité des droits de l'homme aux activités extraterritoriales des Etats", in Barbara Delcourt, Denis Duez et Eric Remacle, L*a guerre d'Irak, prélude d'un nouvel ordre international?*, op. cit., pp. 87 and ff.

[47] Christophe Wasinski, "Généalogie de la guerre dans la pensée stratégique", ibid. pp. 129 and ff.

[48] John A. Gentry, "Doomed to Fail: America's Blind Faith in Military Technology", *Parameters*, Winter 2002-2003, p. 91 (Translated by Christophe Wasinski).

[49] See the critical reflections by James Der Derian, "The Simulation Syndrome: From War Games to Games War", *Social Text*, n°24, 1990, pp. 187-192.

[50] It is also possible to consider that someone fighting a war in the name of humanity

could consider the opponent as "outside of humanity" and consequently does not need to respect the limits that are set up in humanitarian law.

[51] See. Alain Joxe, "Lectures stratégiques: Néolibéralisme de guerre: la nouvelle QDR 06 (*Quadriennal Defense Review*), *Le débat stratégique*, n°84, March 2006.

[52] Sami Makki "Guerre au terrorisme, paramilitarisme et droits de l'homme"*Le débat stratégique*, n°80, summer 2005.

[53] Robert Cooper, "The New Liberal Imperialism", *The Observer Worldview*, 7 April 2002.

[54] See the reflections developed by Benedict Kingsbury, "Sovereignty and Inequality", *European Journal of International Law,*1998, pp. 599-625.

[55] Richard Haass, "Sovereignty: Existing Rights, Evolving Responsibilities", 15 January 2003, available at <http://www.uspolicy.be>

[56] Denis Duez, "Unilatéralisme et militarisation de l'action extérieure: Nouveaux paradigmes de la politique étrangère des Etats-Unis ?", in Karine Bannelier, Théodore Christakis, Olivier Corten, Pierre Klein (Eds.), *L'intervention en Irak et le droit international*, Paris, Pedone, 2004, pp. 129 and ff.

[57] The expression is borrowed from Rudolf El-Kareh in his article published by *Le Monde Diplomatique*, September 2005.

STÈPHANE HESSEL

REFORM OF THE UNITED NATIONS AND INTERNATIONAL HUMANITARIAN LAW

The theme of this meeting is specially important in view of the following facts: one has the feeling, at least at first sight, that no real progress has been made, that the reform of the United Nations is not proceeding, and that international humanitarian law exists in texts, in precious texts, but the way it is applied is frustrating. I would like to personally thank Ramsey Clark for his courage and determination—from the age of 18 (he was then in Nuremberg) up to the present time where he is trying to achieve the removal from office of a US president. What else more courageous, more convincing and at the same time more severe and critical towards his own government, could we expect from a US citizen?

I would like to start by saying the converse. I would like to emphasize that we have an important debt to American civilization, to the United States, not only because we owe it our liberation at the end of World War II (let us not forget that we also owe that debt to the Red Army, not to the US army alone). In my opinion, we have an even more important debt to a US president, and I am thinking naturally of Franklin Roosevelt. As we all know, we would not today have the United Nations without his action. Truly, it is largely his work.

At that time (I was of course much younger than today) the birth of this organization was not guaranteed. There were three main countries, only three, the United States, the United Kingdom and the Soviet Union. Others did not count. Let us not forget that France had been demolished and its power had been drastically weakened. We owe it to General de Gaulle, a man with an extraordinary patriotic arrogance (I dare say it), to have been admitted as one of the five permanent members of the United Nations. We certainly do not owe it to our 1944 military or economic power.

President Roosevelt is the person who imposed the idea of an international organization. Stalin was not very enthusiastic; he would have preferred to pursue his action of progressive domination of the entire world. Churchill did not much believe in it because he thought it would be difficult to reach an accommodation with the communist world. It was therefore Roosevelt who imposed such an international organization. And not any kind of organization, but rather the first one in the history of humanity that founded its Charter on values and not merely on the desire for cooperation between powerful States. One has to read the Charter precisely about the theme I have been asked to develop to see that, for the first time, after all that had happened during World War II, the dignity of the human person and fundamental rights regardless of sex, race, color or political opinion, are inscribed in the founding texts of an international organization.

This is a stage which remains decisive for the functioning of human societies: no society today can forget or deny the existence of a world organization in which all nations are represented. By now, there are 192 such nations, whereas there were only fifty when the United Nations was created. This organization continued to develop, from year to year, and decade to decade. It is now sixty years old. But—and this is always the problem for those who battle for human rights—there is a gap between the texts and their application. I had the privilege of participating in the drafting of the Universal Declaration of Human Rights as a young member of the United Nations administration. Let us not forget that the word "universal" is due to Rene Cassin, who imposed in fact this extraordinary term. One usually speaks about "international" conventions, "international" treaties, but this time no, this time it is "universally" that the rights which make up the thirty articles of the Declaration must be respected: by all citizens, men and women of the whole world.

This declaration was to be the starting point of a long process called the International Bill of Human Rights. It had to include the Declaration as a starting point, which was prodigiously applauded even here in Paris during its adoption at the Chaillot Palace on December, 10, 1948. This first act had to be followed by conventions that would be ratified by all States and which they would be obliged to respect (the Declaration itself had no international judicial value). But this was not all—it was necessary to have a convention on humanitarian law, which had effectively been negotiated in 1949 and gives very precise and ambitious indications on what is permitted or not permitted in armed conflicts. This Convention, the Geneva Convention, is also a very precious document. Other documents, on economic and social rights and on civil and political rights were adopted eighteen years after the Declaration. Such a duration was needed, but we now have an International Covenant on Economic, Social and Cultural Rights (entered into force on January 3, 1976) and an International Covenant on Civil and Political Rights (entered into force on March, 23, 1976).

With more time, I would explore the difference between these two forms of law, but I wish to keep time for questions. Moreover, I do not have the same extraordinary capacity as Ramsey Clark to mobilize your emotions on everything evil that can be said about cultures of violence and impunity. Let me just say that, with regard to these texts and those that were supposed to follow, Declaration, Convention, and measures for applying them (as was the mandate given to the United Nations Commission on Human Rights), due to the state of things, the measures for application could only take a jurisdictional form. A Court was needed, a place where violations of these rights would be judged, and where the persons committing violations could be sentenced.

However, in spite of some steps in that direction, this goal has not been achieved. Let us briefly summarize the situation. First, there was the International Court of Justice in The Hague, whose advisory statements and decisions are important and may be mandatory, but only if States have accepted its jurisdiction, which should in principle apply to all. Many States did not do it, including, but not only, the United States. There is the possibility of examining reports of States on the way rights are applied when they have ratified conventions but, different from those rights from which we benefit inside the European Union, there is no court which might really sanction violations. There are only commissions which examine and make recommendations to those States which committed violations.

We then started to create international criminal tribunals (ex-Yugoslavia, Rwanda and now an international criminal court). However, they may exercise their jurisdiction only to judge persons, and not to judge States. The basic limitation remains the gap between claims in the texts and their application. This gap remains enormous and even increases, due to article 2(7) of the Charter recognizing the sovereignty of each State. In actual fact, there is no longer any sovereign State except one, the United States, because forces present in our societies are more important than States or governments, the latter being at the mercy of economic and financial forces which continue to deepen their power and evolution while neglecting the poor, and accepting an increasing state of injustice as a consequence of the functioning of the international economy. Hence, States are no longer sovereign except one which pretends it is and which has been reinforced in its feeling of sovereignty by history. We mean here recent history. In fact, the United States was already a dominating military and economic power after World War II but there was also the Soviet Union, and later on, there was the China of Mao and there was the process of unification of Europe. Therefore there were various forces in the world that could bring about some degree of equilibrium

Europe found means to reinforce its cooperation in a way which seems miraculous, given the multiplicity of nations which compose it. A European force was created. If it had been done in a better way, if a number of opportunities had not been missed, even recently, Europe would have been, and might still become, a financial, economic, and even to some extent, military power (after all, we have nuclear weapons) in a position to provide a balance to the power of the United States. However, with decolonization on the one hand, including the decolonization of the Soviet Union more recently, the United States presents itself as the only superpower, or hyper-power according to the terminology used by the former French Minister of Foreign Affairs, Hubert Vedrine. We are thus at a point where the gap between the texts and their application is enormous. This is particularly striking with regard to the present situation of the United States. But, whether President Bush is removed from office due to the friends of Ramsey Clark, or goes to the end of his mandate and is then replaced by another president, possibly a Democrat, the fact is that the United States is, and remains, a member of the United Nations.

Many of us had hoped that the summit which took place in New York and gathered 150 heads of state or of governments, would adopt a reform proposed by the Secretary-General of the United Nations, Kofi Annan. It would have increased the legitimacy of the Security Council and contributed to clearly defining terrorism in order to distinguish it from other forms of violence. This would have allowed new institutions which would have reinforced this organization, the only one intended to bring the reign of human dignity, international justice and development—a development which we have failed to accomplish because, over the sixty years during which we claimed we wanted to support the development of those countries which have not yet reached a sufficient economic level, we have not succeeded in doing enough. This is the case in particular of African countries and, beyond, of their nationals who, even when they emigrate, are still neglected persons in our international society. This is a scandal that we can all see here in Paris, every day, since squats in which African people had found an asylum are demolished with the intention of sending these people back to their countries.

What I want to say is that we have an obligation—and I have a great admiration for Monique Chemillier-Gendreau, Mireille Delmas Marty and many others who work with so much energy to ensure an actual jurisdictional translation of decisions on humanitarian law—that the latter should not merely be proclaimed (they are), but applied. This is the task of our present century. We will be satisfied with our human society only when proclaimed rights will also be applied and when financial as well as political powers will have to account and be responsible for the application of these rights. *Accountability* is a nice English word: the presidents, the financial powers, must be made accountable in the exercise of their responsibilities. This is how I see the way we have to achieve the exercise of responsibilities.

It is a fact that impunity has never been strongly contested, because states on the one hand, and financial forces on the other, have never had to face a public opinion sufficiently powerful and well-organized to contest the dominant position that they hold in the world, and among the former, the domination of the United States is at the very first rank. Why shouldn't this change?

I would like to say a further word in favor of the United Nations. It is the first, among intergovernmental organizations, to have stirred up the action of nongovernmental organizations in its very Charter. This word, NGO, comes indeed from the United Nations and was created as a counterpart to inter-governmental action. In the course of the past fifteen years, NGOs and more particularly those involved in the defense of human rights, including Amnesty, OXFAM, ADIF, and many other great organizations, have played an increasing role. Maybe they are about to become one of the forces, maybe they will become THE force which will impose respect for international law on governments. To that end, they need support from all of us.

Each one of us, as a citizen of his or her country and in some way a European citizen if we are in Europe, and also in some way a citizen of the world if we live in an organized world, has the duty, the obligation, to pursue these efforts without respite to ensure that pressure for its actual application—hence for the end of impunity—be added to the proclamation of rights. This proclamation started with the Universal Declaration, then came the Conventions on humanitarian law. We have to work in order to ensure it will become the basis of a less unequal society, with the help of the new forces which have appeared for around twenty years: the forces of inter-communicability, the interdependence that we feel between societies and the modern means of communication which now proliferate in a way which frightens me to some extent, because I am too old to benefit from them, but which may be the crucial resource upon which a great world movement in favor of humanitarian law and against impunity can be founded.

JAN MYRDAL

THE NECESSITY OF DEFENDING THE RULE OF LAW!

Other participants will discuss the economic and geopolitical determinants of the present United States struggle for world supremacy. I want to talk about some consequences this global Pax Americana is having for International law, civic rights and the erosion of what was known as the rule of law in all our countries—even in officially non-aligned countries like Sweden.

In order to make that present development more visible I want to quote from the testimony of Reich Marshal, Defendant Hermann Goering 18 March 1946 at the Nuremberg War Crimes Trial. Mr. Justice Robert H. Jackson, United States chief prosecutor is conducting the interrogation:

> **Mr. Justice Jackson:**: But you are explaining, as the high authority of this system, to men who do not understand it very well, and I want to know what was necessary to run the kind of system that you set up in Germany. The concentration camp was one of the things you found immediately necessary upon coming into power, was it not? And you set them up as a matter of necessity, as you saw it?
>
> **Goering**: That was faultily translated—it went too fast. But I believe I have understood the sense of your remarks. You asked me if I considered it necessary to establish concentration camps immediately in order to eliminate opposition. Is that correct?
>
> **Mr. Justice Jackson**: Your answer is "yes," I take it?
>
> **Goering**: Yes.

Mr. Justice Jackson: Was it also necessary, in operating this system, that you must not have persons entitled to public trials in independent courts? And you immediately issued an order that your political police would not be subject to court review or to court orders, did you not?

Goering: You must differentiate between the two categories; those who had committed some act of treason against the new state, or those who, might be proved to have committed such an act, were naturally turned over to the courts. The others, however, of whom one might expect such acts, but who had not yet committed them, were taken into protective custody, and these were the people who were taken to concentration camps. I am now speaking of what happened at the beginning. Later things changed a great deal. Likewise, if for political reasons—to answer your question—someone was taken into protective custody, that is, purely for reasons of state, this could not be reviewed or stopped by any court. Later, when some people were also taken into protective custody for nonpolitical reasons, people who had opposed the system in some other way, I once, as Prussian Prime Minister and Reich Minister of the Interior, I remember...

Mr. Justice Jackson: Let's omit that. I have not asked for that. If you will just answer my question, we shall save a great deal of time. Your counsel will be permitted to bring out any explanations you want to make.

You did prohibit all court review and considered it necessary to prohibit court review of the causes for taking people into what you called protective custody?

Goering: That I answered very clearly, but I should like to make an explanation in connection with my answer.

/.../

Goering: In connection with your question that these cases could not be reviewed by the court, I want to say that a decree was issued through me and jointly to the effect that those who were turned over to concentration camps were to be informed after 24 hours of the reason for their being turned over, and that after 48 hours, or some short period of time, they should have the right to an attorney. But this by no means rescinded my order that a review was not permitted by the courts of a politically necessary measure of protective custody. These people were simply to be given an opportunity of making a protest.

MR. JUSTICE JACKSON: Protective custody meant that you were taking people into custody who had not committed any crimes but who, you thought, might possibly commit a crime?

Goering: Yes. People were arrested and taken into protective custody who had not yet committed any crime, but who could be expected to do so if they remained free, just as extensive protective measures are being taken in Germany today on a tremendous scale.

In this testimony Herman Goering makes a clear distinction between those who have committed what according to the German law at the time could be considered criminal acts and who - to use his words - were naturally turned over to the courts and those who had not committed any crime but could be suspected of doing so if they remained free and thus for reasons of state were arrested and taken to concentration camps.

Nearly sixty years later president George W. Bush of the United states and his followers like prime minister Tony Blair of the United kingdom —as well as politicians from minor states like the Swedish prime minister Göran Persson and his minister of justice Thomas Bodström—follow the same reasoning.

Even what Hermann Goering said about how the state is to handle the right of the extralegally imprisoned to attorney could now be said by Bush, Blair, Persson or Bodström

I quote Hermann Goering:

But this by no means rescinded my order that a review was not permitted by the courts of a politically necessary measure of protective custody. These people were simply to be given an opportunity of making a protest.

The Guantanamo camp and other prisons outside the ordinary legal framework and the laws being enacted in the so called war against terrorism are held by our governments as necessary for the survival of society. It is a verbiage we who grew up during the thirties' well remember.

The present legal reality can be described by the words of the indictment (count one) at the Nuremberg trial:

They imprisoned such persons without judicial process, holding them in protective custody and concentration camps, and subjected them to prosecution, degradation, despoilment, enslavement, torture and murder....

I am decidedly not asking for Bush, Blair and our local politicians such as Persson and Bodström to be hung according to the Nuremberg precedent but under the existing constitutional laws in our countries they could be held not only politically but legally responsible for the ongoing destruction of basic principles for civic rights and the rule of law. Such indictments of responsible politicians would be positive but seem for the moment to be politically less probable.

But what can—and must—be done is to create such a public awareness of the issues that it will be possible to force through a political change.

It is today once more necessary to state that those civic and legal rights that were acquired by our people during the centuries up to and through the bourgeois revolutions can be called formal but that they are no formality.

In Sweden the legal rule that no man could be imprisoned without due process was formulated in 1350. It was given an even stronger legal structure after the revolution in 1809 (§16 in the Form of government). Today that rule no longer holds.

Of course one can discuss the class structure of Swedish society in 1350 and 1809. But that is not the question. The real political question is that the present Swedish minister of justice—Thomas Bodström—for reasons of state and to keep good relations with the United States is pushing through laws that go against this fundamental right that our forefathers fought for during more than seven centuries. The right to due process is no longer even a formal right, not even a formality if the Security police on the instigation of the United states can get you described as a threat to society.

(If the present laws had been in force forty years ago Olof Palme would have been in danger of being put in prison in a semi-secret trial for his struggle against the racist regime of South Africa and his support for the Vietnamese people in their war against the United States occupiers.)

And what about the right to privacy? Just now the European Union—on the instigation of the United Kingdom and Sweden—is discussing instituting a total control and registration of all our telephone calls, internet contacts and fax messages.

And torture? Not only is torture an official United States policy. Countries like Sweden have accepted that the agents of the United States government act on Swedish national territory and collect people to be sent through their covert CIA-air service to be tortured.

If we are not able to safeguard our rights—in Sweden even the basic civic rights to due procedure from 1350!—the future for our children and grandchildren will be as bleak as if the Reich Marshall had been successful sixty years ago in the Hitlerite Griff nach Weltmacht.

ANTOINE BERNARD

CHALLENGES OF THE NEW SYSTEM OF INTERNATIONAL CRIMINAL JUSTICE

1. Peace through Justice

The preamble of the Rome Statute that has given rise to the creation of the International Criminal Court (ICC), entered into force on July 1st, 2002, and fixes the basic principles and purposes of this first permanent international criminal jurisdiction. Expressed in universal terms, they have an echo that goes beyond the strict domain of action of the Court.

> ...*Mindful* that during this century millions of children, women and men have been victims of unimaginable atrocities that deeply shock the conscience of humanity,
> *Recognizing* that such grave crimes threaten the peace, security and well-being of the world,
> *Affirming* that the most serious crimes of concern to the international community as a whole must not go unpunished and that their effective prosecution must be ensured by taking measures at the national level and by enhancing international cooperation,
> *Determined* to put an end to impunity for the perpetrators of these crimes and thus to contribute to the prevention of such crimes,
> *Recalling* that it is the duty of every State to exercise its criminal jurisdiction over those responsible for international crimes,
> *Reaffirming* the Purposes and Principles of the Charter of

the United Nations, and in particular that all States shall refrain from the threat or use of force against the territorial integrity or political independence of any State, or in any other manner inconsistent with the Purposes of the United Nations,

Emphasizing in this connection that nothing in this Statute shall be taken as authorizing any State Party to intervene in an armed conflict or in the internal affairs of any State,

Determined, to these ends and for the sake of present and future generations, to establish an independent permanent International Criminal Court in relationship with the United Nations system, with jurisdiction over the most serious crimes of concern to the international community as a whole,

Emphasizing that the International Criminal Court established under this Statute shall be complementary to national criminal jurisdictions ...

Getting peace through justice: for many "realistic" people, such a project would be vain in the worst instance, and utopian in the best. Is it not true that peace belongs by definition to a purely political sphere and is the product of relations based on force, with possibly the contribution of a mediator? Is it not true that the marginal or at best subsidiary character of international criminal justice is illustrated by its difficult and late emergence?

This largely predominant view does not take into account the acceleration of history: in a scant fifteen years, international criminal justice has occupied a greater and greater part of the political sphere due to the pressure of public opinions confronted by the perpetration of crimes and the impunity of their executioners, or having recently won the right to demand justice.

Truth, justice, reparation—from the *Velasquez-Rodriguez* decision of the Inter-American Court to the Basic Principles of the United Nations on impunity (the "Joinet" Principles)—these demands have been codified as rights (of the victims) and corollary obligations (of States).

Similarly, the Inter- American Court and other regional and international organizations for the protection of human rights have established the fundamental right of victims to truth, justice and reparation.

The right of victims to an effective recourse to an independent jurisdiction is both the sine qua non condition and the primary avenue for its implementation.

But if, in the last two decades, States did create a number of mechanisms allowing, supposedly, the struggle against impunity at the national and international levels, the tools—(and their mastery) adapted to each situation and political context—are still missing, as is the political will to implement them.

1.1 Genesis of international criminal justice

In 1872, Gustave Moynier, one of the founders of the Red Cross, evoked for the first time the prospect of a universal jurisdiction, in reaction to the cruelty of crimes committed during the French-Prussian conflict. After World War I, the Versailles Treaty had planned a jurisdiction intended to judge Guillaume II, Kaiser of Germany, for a supreme offence against international morale and the sacred authority of treaties. However, the Netherlands, where the Kaiser had found asylum, refused to hand him over.

When the extermination of millions of people by the Nazi regime was revealed in 1945, it led to the creation of the Nuremberg International Military Tribunal. This was the first act of the Allies with a view to the establishment of criminal justice with an international character. A complementary tribunal, the Tokyo Tribunal, was established in 1946 with similar jurisdictional competence.

The idea of creating an international criminal jurisdiction then remained dormant for almost fifty years. This was partly due to the Cold War, to the fact that States were unable to finalize a criminal code and to agree on the definition of aggression. Atrocities committed in former Yugoslavia and in Rwanda at the end of the Cold War, as well as the strong mobilization of civil society and nongovernmental organizations, were among the main factors that led to the acceleration of the efforts towards the creation of an international criminal court in the middle of the '90s.

In 1993 and 1994, the Security Council decided to establish the International Criminal Tribunal for the Former Yugoslavia and the International Criminal Tribunal for Rwanda. The competence of these ad hoc tribunals is limited in time and space. Nevertheless, their activity has brought an essential contribution to the elaboration and development of international criminal law from the viewpoint of both fundamental rules and procedure. Mainly, the creation of these tribunals has played a decisive role in the revival of the idea of a permanent criminal court.

In 1995, the General Assembly of the United Nations then started the process which gave rise, on July 17, 1998, to the adoption of the Rome Statute of the International Criminal Court (ICC) by 120 States.

The close link between justice and peace is already sanctioned in its preamble, as everyone can see. It affirms that impunity for the most terrible crimes is an obstacle to a lasting re-establishment of peace, and it ratifies the premise that the battle against impunity contributes to the prevention of new crimes. The entry into force of the Rome Statute on July 1, 2002, sanctions in that respect a retreat from the arbitrary, through the codification of some basic principles of international criminal law.

1.2 Affirmation of basic principles of International Criminal Law

The Rome Statute is based on a series of basic principles which show a retreat from the all-powerful doctrine of the national interest, or at least of arbitrariness.

Concerning the principle of individual criminal responsibility, the Statute validates the advances of the ad hoc special tribunals by stating that anyone who commits one of the crimes covered in the Statute, orders, solicits or encourages such a crime, or any attempt to commit such a crime, or even facilitates, helps or assists in the commission of a crime or in an attempt to commit such a crime, can be held criminally responsible for these acts. It should be emphasized that, contradictory to the recommendations of some nongovernmental organizations, any responsibility of the body politic has been explicitly ruled out.

Concerning the prohibition of a prosecuted person's invoking immunities linked with his (her) official capacity, the Statute represents a giant advance. Article 27 clearly confirms the theory according to which, when crimes are judged on behalf of the international community, official capacity as a Head of State or Government, a member of a Government or parliament, an elected representative or a government official shall in no case exempt a person from criminal responsibility, nor shall it, in and of itself, constitute a ground for reduction of sentence. Hence, immunities or special procedural rules that might be attached to the official capacity of a person, whether under national or international law, shall not bar the Court from exercising its jurisdiction over such a person.

Concerning the Non-Applicability of Statutory Limitations to crimes within the jurisdiction of the Court, the Statute confirms this principle, which is already part of the 1968 UNO Convention addressing war crimes and crimes against humanity.

Concerning applicable penalties, the ICC explicitly excludes the death penalty: the only penalties that may be imposed are prison sentences, fines, and forfeiture of proceeds, property and assets derived directly or indirectly from the crime.

On all these matters, the very strong involvement of NGOs in the negotiations has led to extremely positive results: the NGOs have indeed succeeded in having a strong influence on the negotiations and obtaining many advances for international law. Besides the principles already mentioned, some other advances are particularly due to the civil society, for example, the definition of sexual crimes, directed in particular against women: this definition has been made precise and definitely confirmed for the first time in the ICC Statute. This is also true concerning the status of victims, their participation in the procedure, and their right to obtain reparation.

2. The consecration of complementarity: national jurisdictions under the spotlight

In contrast to the former special international tribunals, which had primacy over national jurisdictions, the ICC is "complementary" to the latter.

The Rome Statute does not limit itself to the creation of an international jurisdiction. The latter is inserted in an interactive system of international justice including States: the primary responsibility for the guarantee of the rights to truth, justice and reparation is in their hands.

1.1 The challenge of complementarity

The principle of complementarity is stated in the Preamble and in Article 1 of the Statute. It means that judging authors of the crimes of genocide, crimes against humanity and war crimes is primarily the responsibility of States. The Preamble thus affirms that all States have the obligation to themselves punish those crimes within the jurisdiction of the Court.

Hence, the ICC will prosecute and judge a person only if the national jurisdictions "normally qualified" to do it are unwilling or genuinely unable to carry out the investigation or prosecution. The ICC may decide to initiate an investigation if there is an unjustified delay in the action of the national jurisdiction, if this national jurisdiction has started a procedure in a way which shows an intent to shield the person concerned from criminal responsibility or, finally, if the proceedings were not conducted independently or impartially.

In other words, the action of the ICC is subsidiary. The ratification of the ICC Statute by a State thus entails the obligation of prosecuting and judging breaches defined in the Statute at the national level. To implement this responsibility, States must include the definition of crimes within the jurisdiction of the ICC in their national legislation, as well as a number of general principles of international criminal law.

The principle of complementarity relies on a realistic observation: the ICC will not be able to examine all infractions that have been committed and are within its jurisdiction with regard to Articles 5 to 8 of its Statute.

First, its jurisdiction is limited: it may not exercise its functions and powers for crimes that have been committed neither on the territory of a State Party to the Statute nor by a national of a State Party, unless the situation is referred to the Prosecutor by the Security Council (see below). For such crimes, States must take it upon themselves to create conditions such that their national jurisdictions will be in a position to prosecute and judge, themselves.

The experience of international criminal tribunals has shown that international courts are cumbersome machineries. The ICC will not be an exception. The exercise of its jurisdiction is thus appropriate for persons responsible for the gravest crimes, the "top officials", not for second or third rank persons. As a consequence, the latter might elude investigation.

Addressing this "impunity gap" is the major challenge of the coming years: the entry of the ICC into force must impel a significant increase, at the national level, in the repression of international crimes, and public exposure of truth and responsibilities for the purpose of establishing the reparation due. Failing this, the isolation of the ICC would threaten its credibility and reduce the dissuasive effect which might otherwise be expected.

The reduction of this "impunity gap" relies on the action of States which have now a number of tools at their disposal to struggle against impunity and/or encourage the work of memory and reconciliation (see below). But the very application of the principle of complementarity will give the ICC a role in the evaluation of national procedures. It will in fact be the responsibility of the ICC to determine their existence and validity. This evaluation of the capacity and will to treat these problems at the national level will be key to the success or failure of the system of international justice established by the Rome Statute.

2.2 *The challenge of universal jurisdiction*

National jurisdictions have the obligation to prosecute and bring to trial the gravest violations of human rights and of international humanitarian law. This duty is clearly established within international law and has been fully confirmed long before the creation of the ICC: the 1949 Geneva Conventions and the 1984 Convention on Torture oblige States that have ratified them to prosecute and extradite any author of war crimes or acts of torture.

This is the so-called principle of universal jurisdiction: there is universal jurisdiction when a State's jurisdiction can be exercised with regard to acts that do not have any of the links with that State that are usually required. In other words, acts that have been committed neither on the territory of that State, nor by nationals of that State, nor at the expense of its basic interests.

This universal jurisdiction is never general in the sense that it is always established for particular classes of infractions. There are in fact a number of reasons to establish such a principle of universal jurisdiction.

Such reasons appear indeed in the system of complementarity established by the ICC Statute in order to abolish impunity for crimes within its jurisdiction. The main tools to wipe out impunity are the adoption of *national* rules and an improved cooperation between States having adopted such rules. The Statute does not strictly oblige States to establish their universal jurisdiction in this domain but puts forward objectives that are similar to those which usually justify it in international criminal law.

Universal jurisdiction was long considered as a vague theory of interest only to academics until victims and NGOs seized upon it. The case of Pinochet gave rise to a great hope. For the first time, upon the initiative of his victims, a Head of State, though long ago deposed, was in trouble and national interests could not prevent it, at least initially.

After Pinochet was brought back to his country for "humanitarian" reasons, the adventure of the Belgian law of universal jurisdiction, abrogated in 2003, has again illustrated the sensitivity of the subject. In fact, universal jurisdiction raises a number of practical problems (proofs can be found only in foreign countries) as well as financial problems (investigation of mass crimes is expensive). But the true reasons are States' *political and diplomatic* uneasiness at seeing their courts addressing questions in which crimes committed by other governments are brought into public scrutiny.

Some NGOs, like the International Federation for Human Rights, struggle with great determination for an effective application of universal jurisdiction, and at least of territorial jurisdiction of national courts if a person responsible for an international crime is present on their national territory, because they consider it as the only way in many cases for victims to exercise their right to an effective appeal. However, purely judicial mechanisms are not the only ones that might contribute to the establishment of the truth. During some periods of transition, some countries have established special temporary institutions in charge of bringing past crimes to light.

2.3 The challenge of transitional justice

Often, emerging democracies inherit an inoperative system of criminal justice. Furthermore, too often the new regimes are partly composed of persons that were in the previous government during the period of terror. The situation reaches the height of paradox when the very judges corrupted by the previous regime and the very policemen who had practiced torture are now those in charge of the criminal justice system. In such a context, the "truth commissions" can contribute to fill an important void, in order to start to take into account the rights of victims to truth, justice and reparation.

These truth commissions are non-jurisdictional investigatory organs created to shed light on a period of conflict or internal violence, to help the societies to take into account their past in a critical way, to establish a system of (individual and/or collective) reparation for victims and their families, and to prevent any repetition of crimes. They might be either an alternative or a complement to the judicial process. They have the advantage of being able to address a large number of cases in a relatively short time and to fill the void created by a weakened justice system.

These various commissions are very different from each other, in particular because it is essential that their methods of work reflect and take into account the singular aspects of their respective countries.

They have often been opposed to judiciary mechanisms. This opposition is largely due to a deformed perception of the most famous among them: the Truth and Reconciliation Commission (TRC) of South Africa, which has been viewed as distributing amnesties to anyone who agreed to confess his crimes. The articulation between the judicial mechanisms and these truth commissions does raise significant questions, mainly when the latter have quasi-jurisdictional powers or when the chances of their overcoming impunity are negligible.

The first question is, should the truth commissions (which are non-judicial organs) disclose the names of persons responsible of violations of human rights and hence make it possible for justice to act, later? There is no general answer to that question. First, since they are not jurisdictions, these commissions do not necessarily present the needed guarantees of a fair trial and that persons alleged to have committed crimes are able to defend themselves adequately. Then, disclosing names might in some cases be an obstacle to the manifestation of the truth. For example, in El Salvador, when names were made public, a severe government crisis ensued which gave rise to the promulgation of a general amnesty which in turn prevented further investigation and repression. In Argentina, Chile and Guatemala, there was, on the contrary, a disclosure only of the names of institutions responsible for crimes, but this prevented the population from knowing this "other part of the truth" and lodging judicial complaints. Louis Joinet, former United Nations expert on impunity, thus proposes that names of persons be disclosed only after their hearings or at least after they have been summoned to that effect and have been able to exercise their right of reply in writing, their answer being then included in their file.

Arguments in favor of disclosing names arise from those at the origin of these commissions. In a context where proofs are overwhelming and the judicial system is weak or polarized, such a disclosure may be the only chance for justice, at least symbolically, for victims. In Chad, Rwanda and South Africa, names of persons responsible were disclosed.

A second recurrent question when truth commissions are broached is the power to confer amnesty. Let us remind everyone that, according to international law, crimes of genocide, crimes against humanity, grave breaches of the 1948 Geneva Conventions and torture must be prosecuted and cannot be granted amnesty. The jurisprudence of the Inter-American Court and of the United Nations Human Rights Committee is also very clear: according to these bodies, promulgating a law of amnesty is a violation by States of their obligation to guarantee respect of human rights. Nevertheless, the decision to grant amnesty for other crimes, in exchange for peace and global truth, remains a political question arising in general from a compromise between transitional authorities and persons who might be investigated.

For victims and their families, a feeling of incompletion may prevail if persons cited by a truth commission are not prosecuted or if they are granted amnesty before being prosecuted. In practice, if links between truth commissions and justice are different in various situations, there are only a few cases when these commissions have worked in close connection with the judicial process.

Another question is how the ICC will take into account the existence of truth commissions in those countries where it will choose to carry out investigations. Actions carried out by the Prosecutor's Office in Uganda, where a mechanism of amnesty was proposed to rebels that would surrender, and in the Democratic Republic of Congo, where a Truth and Reconciliation Commission was established, might give some further information. In fact, the ICC will probably have to make its judgment on the articulation between its own mandate and those of these transitional mechanisms. In particular, the ICC might have to determine if, and under which conditions, the principle of complementarity might be applicable to them.

3. For an independent and effective ICC: some problems to be overcome

If we now consider the ICC itself, many problems remain to be overcome to guarantee its "independence and effectiveness", as the slogan of the International Coalition of NGOs for the ICC hopes.

3.1 *The ICC and States Parties: founders, controllers, partners?*

Through its permanent character, the ICC is a priori more independent of political hazards than the ad hoc international tribunals directly created by the Security Council. Nevertheless, the ICC remains the result of a compromise between States that founded it. The "political" part of the relation between the ICC and its founders is dealt with in particular in Part 11 of the Rome Statute on prerogatives of the Assembly of States Parties and in Part 12 on the financing of the ICC.

The role of such an organ becomes particularly important in the framework of the ICC: the problem here is not to speak about politics inside a political institution, but to assume political functions inside a *judicial* institution. However, in order to have any credibility, a jurisdiction must be independent of political hazards.

The mandate of the Assembly of States Parties is to give the ICC organs "general orientations" for its administration and to examine and decide the ICC budget (Article 112.2). It may establish "*such subsidiary bodies as may be necessary, including an independent oversight mechanism for inspection, evaluation and investigation of the Court, in order to enhance its efficiency and economy*" (Article 112.4).

Beyond the reasonable purpose of contributing to an efficient and economical administration of the ICC, one sees the paradox in expecting that States possibly involved in problems to be addressed by the Court should give the ICC the financing needed, while preserving its independence in the same time.

The third session of the Assembly, in September 2004 in The Hague, had confirmed this tension: the nervous attention given by many States to the Court they created, to its budget and functioning, confirms that an adequate equilibrium between the judicial and the political has not yet been found.

The risk is therefore that States might attempt to exercise political control over the Court when it shows its independence. At this very moment of truth, judges will show if they are able to get rid of the supervision of its founders and controllers, without depriving the ICC of the political bases necessary for its durability and development. Again, the role of NGOs and public opinion will be needed to prevent possible regressions.

3.2 The ICC and the Security Council: risk of inaction, co-optation or suspension

In addition to the internal political hazards, the ICC also faces an external political hazard, in particular when peace and security are at stake. In fact, the Rome Statute gives two powers to the Security Council. The first one, positive, is to refer to the Prosecutor "a situation in which one or more of such crimes (within the jurisdiction of the Court) appears to have been committed " (Article 13.b), in view of Chapter VII of the Charter of the United Nations. The second one, which is negative, is the power of the Security Council to ask, for a period of 12 months, renewable, that the Court, in virtue of Chapter VII of the Chart, suspend an investigation, or launch or undertake one..

Concerning the first one, three possibilities might be envisaged:

• *Inaction!* This had been the prevailing situation after the entry into force of the Statute. This is not surprising in view of the positions of Russia, China and the United States: all three are permanent members of the Council and did not ratify the Statute. The anti-ICC campaign carried out by the US administration (bilateral agreements on immunity, threat of suspension of military support to many States, immunity for soldiers of States that are not Parties to the Statute involved in UN military operations: see the FIDH report: "No to the US exception", November 2002http://www.fidh.org/justice/rapport/2002/cpi345n8.pdf) is paradoxically a tribute to the potential effectiveness of the ICC: it aims not merely to protect US nationals but also to reduce the capacities of action of the Court.

• *Co-optation*: The Council might activate the Prosecutor according to its political aims and compromises. Highly open to criticism for their selectivity, such seizures of jurisdiction would be comparable to those Council decisions creating special tribunals for ex-Yugoslavia and Rwanda.

• *Integration*: The Council would integrate recourse to the ICC among its tools for the promotion of peace and would refer situations on the basis of objective criteria.

One may hope the Council will not long remain indifferent to the ICC system. Under pressure of public opinion and the media, it had to incorporate the objective of struggle against impunity, and to fix means for that purpose in a number of decisions adopted under Chapter VII. However, only a few of its resolutions on cases presently under the investigation of the Court encourage cooperation with it. The present reticence to include reference to the ICC in the projected resolution on the protection of civilians in armed conflicts illustrates the difficulty in allying the Council with the Court. Resolution 1593 of the Council dated 31 March 2005, referring the case of Darfour to the ICC, illustrates this double tendency. The Council integrates a mechanism for justice into a highly political debate; it qualifies crimes in question, but at the same time, in violation of the Rome Statute, it does not provide UN financing for the action of the Court and then almost congratulates itself on the cooperation of the Khartoum regime with the Court.

For similar reasons, one may hope that the Council will not be tempted to use its power of suspension of an investigation or prosecution: this would mean that, for the Council, the freedom of action of the murderers is necessary for peace or, in a caricatural way, that the crimes are the price of the peace. Between "peace through dialogue", "peace through justice" and "peace through crime", the Council may benefit from the large field of action offered by the two first options to not have to openly assume the third.

It should be especially emphasized that it would be very difficult for States members of the Council to take responsibility for the vote of such a resolution with regard to their respective public opinions. Any government that would submit such a project to the approval of the Council would take the risk of being viewed as trying to protect criminals against humanity. It would moreover be exposed to a negative vote by other States, or possibly a veto.

If, nevertheless, the Council decided to ask for a suspension, a debate would certainly follow on the scope of such a decision: Article 16 indeed mentions a "request" to the Court, so that judges might discuss whether this is an actual order or merely a wish submitted for their approval.

3.3 The uncertainties of the criminal policy of the Prosecutor

Under these conditions, the ICC has two major assets to ensure its credibility and also its apparent and effective independence. They are particularly pertinent in a period of armed conflicts or of reinstatement of peace. The first one is the possibility at its disposal to initiate an investigation *proprio motu* on the basis of information on crimes within the jurisdiction of the Court (Article 15.1). This also opens a way to requests addressed to the Prosecutor by NGOs. The second one is the irrelevance of official capacity as a cause of exemption from individual criminal responsibility (Article 27), thus affirming the principle of equality of all criminals with regard to international justice.

However, the Prosecutor has up to now excluded recourse to this capacity of initiating an investigation and has instead urged States Parties to directly refer relevant situations to him (the third and last way to initiate an investigation: Article 14). His wish to protect the Court from the political interference of its founders in the first months of its entry into force is understandable, as is the hope of obtaining better cooperation from States. However, the Prosecutor would make a major strategic mistake if he were to erect this as a directing principle of his criminal policy.

Such an orientation would deprive him of the basis of his power of judicial dissuasion, that which precisely allows the Court to rein in the armed force of international criminals and to exert its weight in peace negotiations.

It would establish the politicization and instrumentalization of judicial repression, with the initiation of investigations then relying only on States Parties. Of course, the work of justice always takes place in a given political context, and the action of the judge is sometimes the continuation of politics in other ways. But justice here aims at the repression of the gravest crimes, of concern to the entire international community. Its independence, from the very start to investigation, prosecution and judgment, is the very basis of its effectiveness. It is also a sine qua non condition for its appropriation by victims, their families and concerned societies; and experience shows how much this appropriation is itself needed for the lasting success of a peace process.

It thus becomes even more important for the Prosecutor to be able to use Article 27 of the Statute, which affirms "irrelevance of official capacity": in other words, anyone can be prosecuted, including Heads of States or of Governments. If investigations should prove the implication of officials at a high level in the commission of crimes, the Prosecutor would have an occasion to prove his determination.

Whatever will be the strategy finally decided by the Prosecutor, he will have to take into account a new parameter: the capacity, for the victims, to express their views before the Court.

4. The challenge of appropriation by victims of the tools of struggle against impunity

The Statute is an historical advance in the recognition of rights of victims. In fact, in contrast to the statutes of international criminal tribunals, mainly influenced by Anglo-Saxon law, the ICC Statute is the result of a compromise between Romano-German law and Common Law, and it affirms, for the benefit of victims, the rights to be protected, including to participate in procedures and to get reparation. These two last rights were absent from the statutes of previous international tribunals.

Who are the victims ?

Article 85 of the Rules of Procedure and Evidence defines "Victims" as *"natural persons who have suffered harm as a result of the commission of any crime within the jurisdiction of the Court"*. It adds that *"Victims may include organizations or institutions that have sustained direct harm to any of their property which is dedicated to religion, education, art or science or charitable purposes, and to their historic monuments, hospitals and other places and objects for humanitarian purposes"*.

Protection

All ICC organs have the obligation of protecting victims and witnesses: "The Court shall take appropriate measures to protect the safety, physical and psychological well-being, dignity and privacy of victims and witnesses… The Prosecutor shall take such measures particularly during the investigation and prosecution …". This general principle, stated in Article 68.1 of the Statute, is made more precise in rules 87 and 88 of the Rules of Procedure and Evidence.

The ICC thus has an obligation to elaborate short and long term programs ensuring an effective protection of victims and witnesses. It must guarantee their access to the Court and ensure means for their cooperation. As a consequence, and although investigations take place in the countries of the conflicts, the Court must strictly reduce the risks of reprisals. Otherwise, victims and witnesses will not be in a position to use their right to participation and reparation. Absence of the protection planned by the Rome Statute would thus destroy one of the basic advances of this text and would highly damage the credibility of the Court and the efficiency of its investigations.

Participation

The ICC Statute affirms the right to participation in procedures: "*Where the personal interests of the victims are affected, the Court shall permit their views and concerns to be presented and considered at stages of the proceedings determined to be appropriate by the Court and in a manner which is not prejudicial to or inconsistent with the rights of the accused and a fair and impartial trial. Such views and concerns may be presented by the legal representatives of the victims where the Court considers it appropriate, in accordance with the Rules of Procedure and Evidence*" (Article 68.3).

To make their participation easier, victims are free to choose a representative, possibly on a list at their disposal. The legal representative of victims will guarantee their participation in the proceedings, often exclusively. In fact, if there are many victims, the Court might ask them to choose a common representative.

The effective participation of victims will then be possible under two conditions: they should be effectively informed of their rights and represented adequately.

Victims, in particular those living in rural regions, often will have no knowledge of their right to participate. Some of them might moreover fear to appear before the Court if they are not aware of precise conditions of their participation. Most often, they will not know any one of the languages used by the Court and will not be able to write. The section on participation of the victims and reparations, in charge of organizing their participation before the Court, will thus have to develop a very important groundwork. It will have to inform victims about their precise rights and explain consequences, modalities and limits of such a participation, in order to avoid creating false hopes.

Reparations

A Fund for victims and their families has thus been created. It will play a double role. First it will be at the disposal of the ICC to execute the reparations ordered and all measures of confiscations and fines decided by the Court. It will also, under certain conditions, use its own resources, the product of voluntary contributions, for programs of assistance to victims, for instance by allocating some sums of money to institutions (including inter-governmental, international and national ones) for activities and projects benefiting victims and their families.

The use of such mechanisms would give the ICC a new aspect: while victims could only be witnesses before ad hoc tribunals, they would now have the possibility of becoming actual actors in the judicial process. The expression of their preoccupations and expectations must contribute to the making of an international justice that will be more closely connected to actual situations. It will therefore be in a better position to explore them and better accepted by all those who suffered from the crimes it will examine.

Conclusion: reconciling peace and responsibility

The expectations placed on the ICC are even greater in the context of the post September 11 events, a period in which respect of international norms concerning human rights has decreased. Many opportunist States have seized this occasion—symbolized by Guantanamo and Abu Ghraib, and by the doctrine of preventive war—to reinforce their authoritarianism under the pretext of the war against terror. Under such conditions, the consolidation of a system of international criminal justice is one of the rare reasons for hope in the construction of peace through law and justice.

Peace remains of course the domain of excellence of politics. But the emergence of a system of prevention, repression and reparation, as embodied in the ICC, will highly reduce arbitrariness. The potential of effective action by an independent judge in the political procedures for reinstatement and consolidation of peace is, above all, good news for victims whose interests and rights (to truth, justice and reparation) were often sacrificed in the name of the falsely alleged viability of peace agreements. While this may not be a priori apparent, it is in fact at the local level that, with the emergence of the ICC system, new opportunities for the consolidation of peace and democracy may be found.

NURI ALBALA

UNIVERSAL JURISDICTION UNACCEPTABLE TO THE MOST POWERFUL *

The principle of universal jurisdiction to judge crimes against humanity, or in actual fact criminals against humanity (tribunals do not judge crimes but criminals; the latter are those who will possibly be sentenced) relies on an observation which is as simple as it is obvious: if there is a crime against humanity, the victim of the crime is humanity; hence judgment of the criminal should be within the jurisdiction of any tribunal, in any district of any country. That's the fundamental observation.

What were the forerunners of this notion and what is its present situation? The Nuremberg and Tokyo proceedings are often presented as the first concrete application of the principle. Without going into too many details, it suffices to note that the victors of the Second World War organized the proceedings against Nazi or Japanese war criminals in Germany or Japan in a very deliberate manner. These proceedings were organized by powers who, at the time, held political authority in Germany and Japan, namely the Allies. To say that these trials were the beginning of universal jurisdiction is thus a little—or even very—debatable, since they were being judged by competent courts, even though these courts had been improvised, of the countries in which the crimes had been committed. On the other hand, what was new and audacious, and somewhat problematical for lawyers, was the idea that the criminals would be judged before courts that did not exist at the time of the crimes. But this is a different story.

During the years following World War II, some states, not so many— Australia, Israel (with the proceedings against Eichmann), Canada—had equally applied the notion of universal jurisdiction to judge war criminals for acts committed during that war, and only for those. The difference between

---

* The original title for this article was "Universal Jurisdiction to Judge Crimes Against Humanity: An Unacceptable Principle for the Most Powerful."

these two types of jurisdiction, Nuremberg and Tokyo on the one hand, and those that have just been mentioned on the other hand, is the fact that the criminals were respectively judged in the countries where they had committed their crimes, and the countries where they had been arrested. Nothing like at Guantanamo…

What is fundamental to universal jurisdiction is the fact that all of humanity is victimized by crimes against humanity, and hence that these crimes can be judged everywhere. This is the theory. In the period following World War II up to the present date, a number of international treaties have included this principle with more or less important variations. The first one, in 1948, is the Convention on the Prevention and Punishment of the Crime of Genocide, which projected a field of jurisdiction somewhat beyond strictly national jurisdiction, but did not yet arrive at the universal jurisdiction expressly planned by the 1949 Geneva Conventions. A basic article of the latter is as follows:

> Each High Contracting Party shall be under the obligation to search for persons alleged to have committed, or to have ordered to be committed, such grave breaches, and shall bring such persons, regardless of their nationality, before its own courts. It may also, if it prefers, and in accordance with the provisions of its own legislation, hand such persons over for trial to another High Contracting Party concerned, provided such High Contracting Party has made out a prima facie case.

This is something really concrete in an international convention, and as a matter of fact, universal jurisdiction is indeed admitted for the first time in a systematic way in the four Geneva Conventions (except that on war prisoners, for particular reasons).

Then there was the 1984 Convention on Torture. It gives a somewhat different, but nevertheless interesting, definition: "The offences shall be deemed to be included as extraditable offences in any extradition treaty existing between States Parties". In addition, the Convention directly allows extradition even if there is no extradition treaty between two States. This is a good way to prevent a state from which extradition is requested from using the absence of an extradition treaty to reject the request. The tribunals of the country from which the request is addressed will just answer: "since we have ratified the Convention, whether there is an extradition treaty or not, the Convention is sufficient to grant that extradition". This is indeed considerable progress.

We should also consider, here, a very targeted convention, the Convention on Repression of Illicit Captures of Aircrafts—a convention on hijacking. The range of its judgments are large enough, but here, one is no longer in the framework of the generous ideas of the original principle of universal jurisdiction, but more addressing security ideas which are starting to be applied.

As far as France is concerned, it has been possible for more than ten years to judge and extradite people, or to judge them in France, when they have committed crimes against humanity, war crimes, or crimes of genocide outside the French territory. This legislation was applied in the famous case of the Mauritanian, Colonel Ely Ould Dah, for torture and acts of barbarity committed in Mauritania in 1990. Thanks to this legislation, he was condemned to ten years imprisonment by the Court of Appeal of Nîmes.

Should one then believe that universal jurisdiction for war crimes or crimes against humanity is now a reality?

I have here a document of the Sub-Commission on Human Rights of the United Nations which surprisingly has remained unknown; it's a resolution that was adopted unanimously without vote on August 18, 2000. At a time when the extradition and judgment of General Pinochet was being discussed, the Sub-Commission adopted this resolution, which states: "*Reaffirming equally the principle of universal jurisdiction for crimes against humanity and for war crimes as recognized by law and practice...*" This is interesting, because here are the experts of the Sub-Commission unanimously referring to something which, as a matter of fact, is very far from being a universally recognized principle. Just between ourselves, what the Sub-Commission says is just not true! If it speaks of this principle as something recognized whereas it is not, or not really or not yet, let us say that it does so to push the issue in the right direction (and we will not complain about it even though it is not in accord with actual facts). At the same time, it invites all governments to cooperate, whether by acting in the framework of universal jurisdiction "as recognized by international law"—ladies and gentlemen internationalists, back to your books—or by an internal law establishing a rule of extraterritorial jurisdiction. In other words, this would mean that the experts of the Sub-Commission encourage States to establish rules of universal jurisdiction even outside the framework of conventions. We are making progress, it would seem!

But, alas, on February 2002, the UN International Court of Justice had to rule on a warrant for arrest delivered by a Belgian judge against a former Minister of the Democratic Republic of Congo: the Court first had to decide whether Belgian law on universal jurisdiction for war crimes and crimes against humanity is lawful or not. Because it seemed to have a better chance of success, the government of the DR of Congo abandoned that question and decided to stick to immunity by claiming that a Minister cannot be extradited, cannot be prosecuted even on the basis of extraterritorial law. In that way, the Court was no longer obliged, for purely technical procedural reasons, to say if universal jurisdiction as established by the Belgian law is legitimate or not. While this was regrettable, the President of the Court, Mister Guillaume, with the authority attached to his function, moreover felt the need, in addition to the decision of the Court, to state his own opinion on universal jurisdiction, and it is exactly the contrary of what the UN Sub-Commission on Human Rights had claimed.

A State may usually examine an infraction committed in a foreign country only if the person responsible for that infraction or possibly the victim is a national of that State, or if the crime undermines its internal or external security. States may also examine it under the provisions of the few special international conventions I mentioned earlier (convention on highjacking and a few similar ones). But, apart from these situations, international law does not admit universal jurisdiction.

It is thus a titanic battle. The Sub-Commission says this is a generally accepted principle, and the President of the International Court of Justice says the principle is absolutely not accepted.

Let me now turn to the Belgian law. Belgium has had, since 1993, for reasons which one might debate or question, a law providing for Belgian jurisdiction for war crimes, wherever they may have been committed. This law, moreover, in 1994 was extended beyond war crimes to cover crimes against humanity: this is the 1999 law. Since then, a number of complaints have been lodged against various people, some of which attracted a lot of attention, while others went unnoticed... There was a particular provision in the Belgian law: it allowed the Belgian government, through its Council of Ministers, to decide that someone being prosecuted according to universal jurisdiction could be sent back to their national country, but under two conditions:

i) That the country of origin would judge that person and

ii) That the country of origin would guarantee the conditions needed for a fair trial.

Why such reserve? In fact, while it had established this law of universal jurisdiction, Belgium was aware of the political problems involved in its relations with powerful countries, whose nationals it would very much like to see come to judgment. We are here truly at the heart of the problem of impunity of powerful States, of their nationals and allies.

However, in May 2003, Jan Fermon lodged a complaint on behalf of a number of Iraqi and Jordanian victims against General Tommy Franks and some members of his staff for war crimes. The complaint addressed acts which were very grave: bombardment of civilian targets which had nothing to do with military objectives, use of fragmentation bombs with their well known horrible consequences, firing on the Palestine Hotel where only journalists stayed, as was well known. (It was later claimed that the soldiers responsible for the shooting had observed "enemy binoculars" observing them... Legitimate defense against binoculars is something that had to be invented.) There were also attacks against medical infrastructure and pillaging.

Immediately the American administration's blackmail machinery was activated against Belgium with an absolutely extraordinary power. First, a law passed by the US Senate permitted the Pentagon and the US President to start military operations against anyone who would detain members of US military forces, and it is claimed this could be applied to Belgium! Then it is explained to Belgium that NATO headquarters were presently located in Brussels, and represent a large number of jobs and that, if the complaint were not immediately rejected, NATO headquarters would be transferred outside Belgium, which would result in some thousands of unemployed.

This led to a series of meetings and a decision by the Belgian government in rather difficult conditions, since that government had resigned at that precise time. As we already mentioned, the law allowed the Council of Ministers to decide whether the proceedings could take place before the national courts of the persons prosecuted; hence the Council could decide to send the matter, for example, to the US courts.

However, this was a priori not possible since the government had resigned: hence it could only address ordinary problems and could not meet as an actual "Council of Ministers". Well, one might say this is pure formalism. But the law said, moreover, that there was the possibility of sending the matter to the national jurisdiction of the persons under pursuit, provided verification could be obtained that:

• the State of which they are nationals is indeed willing to prosecute them. (I very much doubt it was checked whether the US would consider prosecuting General Franks) and

• that the State would guarantee the conditions of a fair trial. Can you really imagine a fair trial in the US for Iraqi people saying: "I am a victim of war crimes committed by US military forces in Iraq"? There is no need to comment.

We thus have a decision where the Belgian government simply grovels before the US.

Does that end the story? No. The US authorities say, "Just wait. All that is good but is only temporary. What we demand is that this be totally impossible, forever. What we demand is purely and simply the abrogation of the law, or at least the universal jurisdiction part of it." And not only will Belgium do it, abrogate its law, but moreover, during the course of debates in Parliament, several members will ask representatives of the government: "Are you very sure that prosecution against General Franks will be automatically stopped if we adopt that law?"

The government gives that guarantee and the law is adopted. And when Jan Fermon and I go to the Court of Appeal in Brussels, we are just told that, since Parliament and the government consider that prosecution is no longer possible, we have nothing to do before the Appeal Court: since the new law has been voted, all possibilities of prosecution are definitely excluded.

What possibilities remain?

Can the International Criminal Court (ICC) do anything ? In the ICC Statute there are extraordinary provisions for the impunity of powerful States and their allies. Here is Article 16:

> No investigation or prosecution may be commenced or proceeded with under this Statute for a period of 12 months after the Security Council, in a resolution adopted under Chapter VII of the Charter of the United Nations, has requested the Court to that effect; that request may be renewed by the Council under the same conditions.

In other words, the Council may ask the ICC to stop its investigations for a period of one year and this request entails obligation. Then the request may be renewed not just once, or ten or a hundred times, but without any limits.

In other words, the ICC cannot exercise its jurisdiction if the Security Council does not so wish. And, as if this were not enough, the US has threatened various countries with economic sanctions and termination of military assistance (in particular, in the case of Colombia), if these countries did not guarantee they would never extradite members of US military forces to the ICC in case the ICC should request it. There are by now around 100 bilateral treaties according to which 100 states have made such commitments in exchange for economic or other advantages.

Let me end by a preliminary, not an actual, conclusion. The impunity of criminals is what we wish to avoid. Affirming the priority of law, I do not come back to that, is clearly not enough. This is not the way to reach that goal. On the other hand, the demand for justice by people is not an illusion, nor vain words: it does exist. The case of Argentina has been mentioned. There is also the case of South Africa, where the Truth and Reconciliation Commission battles against impunity in a rather original way. The peoples' demands have been manifested in all the large cities of the world where millions and millions of people from all over the entire planet have carried out huge demonstrations against the war in Iraq, or against the participation of their countries in that war. Can peoples carry out effective action? I believe that there are some possibilities. The very fact that the UN Sub-Commission on Human Rights has adopted the position we mentioned confirms there are possible alliances. NGOs have been mentioned but there are also less powerful states, because, while the theory affirms the equality and equal sovereignty of nations, in practice less powerful States and organizations that represent peoples and their populations do not have the same power. Among all of these, alliances are possible in the battle against iniquity. They have started and I believe that this is what we need to do: develop these advances in order to progress.

PART III

IN PURSUIT OF
AN END TO IMPUNITY

ROLAND WEYL

ON HUMANITARIAN LAW

1. The Risk of Reduction

The notion of "humanitarian law" has in itself a doubly reductive connotation:

- · It infers feelings of protection and pity which nourish the idea of a human being as an object which should be treated "in a human way", just as one should not inflict suffering on animals.

- · Mainly, creating a judicial category labeled as humanitarian seems to imply that only physical attacks against human beings are inhuman. But when an embargo leads to the death of thousands of children, this should also be part of humanitarian law, as well as when there is starvation in Niger or when the United States refuses to ratify the Kyoto Protocol when the warming of the planet through a wild industrialization obeying only the law of profit yields well-known humanitarian disasters, including disasters in the United States itself.

Nevertheless, it is true that at the Malta 1980 Congress of the IADL, when lawyers of European socialist countries and those of Western countries were learnedly discussing the respective hierarchy or the indivisibility of political and economic rights, a representative of Uruguay reminded everyone that all that was rather academic when, in his country, the first right one had to claim was that of not being killed on the street corner. And a lawyer from Bangladesh added the mere right of not dying from hunger.

Therefore, there does exist a right to a minimal security and, even though human ambitions of justice and security must go much beyond, special attention should be paid to these minimal rights, the only condition being that one should not forget this is only an elementary minimum.

2. Repression and Impunity

Attention is currently focused on the way persons responsible for the worst breaches of humanitarian rights are able to defy law and ethics because they never have to account for their crimes. This leads to a failure of humanitarian law, since it cannot be applied. An intense demand for the repression of crimes again humanitarian law resulted, and judicial means have been created in the form of various tribunals. But the exasperation previously caused by the absence of tools for the repression of impunity is now caused by the ineffectiveness of these tools of repression.

In fact, when the idea of creating an international criminal court was put forward, some expressed reservations because a law cannot exist if it is not equal and universal, and it was very doubtful that we would see representatives from the most powerful countries or their allies prosecuted before such a court. This in turn would worsen the division in the world between the powerful and the others. This is indeed what we see today where there is no prosecution of US torturers in Afghanistan or Iraq, or of the jailers of Guantanamo, or the Israeli persons responsible for State terrorism, for instance for the crimes of Sabra and Shatilla, or Jenin, and when the United States is not obliged to pay reparations for the crime of biocide committed in Vietnam through the use of Agent Oame United States institutionalizes impunity when it exerts pressure on Belgium to oblige it to abandon its law of "universal jurisdiction" which had led to proceedings in Brussels against General Franks, or when it exerts pressure on all States in order to obtain their official and judicial guarantees that US torturers will not be handed over to the ICC.

A repressive institution is possible only if there are guarantees and certainties about its *erga omnes* effectiveness.

3. The Perverse Effects

Not only is humanitarian law applied in an unequal way, but it can also be diverted and have inverse, anti-humanitarian effects.

There is no need to demonstrate how much this has been the case in Iraq, but also in Afghanistan where, without any regret for the Taliban, one can nevertheless question the humanitarian effects of the extensive resumption of the cultivation of opium. The bombardment in Belgrade of electric power production at the expense of hospitals, and the destruction of drinking water networks, were not particularly humanitarian. And the secret clause of the Rambouillet Agreements demanding the privatization of the Serb economy did not have much to do with the alleged aims of defense of human rights.

International criminal tribunals are notorious for their rules not being models of respect for the rights of the defense. It is also known that, of those who have been handed over to these tribunals, not all are necessarily guilty. But "Humanitarian Law" enjoys such a sacred image that it is not possible to express any doubt without being accused of approving of torture or genocide.

4. Repression and Prevention

One should be clearly aware that the obligation to resort to repression, even when it cannot be avoided, is merely an *a posteriori* remedy to a failure of law. It is comparable to surgery, which is a failure of medicine, and to curative medicine, which is a failure of preventive medicine. And the complaints about the ineffectiveness of the texts and organs of repression are the same as those on the ineffectiveness of law and of international institutions. The ineffectiveness of the institutions or texts can be resolved only by the creation of other texts and institutions addressing the question of effectiveness.

The great alternative of our time, which sets out the stakes at this turning point in human history, is between the sharing among the powerful of their power over the peoples, and the power of the peoples themselves over their own affairs. The preamble of the Charter of the United Nations proclaims the advent a new order of the world when it states: "*We, Peoples of the United Nations...have resolved...Accordingly our Governments...*" and places the new International Law under the sign of the sovereignty of Peoples in a universalism which cannot be dissociated from their plurality, their equality and their mutual respect.

These principles have been at the origin of subsequent texts which, through their definition of the rights to be recognized as adhering to the human being, *a contrario* define what their negation contains as inhumanity. It is sufficient to refer to the 1966 Covenants, the Covenant on Civil and Political Rights but also the Covenant on Economic, Social and Cultural Rights which the United States did not ratify: it considered that the latter are not human rights. These treaties are written in a way which entails a judicial obligation by States with regard to their nationals, but they are unfortunately largely ignored.

The "rulers of the world" do not intend to bow, and they work for a durable continuation of the old logic of their domination. Law is thus what is at stake in the struggle, as are the institutions in charge of applying it. This struggle relies essentially on the action of peoples, hence on their knowledge of their rights and of the ways of obtaining respect for same. It is the noble mission of lawyers to help them.

One cannot forget that, even though the most powerful States have later prosecuted authors of crimes against humanitarian law, this occurred only after they had given power to these persons or supported them against their peoples to the benefit of their own domination.

The impunity of these criminals cannot be tolerated, particularly when they are the agents or leaders of countries for whom this serves as a way of domination. They must account for their crimes, and everything must be done to that purpose, both at the international level and before the tribunals of each country, where universal jurisdiction must be applied. But the ambition must be the advent of humanitarian law as a standard of life and civilization such that repression will no longer be needed for its universal application. To that end, an investment must be made in the consciences of peoples and therefore in education programs, in the deontology of media and of course in the eradication of the law of plunder and the world gangsterism of inhuman forces which still today impose their law upon peoples.

AMY BARTHOLOMEW

"STRATEGIES OF THE WEAK"?

CONTESTING EMPIRE THROUGH LITIGATION UNDER INTERNATIONAL HUMANITARIAN LAW

International law and international humanitarian law, in particular, are often viewed as little more than words on paper. Yet, the *National Defense Strategy of the United States of America* released in March 2005 declares that the 'changing security environment' post 9/11 requires 'global freedom of action' for the US aimed at securing and promoting its interests. It asserts that the current milieu reveals both American strengths and vulnerabilities in the coming decade. Among the strengths it outlines are its preeminent military power and the 'leading roles' of the US on matters of international concern. Among its vulnerabilities one finds the apparently astonishing claim that: 'Our strength as a nation state will continue to be challenged by those who employ a *strategy of the weak* using international fora, judicial processes, and terrorism.'[1]

Commenting on this 'vulnerability' at a press conference, Douglas Feith, who was then the Under Secretary of Defense for Policy, said "There are various actors around the world that are looking to either attack or constrain the United States, and they are going to find creative ways of doing that, that are not the obvious conventional military attacks." He went on to identify 'legal lines of attack' along with diplomatic and technological ones while indicating that all of these are 'kinds of asymmetrical warfare' that may be deployed in attempts to constrain America's 'global freedom of action.' When pressed to provide an example of what might be considered a 'legal line of attack' Feith identified "arguments that some people make to try to, in effect, criminalize foreign policy and bring prosecutions where there is no proper basis for jurisdiction under international law as a way of trying to pressure American officials."[2]

How interesting and perverse that the Bush Administration—the pinnacle of the American Empire—should view international law and international institutions as 'strategies of the weak' about which they should be concerned. Is the Bush administration onto something here? Do legal strategies aimed at 'constraining' America's 'global freedom of action' have the potential to be *political* strategies that ought to worry American Empire?

Radical scholars of international politics ranging from Marxists to critical legal scholars and 'neo-Schmittians' have insisted that international institutions like the UN and international law function as a "butler to the master",[3] as a mere instrument of American imperium, or they have argued, as Giorgio Agamben has in good Schmittian fashion, that humanitarianism has fostered *increased* aggression and undermined limitations on war. Agreeing with those who view the US as *the* imperial power, the global state.[4] and agreeing with them that humanitarianism is an 'open signifier' that *may*, in fact, promote aggression, the question is: Why doesn't the Bush administration recognize that it fully controls international law and institutions, that they function as its 'butler' and that it unilaterally can provide the content of the meaning of humanitarianism under such conditions? Is it the case, contrary to the claims of some radical critics, that international law, in general, and international humanitarian law, in particular, under the general sway of the discourses of human rights which have taken hold since the end of the Cold War, *may in fact* function as a 'strategy of the weak' against American eEmpire, constraining and attacking it?

An affirmative answer to these questions may seem surprising since we know that the US regularly flouts international law and has now developed, under Bush and since 9/11, an explicit doctrine [the Bush Doctrine] justifying doing so, and since we also know that international law against the use of force and international humanitarian law are recognized far more in the breach than in observance. Yet, I want to argue that, far from the critique that is formulated by some of the most radical critics (as well as by liberal *supporters* of American empire, like Anne Marie Slaughter), the defense, deployment and development of international law—the promotion of 'law's empire'[5]—is something that radical forces (that is, those of us who want to contest the impunity of the American Empire in the interests of human rights and anti-capitalism) should promote. If this is so, the Bush Administration may have rationally identified international law as a potential 'strategy of the weak.'[6]

This general starting point means that we must carefully consider the possibilities and pitfalls of mobilizing international humanitarian law for progressive purposes, for contesting and binding (as that liberal enemy of international law, Michael Ignatieff, has put it) Gulliver with a thousand legal strings. Of course there are multiple avenues for such efforts,[7] one of which is litigation over abuses of international humanitarian law including torture, illegal detention and the illegal use of (illegal) weapons. It is this that I will use as my referent in the context of the (illegal) war against Iraq.

Before considering this, however, a caveat should be entered. As radical scholars like Michael Mandel have insisted (and I suspect that Jean Bricmont would agree) the *key principle* upon which we must insist is the international rule against the use of force. We may take as our support here the astonishingly powerful statement by the Nuremberg Tribunal which famously claimed that 'To initiate a war of aggression…is not only an international crime; it is the supreme international crime differing only from other war crimes in that it contains within itself the accumulated evil of the whole.'[8]

But, even with that recognition, we must still think about other legal/political strategies aimed at attempting to constrain empire, to undermine its impunity. And the concept of impunity, itself, must be thought in a wider than usual context. It is not just legal impunity, but political impunity that must be contested. That is, we must contest the ability and willingness of the United States to act, as the OED puts it, without 'having to suffer the normal injurious consequences (of an action)."

Contesting American empire's impunity through politically astute and inspired litigation is the work that progressive international lawyers have been undertaking recently. It may be considered a desperate tactic if one assesses it only from the point of view of the likelihood of actually *winning* such litigation[9] or at least having dreams of winning in anything short of the long run. Witness the attempts by the Center for Constitutional Rights (US) to bring Donald Rumsfeld *et al* to justice under Germany's universal jurisdiction law of which Andreas Fischer-Loscano, a supporter of that action, maintained "no one seriously believed in the Chief Prosecutor['s] willingness to conduct investigations against the U.S. military in the case of Abu Ghraib".[10] Also witness the important attempts by Jan Fermon to bring Tommy Franks to justice in Belgium and the case submitted to the OAS by the Humanitarian Law Project/International Educational Development and the Association of Humanitarian Lawyers (US) requesting the OAS to investigate violations of humanitarian law in the assaults on medical facilities in Fallujah brought by Karen Parker.

The Franks case very clearly illustrated what we can expect of an American empire when it is confronted with attempts to call it to account transnationally when it demanded (and prevailed) that Belgium change its universal jurisdiction law or else it would insist on moving NATO headquarters elsewhere.[11]

The question of what we may hope for in challenging an *Empire's* impunity through legal action is an important one, I think. But, the cynical (and I think ultimately unpolitical) answer that we should not do our fighting on the sort of universalist grounds that law implies, can be disposed of rather handily by relying on Franz Neumann who emphasized the importance of universality in the face of imperialism. Neumann argued:

Hardly any other ideological element is held in such profound contempt in our civilization as international law. Every generation has seen it break down as an instrument for organizing peace, and a theory that disposes of its universalist claims has the obvious advantage of appearing to be realistic. The fallacy should be equally obvious, however. To abandon universalism because of its failures is like rejecting civil rights because they help legitimize and veil class exploitation, or democracy because it conceals boss control, or Christianity because churches have corrupted Christian morals. Faced with a corrupt administration of justice, the reasonable person does not demand a return to the war of each against all, but fights for an honest system. Likewise, when we have shown that international law has been misused for imperialistic aims, our task has begun, not ended. We must fight against imperialism.[12]

I agree with Neumann and will argue that, despite the power of American empire that is vividly obvious, in fact, in the *face* of American empire, those legal cases that deploy international humanitarian law as a spring board may be viewed as potentially farsighted attempts to defend and strengthen global law (or 'law's empire' globally). They may be important to both encouraging and 'disciplining' cosmopolitan desire (morality/ moralization). And I will argue, more specifically, that such attempts may contribute to (1) the investigation, publicity and constitution of the crimes of empire as crimes, (2) the political responsibility for contesting a criminal empire, and (3) further develop the juridical potentials of international humanitarian law as *one* weapon among others that may be deployed against American empire.

Efforts to defend and to develop what we might call '*law's* empire' are especially important under conditions in which an imperial power asserts for itself an exception, a 'special law', a 'right of empire' that it may impose upon others, demand of others, reserve for itself and so on, on the one hand, and where, in concert with human rights hawks, it moralizes politics in lieu of legality, on the other hand. That is, my contention is that where the American empire attempts to crystallize '*empire's* law',[13] the counterforce of radical litigation is *one* possible tactic against that deeply threatening politics of empire. It is, at least potentially, *political, not just legal,* work and as such it should be developed within and connected to the work of the anti-empire and anti-war movements, not eschewed as merely 'liberal' justice.

Before turning to these arguments one should define empire's law and rehearse, even if very briefly, a few of the key findings by major human rights organizations and litigation centers regarding the Bush administration's attempts to develop and deploy 'empire's law'.

I am calling empire's law those attempts by the US to undermine the regime of 'law's empire', that is, the post World War II development of human rights and international law that foreshadowed (however imperfectly) a future order of democratic cosmopolitan law. 'Empire's law', on the other hand, aims to derail that project and seeks to do so unilaterally, brutally, and by the projection of military as well as economic, cultural, political and even legal power across the globe. The proliferation of war crimes committed by the United States and the legal and ideological work it does to constitute those actions as *not* illegal is part of this threatening process. This is crucial, I think: To recognize that the crimes we are witnessing are not *just* egregious *violations* of the law, but rather are part of a broader strategy to *reconstitute* the law itself.[14]

In its report entitled 'Guantanamo and Beyond: The Continuing Pursuit of Unchecked Executive Power', Amnesty International said of US Attorney General Alberto Gonzalez who, because of his key role in writing the Justice Department memos on torture, is considered by many to be one of the leading 'legal architects of the torture policies' that he may have been involved in '"a conspiracy to immunize U.S. agents from criminal liability for torture and war crimes under U.S. law"'.[15] And this, it should be noted, is part of the process of reconstituting the law: *redefining* torture and the rules against it, not just violating those rules.

As for Donald Rumsfeld, Amnesty International USA and Human Rights Watch maintain that there is sufficient evidence against him of having committed war crimes that an official investigation should be launched in the US and if it is not, other countries should fulfill their obligations under universal jurisdiction to investigate him for abuses.[16]

A writer for *The Progressive* concludes about these two 'cases' that 'when these two leading human rights organizations make such bold claims about the President and the US Secretary of Defense, we need to take the question of executive criminality seriously.'[17] This is interesting both because of the implication that these are usually mild-mannered liberal organizations that have been hesitant to call the US to account and because of the livid responses that the most recent Amnesty report (the Yearly Report 2005) elicited from Bush administration officials (absurd, etc. Cheney, Bush, Rumsfeld) suggesting that they 'protest too much.'

Little bears out the theme of American impunity more forcefully than the statements of Bush administration officials in the aftermath of the Amnesty Report. For example, the Chairman of the Joint Chiefs of Staff, General Richard B. Myers, proclaimed the Report which, in addition to calling the system of incarceration 'the gulag of our times' demanded that government officials, including Bush, Cheney, Rumsfeld and Tenet, should be investigated (and possibly prosecuted), '"absolutely irresponsible"' adding that while some 100 of 68,000 detainees held in the war against terrorism had been abused (according to the government's reckoning), "'[I]t's very small compared to the population of detainees we've handled...'" He also pointed out that "'many of the abuses have produced courts-martial and other punishments'" refusing, of course, to comment on the fact that virtually no official has been held responsible. Vice-President Dick Cheney said the Amnesty Report 'disgusted' him. Meanwhile, George W. Bush called the report 'absurd'. He maintained that Amnesty seemed to have based some of its Report on "the word and allegations by...people who hate America, people who have been trained in some instances to disassemble [*sic*], that means not tell the truth. So its an absurd report. It just is."[18]

So, what might be the potentials of litigation against empire that take the form of demands for investigation under universal jurisdiction as in the case against Rumsfeld in Germany and that brought by Peacerights (UK) against the Blair Administration at the ICC? My suggestion (ignoring for now the risks involved, which are plenty) is that, in addition to legally challenging impunity and potentially isolating the leaders of empire territorially, such litigation could contribute to:

(1) investigating, publicizing and constituting empire's crimes,

(2) developing a sense of political responsibility among Empire's citizens that demands political action while disciplining the excesses of cosmopolitan morality, and

(3) developing further global law that itself holds the potential to contribute to further challenges to empire.

Investigation, Publicity and the Constitution of the Empire as Criminal

My hypothesis is that the acts of demanding legal investigations, litigating (not necessarily winning) and asserting possible legal guilt may contribute to the sense of 'political' responsibility that extends far beyond the parties to the immediate dispute. Such litigation is one form of *investigation* and *publicity* that may aim at the transformation of relations of responsibility and solidarity. What is potentially interesting about such litigation is that it is *not* just about pinning an isolated powerful actor with legal responsibility. It is not aimed just at "hounding particular culprits of particular misdeeds"[19] as Zygmunt Bauman contends, for example. Nor is it just about attempting to isolate them territorially, although this, too, is important.[20] Rather, it may function to *expose* and *publicize* their crimes, and constitute them *as crimes* rather than as the *right of Empire as Empire itself asserts*. By constituting the actions of Empire as crimes that specifically contradict what it claims it is doing—acting benevolently to spread human rights and democracy—and in that way by contributing to the unveiling of the Empire, contributing to an 'unconcealed Empire' (Panitch and Gindin), such actions may contribute to delegitimization of it by attempting to intervene in the DNA of that project (of course, it could legitimate it too if every action is rebuffed!) This is particularly the case where the empire pretends to be 'benevolent', as in the case of the US.

Such cases may thus contribute to publicity. But publicity in simple terms of 'revelation' is not enough. Revelation of egregious acts committed is both necessary and insufficient to the task, of course. One reason for this is identified by Mike Davis who argues:

> Let's face it, a tolerance for atrocity is now enshrined at every level of American culture. And because we are unmoved by the war crimes of the past, we are passive in the face of the monstrous acts being committed in our names today. Where are the congressional investigations, the public outcrys, and the campus protests in the wake of the revelations about the torture regimes at Abu Ghraib, Bagram Air Base in Afghanistan, and Guantanamo?[21]

It seems to me that Davis's position suggests both that a call for *more* publicity and an acknowledgment that something *more than* publicity in terms of 'revelation' is required. This may especially be so in cases where, as Hannah Arendt put it of the Third Reich, the "aura of mendacity" has "constituted the general, and generally accepted atmosphere".[22] We can think of no time since then that, at least in the western liberal democracies, this 'aura of mendacity' has more stained our societies than now.

So the publicity that is required seems to be of a certain type. Despite our well-grounded criticisms of the mass media, even it is now joining human rights organizations, as *The New York Times* and *Wall Street Journal* have, in calling for investigations into the possibly criminal activity of America's leaders. And *still*, we do not seem to see a groundswell of concerted opposition to the Bush administration in the US or a widespread call for an end to their impunity on the part of the citizenry of Empire, much less do we see 'public outcrys and campus protests'. My suggestion is that the sort of publicity that could come from successful litigations—successful in the sense of even just getting on the docket—may be significant, particularly in an American culture that holds courts and litigation in fairly high esteem.

And yet, cultivating a counter-discourse that fights the mendacity and hypocrisy of a self-proclaimedly benevolent empire will require enormous political organizing, imagination and effort in a context in which the mainstream media remains not very interested, despite its recent calls for investigations. An example of such disinterest is provided by Michael Ratner, the lead lawyer in the Guantanamo cases that made their way to the US Supreme Court and the Rumsfeld case in Germany. Ratner reported that, even upon winning the Supreme Court cases, "I have seen very little coverage of people who had been released from Guantanamo. Similarly, I don't understand why the media didn't cover the German case we brought. I was willing to give the *[New York] Times* an exclusive *and they wouldn't cover it*, neither would the *Wall Street Journal*."[23]

Despite such difficulties, what is important, in part, about such litigation in the context of post 9/11 was well identified by Mark Danner. Danner suggests that, prior to 9/11, the 'narrative of scandal' typically took the following form: first, revelation, next, investigation, and last, expatiation in which "when the judges hand down sentences, the evildoers are punished, and the society returns to a state of grace." Now, of course, this narrative has its weaknesses—chief among them the idea of returning to a state of grace after 'expiation'. But, Danner argues that even this narrative is now short-circuited. Now we witness the first step of *revelation* such as the revelation of torture and ghost prisoners, the construction of a world-wide penal colony by and under the control of the US, called by the normally very careful Amnesty International 'the gulag of our times.' But, there is very little in the way of serious *investigation*. We are, Danner says, 'stuck at step one.' Being 'stuck at step one' fails to challenge impunity in any meaningful way for revelation itself has little meaning.[24]

If covering up, then lying about and denying American war crimes or, when necessary, shifting the responsibility for them far down the chain of command, has proved a thoroughly bipartisan business going back for decades, if we are suffering a systematically produced 'aura of mendacity', as surely we are, and if we are stuck at the level of *revelations* rather than investigation and publicity in the wider sense, it is surely the time to force the lid off the box.[25] Investigation and publicity through litigation against political and military leaders is *one* of the means to do this.

But, the political potential of such litigation absolutely depends on linkages between litigators and political movements. While litigators can mobilize the resources of law (something near and dear to Americans with their constitutional traditions), the political movements must work to publicize and to politicize their efforts.[26]

Political Responsibility and the Delegitimization of Empire

Such investigation and publicity is necessary but not sufficient to contesting empire, of course. We must also attempt to develop a sense of *political responsibility among the citizens of empire*. The potential for developing a sense of political responsibility is based on an argument that legal attempts at holding American Empire accountable may contribute to a sense of wrong having been inflicted and of being *implicated* in the injustices that have been inflicted by its leaders, and an associated sense of *outrage* of the sort that seems currently to be missing even in the face of widespread revelations of egregious violations of human rights and international humanitarian law. Such a felt sense of *political responsibility* for Empire's actions by its citizens is dependent on viewing oneself not as an innocent or impotent bystander but rather as an implicated agent.[27] And such an implicated agent may come to view oneself as *politically responsible,* by which I mean, in the first instance, displaying a willingness to judge, a 'thoughtfulness', as Hannah Arendt puts it.

Arendt famously said of Adolph Eichmann that he was 'thoughtless' in his actions—that he displayed an "inability to *think,* namely *to think from the standpoint of someone else.* No communication was possible with him, not because he lied but because he was surrounded by the most reliable of all safeguards against the words and the presence of others, and hence against reality as such."[28] What if the inability to think in this sense, that 'thoughtlessness' that Arendt so well describes, characterizes much of the citizenry of American empire? What if, through its various means of propaganda, poor education, inequality, insecurity, coercion, the politics of fear and anxiety and a sense of cultural and political superiority, it breeds such 'thoughtlessness'?[29]

Following Arendt, political responsibility entails judging actions from the point of view of justice.[30] If, for her, "authentic political action and judgement...require us to act and judge for the sake of the world rather than the self",[31] the encouragement of such political responsibility must be promoted to overcome not just the hubris but also the self-interestedness, the 'thoughtlessness', of empire.

But, it must immediately be acknowledged that the invocation of political responsibility aimed at overcoming 'bystander' status based on political responsibility and thus imploring action also has its dangers. [This is why it must be embedded within anti-empire politics]

Zygmunt Bauman provides a compelling argument, I believe, with regard to the relationship between perpetrators and bystanders but it is also representative of a problem in post holocaust political theory as it pertains to Empire. Bauman argues that modernity has treated the issue of responsibility triadically: as a relationship of *perpetrators* of atrocities liable for legal prosecution for having committed crimes of commission, their innocent and violated *victims,* and *bystanders* who may be viewed, at most, as culpable of sins of omission, morally guilty of the "excusable and forgivable *misdeed* of 'bystanding'". This approach, Bauman argues, misses the fact that there is a necessary relationship—a "grey area"—between perpetrators and 'bystanders'. But by constituting them as distinct categories we miss the fact that there may be "common ground to both", an "affinity between 'evil doing' and 'non-resistance to evil'" and this needs not just to be recognized but also to be the object of our political efforts to bring these two categories under the lens of moral and political concern.[32]

I think this analysis is apt. And we can surely use it to argue that the 'non-resistance' to empire is a moral and political failing. But, as with much of post holocaust political theory, by focusing on the *problem of inaction* or 'bystanding' and by asserting that political responsibility entails the obligation to act, it fails to emphasize (though Bauman does recognize this problem) that under current conditions[33] we may be more inclined to view ourselves as cosmopolitan actors rather than as bystanders. Because of the obvious horrors of bystanding and inaction, increasingly the argument has been made, since the holocaust, that we must act and that when we do so we are *liberating* the human rights victims from egregious abuses. This, of course, is one of the main justifications put forward by the Bush and Blair administrations and human rights hawks alike for the invasions of Afghanistan and Iraq.

This is one of the reasons that the Left often eschews claims of cosmopolitan morality. It leads, too often, to the moralization of politics and this often *fuels empire*. Perhaps in the context of an empire that justifies its violations as necessary to its larger benevolent aims—spreading democracy and human rights 'by fire and sword'—it is in fact *better* to be a bystander. But, surely, bystanding also remains a problem.

So we have the problem of inaction—bystanding—*and* the problem of action—of a moral cosmopolitanism that supports military humanism/ empire. What are we to do and how can such cases help us with this difficulty?

Rather than accept bystander status as our fallback position—a moral failing that we cannot, after the holocaust, accept as justified—it seems to me that we require a much more differentiated and necessarily political analysis of the obligations attached to implicated agency and political responsibility. We want to *encourage* empire's citizens not to view themselves as innocent bystanders of American Empire's wreckage. But we *do not* want them to conclude that 'something must be done', that American empire is the only vehicle to do it, that the 'lesser evil' may justify torture, that Empire must act, that military humanism is 'worth the cost' and so on. What I take from this is that the indeterminacy of the action implications of political responsibility suggests that the categories being used are too abstract.

The leap from political responsibility to political action/inaction requires, instead, a more pragmatic political analysis. 'Thoughtfulness', the ability and inclination to judge and show concern for others across borders is simply too abstract to guide politics progressively. The call to action—such as resistance to empire—depends on particular arguments in favor of it.

The analysis above provides a more pragmatic stance by suggesting that the citizens of empire *do* have the responsibility to act to resist empire. This is based on an analysis of the *impunity of empire* for it is the idea that there is a *nonreciprocal right of Empire to run roughshod over everyone else in the name of spreading its own values and its own conception of security globally—one of the essential hallmarks of 'empire's law'*—that must be contested. And one of the important targets of this sentiment must be Americans themselves.

Forging such an anti-empire sense of responsibility is important in order to broaden within the United States, in particular, and across the world, the constituency that may come to view the 'global war on terror', in general, and its violations of international humanitarian law, in particular, as assaults both on humanity *and* on legal principles: impunity in a very broad sense. The necessity for widening that constituency is obvious, I suppose, but it can be illuminated with reference to the World Tribunal on Iraq, of which I have been part. While aimed at investigation and publicity, and while very successful in the senses of articulating sophisticated analyses of empire's impunity and developing a serious, politically engaged network of anti-war and (slightly less so) anti-empire activists, one had the persistent sense that one was 'preaching to the converted' at the tribunals. The same could be said, of course, for networks like the World Social Forum. Speaking and struggling in such self-selected 'subaltern public spheres' has its deficits as well as its strengths. What we need, of course, is a proliferation of strategies, of which citizens' tribunals and social forums are one form, to widen the anti-empire structure of feeling, to sharpen our 'thoughtfulness'. But politically inspired litigation may be another one of the strategies that we can deploy. And it may have the distinct advantage of gathering support, through investigation and publicity, and through the constitution (the discursive and legal construction) of the leading figures in the American empire literally as criminal in their actions and thus may speak, through the legitimacy that law and legal institutions still have to offer, to wider segments of the population. It may have a special potential, in other words, to delegitimate empire—particularly one that claims to be 'benevolent'—and thus contribute to a sense of the political responsibility that its citizens bear for its crimes.

Here, I must distinguish my position (again) from a variety of other critical positions. One of these is Arendt's position in relation to the Nuremberg Trials—that criminal and moral guilt would problematically "exonerate not only Germans but humanity from the need for a more profound ethical and political response."[34] Another is Heidegger's—that prosecuting war criminals just "reinstates conventional notions of guilt and innocence" while affirming "humanity without acknowledging the complicity of humanity."[35] Finally, is Zygmunt Bauman's contention (raised above) that "hounding particular culprits of particular misdeeds" "bring at best temporary and local relief." He goes further to contend that such actions typically just "alleviate the most painful symptoms of the disease only to detract urgency from its cure."[36]

Rather than following these critical inclinations it is more productive to accept the sort of position that Arendt articulated fifteen years after her statements on the Nuremberg Trials when, in *Eichmann in Jerusalem,* she argued that the legal case "encouraged the prosecution of leading Nazis in

West Germany, it publicized the Holocaust to the world, it offered a forum for the testimony of victims, it accomplished a touch of justice."[37] And her enduring criticism that it constructed a much too simplistic division between us and them, between perpetrators and bystanders, thus denying the nuance and complexity of responsibility, is just what I want to argue can be (but isn't necessarily) addressed in legal justice pursued under the umbrella of a political analysis.

The standard critical depiction of the use of criminal law in political cases is, in fact, that it individualizes justice thus severing the tie between the perpetrator and politics. This is viewed by some, like Arendt, as necessary to the legal quality of the case. It is criticized by others as passing over the main problem in political justice cases—the wider circumstances that make particular "'human rights violations' particularly atrocious."[38] So, for example, Fernando Atria argues that the individualization of political justice in trials for human rights abuses has had the effect in Chile of severing the tie between individual legal responsibility and the larger political context of impunity. When we are dealing with state-sponsored terrorism, he argues, mechanisms like truth and reconciliation commissions are more apt than criminal trials for criminal courts could put individuals on trial but not, for example, the national intelligence agency of which they were a part.[39] The claim, then, put forward by some critics is that litigation depoliticizes by individualizing and by attending to symptoms rather than causes of human rights abuses. And this may indeed often be the case. But two important caveats must be registered. First, as lawyers like France's Jacques Verges show, even individualized justice in the courtroom can be turned into radical political analysis in skilled hands under favorable circumstances. Second, and more important to my argument, one can recognize the largely individualized conception of legal responsibility and still make the argument that such cases can be enveloped within, and contribute to, a broader network of arguments and political actions that take it far beyond the initial context of the legal case. Asserting legal responsibility can contribute to the development of a sense of political responsibility. It is this work that aims at both legalization and politicization[40] that I think we should pursue and this is why I think it is crucial that such cases be closely aligned with anti-empire movements which can play crucial roles in contextualizing the legal case.

So, my argument is that political litigation like that being pursued in Germany and at the ICC against the US and UK may contribute to the sense of political responsibility for Empire's impunity, thus potentially widening the constituency willing to contest it. If one's political leaders in a democracy (as formal and shot through with weaknesses and contradictions as it may be) are legally responsible for developing policies, practices and laws that egregiously violate fundamental human rights and international humanitarian law—torture, incarceration without trial, the use of illegal weapons—why wouldn't the citizens of empire be called upon to accept some political responsibility for this state of affairs? For *critics and radicals* who already contest empire from within it, such litigation would add fuel to the fire of their critique of and resistance to empire. For *liberals* who support American empire on the assumption that it is acting benevolently or in the name of humanitarian values and engaged in the 'lesser evil' or supporting human rights in a way that breaks with the 'contract of mutual indifference' such a legal judgment should produce a sense of cognitive dissonance as they would surely be forced to face up to the fact that their 'benevolent' empire is self-contradictory. And, for the disenfranchised and suffering populations at home within empire's core, the basis for solidarity with its victims abroad should be made even more clear insofar as both suffer the injustices of a hypocritical and vicious empire.

Political Responsibility, Political Action and Disciplining Cosmopolitan Desire

I want further to suggest that a defensible conception of political responsibility in the context of empire requires a 'critical cosmopolitanism' that has two dimensions. First, it is *cosmopolitan* because it exhibits moral and political responsibility for others across borders and it is *critical* insofar as it *judges the actions of empire* and tempers cosmopolitan excess with a radical political analysis and action. Action must not only be based on cosmopolitanism, aimed at responding to the "needs of strangers" and ending the "contract of mutual indifference",[41] as moral cosmopolitans insist. Rather, it must be based on an *anti-empire solidarity* that accepts political responsibility *to resist, contest and seek to undermine Empire,* and does so in solidarity *with its victims* across borders. Second, it acknowledges the role that a reinvigoration of global law—of law's empire—might play in this project. Both of these dimensions may contribute to 'disciplining' cosmopolitan morality's excesses and political responsibility's overextension while contributing to resistance against Empire's impunity.

The question is whether we can politically build a sense of *critical* cosmopolitanism, in part, on the back of such legal strategies.

To think about this, we might return to Bauman who argues that we need much more seriously to "chase the 'political moment' in a globalized world".[42] Turning to economic globalization, Bauman suggests that, while capitalism is unleashed and "economic forces are free to act globally", "there are at best only germs and premonitions of a globally binding legal and juridical system, global democracy or globally binding, enforceable and obeyed ethical code." He goes on: "Ethically motivated and informed global action has no adequately global instruments."[43] In the absence of this, we all appear to be stuck as bystanders. Political action, he argues, requires a 'steady, long-term commitment' to achieve the political moment par excellence' the 'act that transforms spectator into actor.'[44] Bauman contrasts this with other, more typical, responses to atrocity and suffering like "hounding particular culprits of particular misdeeds" which, he suggests, "brings at best only temporary and local relief". "Most commonly, they [such actions] alleviate the most painful symptoms of the disease only to detract urgency from its cure." They may, far too often, function as a 'fig leaf'. But I suggest, that Bauman fails to recognize or theorize the possible (not necessary) link between 'hounding particular culprits' and developing a sense, not just of implicated agency, but also a mode of politics that can contribute to tempering the cosmopolitan risk of 'bombing for humanity', the "traps and ambushes" of action. It is a way of developing the political institutions—including global law —that Bauman also thinks are necessary.[45] But if this is so, we should be much more attentive to the possibilities of litigation in this context than Bauman is, which he appears to write off in advance as a mere 'fig leaf'.

Global Law

The commitment to the necessity of political responsibility and political action does not (or it should not) detract from the importance of the *juridical itself*. In fact, it is integrally tied to it.

Even where responsibility is accepted, the global field of law is underdeveloped and the power of American Empire seems committed to fight every attempt to develop it as we can now see, going as far as to associate it with 'asymmetrical warfare' by the weak against the strong. Yet, legality is crucial, and radical movements must, in my opinion, realize this.

But, even 'prior to this' project of extending the global field of law is the need to *defend* what has been in place but which is currently under egregious attack—the Geneva Conventions etc. which, as Karen Parker has put it, face likely "death ...if other States do not rally."[46] It is the defense and the extension of law's empire that American Empire currently seeks to undermine.

Empire's law seeks exceptions, evasions and legal arrangements that accommodate its needs and desires while *in principle* marginalizing others—treating them as law's mere objects, not its equal subjects or authors. That the American Empire seeks to reconstitute and refound the law virtually by unilateral fiat, with enormous pressure placed on its 'coalition' and 'allies', to say nothing of its enemies, both attacks the *internal* legitimacy of law—its egalitarian universalism—and further degrades its *procedural* (or democratic) legitimacy. It is, therefore, inadequate, as the National Defense Strategy illustrates, to assume that the Bush Administration's position in relation to law is one merely of acting 'lawlessly'. Its implications are much more threatening than this. Its violations of international humanitarian law are being underwritten by policy and legal arguments that *justify* this impunity. This is why, as Andreas Fischer-Lescano puts it (in relation to a discussion of the so far unsuccessful attempt to have Donald Rumsfeld and others investigated under Germany's universal jurisdiction law), the question is whether the 'fundamental constitutional idea of a legal construction and limitation of power can be asserted or whether global law will be pushed back by the totalizing demands of the international political system to perpetuate a global state of exception.'[47]

This is what is at stake. And, it seems to me that concerted efforts to litigate against Empire can be one part of our effort to contest this form of impunity.

Martin Shaw makes an important argument here, one that I think is deserving of our serious attention. Shaw suggests that the "political ethics of human rights" may be changing our view of the rules of war. As one piece of evidence to support this suggestion, Shaw notes the case of nine British troops who were mistakenly killed by the US in the first Gulf War. The families took the British Defense Department to court, and attempted to have the US soldiers called as witnesses, 'in an effort to hold the state accountable for the avoidable accident of their sons' deaths. They did not fully succeed in their aims, but they did make the matter a cause of public debate.' Shaw concludes that: 'It is difficult to imagine any comparable concern over the lives of soldiers in similar incidents in earlier wars....' 'In an age of human rights, this concern for individuals is in principle extended to individual civilians, and may even begin to apply to enemy soldiers too.' From this, he further contends that, in this context, it isn't surprising that the US is worried about the ICC. 'The laws of war were never intended to be applied in criminal courts in this manner. The drive to do this stems from general trends towards intensified legal regulation, heightened awareness of individual rights and extensive litigation—trends that derive much of their momentum (ironically) from U.S. society.'[48] The criminalization of war, he argues, makes it like any other activity: it is no longer exempt from the norms of human rights.

'If the means of war are generally picked over with a fine toothcomb [*sic*], in the courts, in the press and (indeed) in academia, then the legitimacy of war will be regularly undermined.'[49]

In these ways it seems that the new legitimation of war which has taken place under cosmopolitan morality and the pretext of humanitarian intervention may be challenged or even undermined. There may, indeed, be a delegitimation of it under the sign of human rights.[50]

I would hypothesize, if current litigation can gain sufficient weight, sufficient publicity and pull, it will contribute to this. It is for these reasons of encouraging a critical political responsibility, contribution to politics and development of the norms of international law and human rights precisely when American Empire asserts the right of Empire to undermine and reconstitute them, that these 'strategies of the weak' may be haunting to the Bush administration. We should pursue and support such strategies in recognition of their potential—not as starry-eyed and 'benevolent' liberals or mere moral cosmopolitans who so often tend to turn into benevolent imperialists, but rather as steely radicals who seek to tie Gulliver down with a thousand legal strings *and then use our political might to vanquish him.* The Bush administration is not deluded in this one respect: international law and international humanitarian law, as well, as human rights more generally, *are* strategies of 'the weak'. What the American Empire fears, and I think rightly, is that such strategies may contribute to our capacities to become 'the strong.

In conclusion, my claim is that such politically inspired attempts at litigating against American Empire under international humanitarian law may contribute to the goals of cultivating a sense of political responsibility, while both depending on political action for their broad effectivity and contributing to further political action. Both are also dependent on legality and aimed at further legal development of global law (which is crucial to 'taming' moralization).[51] In these ways they can be viewed as contributing to the reflexive development of global law, progressive politics and solidarity—resources that, while obviously highly fraught and providing absolutely no guarantees of justice, are crucial for contesting the impunity of American Empire. So, the anti-war and anti-empire movements should expend energy and resources supporting these efforts rather than detracting from them as a traditional left hostility to rights and law recommend.[52] And yet, and yet: it is equally important to hang onto the realist idea that it is not as if the development of cosmopolitan law, of global law, "will provide the key to perpetual peace and universal freedom".[53] This illusion must be rejected. But, even a contaminated law is still one that can contribute, if we use it politically and intelligently enough, to our struggles against the broad-based impunity of empire.

ENDNOTES

[1] United States of America, 'The National Defense Strategy of the United States of America,' 1 March 2005, issued by the Secretary of Defense, Donald H Rumsfeld. Available on line at: <http://www.globalsecurity.org/military/library/policy/dod/nds-usa_mar2005.htm> Accessed 13 May 2005. Emphasis added.

[2] Quoted in John J. Lumpkin, 'American at War: Terrorism Report Decries "Strategy of the Weak"' 19 March 2005, <http://www.capitolhillblue.com/artman/publisher/printer_6428.shtml> Accessed 25 March 2005. Also see John Hendren, 'Policy OK's First Strike to Protect US' *Los Angeles Times*, 19 March 2005, <http://www.commondreams.org/cgi-bin/print.cgi?file=/headlines05/0319-01.htm> Accessed 25 March 2005. This was after Feith announced in late January that he intended to step down.

[3] Tariq Ali, 'Re-colonizing Iraq', *New Left Review* 21 (May-June 2003): 5-19, 15.

[4] See Leo Panitch and Sam Gindin, 'Theorising American Empire', in Amy Bartholomew (ed.), *Empire's Law: The American Imperial Project and the 'War to Remake the World'* (London: Pluto Press: 2006).

5   The idea of 'law's empire' is borrowed from Ronald Dworkin, but also from the Martens Clause in international humanitarian law (Hague conferences of 1898 and 1907) which states that 'Until a more complete code of the laws of war is issued, the high contracting Parties ...declare that in cases not included in the Regulations adopted by them, populations and belligerents remain under the protection and empire of the principles of international law.' Quoted in Michael Byers, 'The Laws of War, US-Style,' *London Review of Books*, vol. 25, no. 4, 20 February 2003. <http://www.lbr.co.uk/v25/n04/print/byer01.html> Accessed 14 May 2005.

6   The above paragraphs are taken, in part, from Amy Bartholomew, "Empire's Law and the Contradictory Politics of Human Rights" in Amy Bartholomew editor, *Empire's Law: The American Imperial Project and the 'War to Remake the World'* (London: Pluto Press, 2006).

7   Such as calls for a special prosecutor in the US, for an independent commission to be appointed in the US etc.

8   Available on line at <http://www.yale.edu/lawweb/avalon/imt/procjudnazi.htm>. Still, in my opinion, a robust rule against the arbitrary use of force does not rule out humanitarian intervention in principle. The problem is humanitarian intervention in practice. See Amy Bartholomew and Jennifer Breakspear, "Human Rights as Swords of Emoire", in Leo Panitch and Colin Leys, (eds.), *The New Imperial Challenge: The Socialist Register 2004* (London: Merlin Press 2003) and Fuyuki Kurasawa, ""the Uses and Abuses of Humanitarian Intervention in the Wake of Empire", in Bartholomew, (ed). *Empire's Law*.

9   Cf. Volker Heins, "Giorgio Agamben and the Current State of Affairs in Humanitarian Law and Human Rights Policy," *German Law Journal*, 6 (5) (2005): 845-860, at 849: 'it is much more difficult to ensure compliance with humanitarian law' than human rights law. '[T]o the present, charges filed by war victims or their relatives against individual countries have always been rejected.'

10   For an excellent analysis of this see Andreas Fischer-Lescano, 'Torture in Abu Ghraib: The Complaint against Donald Rumsfeld under the German Code of Crimes against International Law,' *German Law Journal* 6(3): 689-724,at 718.

11   Andreas Fischer-Lescano, 'Torture in Abu Ghraib'. Fischer-Lescano discusses the 'scandalous' (727) refusal of the German Prosecutor to open an investigation into the complaint filed against Donald Rumsfeld and others in a case brought under Germany's universal jurisdiction law by the Center for Constitutional Rights (New York) and others (including the predominantly Canadian organization, Lawyers Against the War) on charges of torture and mistreatment of prisoners at Abu Ghraib prison by allied forces. He concludes that it was 'no accident that...the German judiciary has been very reluctant to become involved in criminal cases with a transnational dimension' (716) despite the fact the law was introduced in Germany in 2002 with much praise for its role in establishing a 'global model' of the transnational rule of law (718). Like Belgium before it (in the Tommy Franks cases and others) Germany appears to have been pressured. Donald Rumsfeld described the Belgium cases as 'absurd' and went on to say that 'Belgium needs to realize that there are consequences to its actions.' He says the Belgium law fails to respect the US's sovereignty and 'this law calls into serious question whether NATO can continue to hold meetings in Belgium...If the civilian and military leaders of member countries cannot come to Belgium without fear of harassment by Belgian courts entertaining spurious charges by politicized prosecutors, then it calls into question Belgium's attitude about its responsibilities as a host nation for NATO and Allied forces.' 718-719, footnote 113. Belgium 'gave in' and redrafted its new law shortly thereafter. (719)

12   Franz Neumann, *Behemoth: The Structure and Practice of National Socialism 1933-1944.*

13   Bartholomew, 'Empire's Law' and Bartholomew and Breakspear, 'Human Rights as Swords of Empire.'

14   Bartholomew, 'Empire's Law'.

15   Matthew Rothschild, 'Stripping Rumsfeld and Bush of Impunity', *The Progressive,* available at <http://www.alternet.org> 31 May 2005. The subquote is from Am-

nesty International's report. This is now recognised as well in the Center for Constitutional Rights' efforts to join Gonzalez to the case it is attempting to bring in Germany.

[16] William Schultz, head of Amnesty International USA, ... (see Democracy Now discussion around May 31 2005).

[17] Rothschild, 'Stripping Rumsfeld and Bush of Impunity.'

[18] Quoted in 'General Slams Amnesty Report,' *The Washington Times* 30 May 2005. Dick Cheney was, according to CNN, 'offended' by the report. See 'Cheney Offended by Amnesty Criticism,' 31 May 2005. <http://www.cnn.com/2005/US/05/30/cheney.amnestyintl/index.html> Accessed 1 June 2005.

According to the *Asian Times*:

> 'In Washington, the White House said the report was "ridiculous and unsupported by the facts."
>
> "The United States is leading the way when it comes to protecting human rights and promoting human dignity. We have liberated 50 million people in Iraq and Afghanistan, we have worked to advance freedom and democracy in the world ...," said spokesman Scott McClellan.
>
> And while US Defense Secretary Donald Rumsfeld did not address the Amnesty report he said in response to questions after a speech to the World Affairs Council yesterday: "It (Abu Ghraib) clearly damaged the U.S. image in the world."[1]
>
> 'US Undermines Rights, Guantanamo like 'gulag' —Amnesty' 26 May 2005. <http://www.asianetglobal.com:8080/asianet/2004/news/detailedstory.jsp?catId=3&newsId=1185> Accessed 1 June 2005.

The Bush quote can be found on Democracynow.org 1 June 2005. 'Guantanamo Bay: A 'Gulag of our times' or 'a model facility'? A debate on the U.S. Prison and Amnesty International'. Bush apparently meant 'dissemble'. He should know.

[19] Zygmunt Bauman, 'From Bystander to Actor,' *Journal of Human Rights* 2(2) (2003): 137-151, at 148.

[20] So, I reject the notion that the prosecution of leaders will necessarily lead to a sense of exoneration on the part of the population. See Andrew Schaap, "Guilty Subjects and Political Responsibility: Arendt, Jaspers and the Resonance of the 'German Question' in Politics of Reconciliation," *Political Studies* 49 (2001) :749-766, at 751. This depends on the political context and political work that is done around it.

[21] Mike Davis, (2003). 'The Scalping Party,' TomDispatch <http://www.tomdispatch.com/index.mhtml?pid=3241> (HC)

[22] Arendt argues:

> 'German society of eighty million people had been shielded against reality and factuality by exactly the same means, the same self-deception, lies and stupidity that had now become ingrained in Eichmann's mentality. These lies changed from year to year, and they frequently contradicted each other; moreover, they were not necessarily the same for the various branches of the Party hierarchy or the people at large. But the *practices of self-deception* had become so common, almost a moral prerequisite for survival, that even now, eighteen years after the collapse of the Nazi regime, when most of the specific content of its lies has been forgotten, *it is sometimes difficult not to believe that mendacity has become an integral part of the German national character*. During the war, the lie most effective with the whole of the German people was the slogan of 'the battle of destiny for the German people'..., which made self-deception easier on three counts: it suggested, first, that the war was no war; second, that it was started by destiny

and not by Germany; and, third, that it was a matter of life and death for the Germans, who must annihilate their enemies or be annihilated.'

....'the aura of systematic mendacity ...had constituted the general, and generally accepted , atmosphere of the Third Reich.' *Eichmann in Jerusalem*, 52.

23 Onnesha Roychoudhrui interviews Michael Ratner in 'The Torn Fabric of the Law: An Interview with Michael Ratner,' *Mother Jones.* <http://www.motherjones.com/cgi-bin/print_article.pl?url=http://www.motherjones.com/ne>... Accessed 3 May 2005.

24 Compare with Bauman.

25 Mike Davis.

26 One risk that must be considered is whether relying, for example, on Germany's universal jurisdiction law would make it easier for citizens of Empire to dismiss.

27 Bauman, "From Bystander to Actor." On bystander status also see Geras, Norman. 1998. *The Contract of Mutual Indifference: Political Philosophy After the Holocaust.* London: Verso.

28 Quoted in Richard J. Bernstein, *Radical Evil: A Philosophical Interrogation*, p. 221, *Eichmann in Jerusalem*, p. 49 emph added by Bernstein.

29 In the *Guardian* there is a report of a discussion with Zygmunt Bauman that expresses this idea of thoughtlessness very movingly with regard to the holocaust. "The Holocaust triggered the ethical preoccupations of his books of the early to mid-90s: 'What is it in our society which makes this sort of thing possible? The real problem is why, under certain circumstances, decent people who are good husbands, neighbours and so on, participate in atrocities. That's the real heart of the problem. There are not so many psychologically corrupted people in the world to account for all the many atrocities around the world. So that was my problem: people who, under other circumstances, would be exemplary members of society, participate in monstrous things—though it's difficult to say if they become monsters.'"

30 Schaap on Arendt 754.

31 Schaap, "Guilty Subjects and Political Responsibility", 757. A possible problem with Arendt's position is her insistence that individual legal justice—that neither history, nor context, nor ideology is or *should* be on trial in a legal case. Rather, that the individual as the liberal individual under law is:

> ''For, as the judges took pains to point out, in a court-room there is no system on trial, no history or historical trend, no 'ism', anti-Semitism for instance, but a person: and if the defendant happens to be a functionary, he stands accused precisely because even a functionary is still a human being, and it is in this capacity that he stands trial.'

32 Bauman, "From Bystander to Actor", 137-138.

33 Which Beck aptly diagnoses as the 'second age of modernity' in which human rights threaten to trump international law.

34 Quoted in Robert Fine. "Crimes Against Humanity: Hannah Arendt and the Nuremberg Debates." *European Journal of Social Theory* 3 (2000).:293-311, at 296.

35 Fine, "Crimes Against Humanity", 303.

36 Bauman, "From Bystander to Actor", 148.

37 Fine, "Crimes Against Humanity", 299.

38 Fernando Atria, "The Time of Law: Human Rights Between Law and Politics" *Law and Critique* 16 (2005):137-159, 151. A point that, as Atria emphasizes, Otto Kirchheimer recognized. Kirchheimer claimed "'there is an intrinsic contradiction between judicial means and the political goal. Political action is directed toward changing or confirming power relations; the apparatus of justice serves to resolve limited conflicts between the individuals and the community, or between individuals, according to preordained community rules'". Quoted in Atria, 151 n. 36.

39 Atria, "The Time of Law', 152. DINA refers to the Direccion de Inteligencia Nacional or the National Intelligence Agency of Chile.

[40]   Atria also argues: "Exceptional times are not the times of forgiveness nor punishment, not even understanding: they are not political times. They are times to fight. The time to think about forgiveness, punishment and understanding, the time of law and the time of politics will come later, with normality. This is the deep reason why our normal political language cannot grasp the exception." 156
        [notice how this plays precisely into Bush's hands]

[41]   Norman Geras. *The Contract of Mutual Indifference.*

[42]   Bauman, "From Bystander to Actor",148.

[43]   Bauman, "From Bystander to Actor",148.

[44]   Bauman, "From Bystander to Actor",148, drawing on Boltansky.

[45]   Bauman, "From Bystander to Actor",149.

[46]   Karen Parker 'Report from Geneva: U.N. Commission on Human Rights Session, March-April, 2005. http://www.webcom.com/hrin/parker/unreport2005.html Accessed May 13, 2005.

[47]   Fischer-Lescano, 'Torture in Abu Ghraib', 690-691. This paragraph comes (slightly altered) from Bartholomew, "Empire's Law".

[48]   Shaw, 'Risk Transfer Militarism', 10.

[49]   Shaw, 'Risk Transfer Militarism', 11.

[50]   Contrast with Danilo Zolo, *Invoking Humanity: War, Law and Global Order* (London: Continuum, 2002).

[51]   As Andreas Fischer-Loscano compellingly argues in 'Torture in Abu Ghraib'.

[52]   See, for example, Zolo, *Invoking Humanity.*

[53]   Fine, "Crimes against Humanity", 306.

KAREN PARKER

ON THE DRAFT UN PRINCIPLES AND GUIDELINES ON HUMAN RIGHTS AND TERRORISM

1.   The Sub-Commission, in its resolution 2003/15 entitled "Effects of measures to combat terrorism on the enjoyment of human rights", requested that the Sub-Commission review the compatibility of counter-terrorism measures adopted at the national, regional, and international level with existing international standards "with a view to elaborating detailed guidelines" (op. para. 5). It further appointed its Special Rapporteur on "Terrorism and Human Rights" as the coordinator of this effort (op.para.6).

2.   Subsequent to that decision, the Commission on Human Rights, in its resolution 2004/87 entitled "Protection of human rights and fundamental freedoms while countering terrorism" did not include the elaboration of guidelines by that body, thereby ensuring that there would not be ongoing efforts at both the Commission and Sub-Commission on the same topic. The [Coordinator][Special Rapporteur] therefore, assumed that the Commission wanted the Sub-Commission to proceed to draft guidelines.

3.   Aware of the urgency of the Sub-Commission on this matter, the [Coordinator][Special Rapporteur] submitted a working paper, entitled "A preliminary framework draft of principles and guidelines concerning human

rights and terrorism" ("Draft Principles") to the Sub-Commission at its fifty-sixth session (E/CN.4/Sub.4/2004/47). That paper contains a brief note on Sub-Commission resolution 2003/15 as well as the preliminary draft principles themselves. The note comments on the traditional role of the Sub-Commission as an expert body to draft "guidelines" or "principles" regarding the many human rights issues that have come before it. The note also identified the overall sources of legal norms, distinguishing those derived from international law as a whole (for example, *jus cogens* and *erga omnes*) and those derived from specific human rights provisions (for example, the concept of non-derogability of certain rights coupled with some limitations of rights allowed in wartime). The [Coordinator][Special Rapporteur] also pointed out specific issues that would have to be addressed in the most important area of the administration of justice where there is great potential that counter-terrorism measures will overtake long accepted norms and principles. She concluded her preliminary review of issues to be addressed with the need to address the situation of vulnerable groups and the importance of certain principles (for example *non-refoulement)* to them.

4.   The Draft Principles themselves were divided into six areas: general principles; terrorist acts and human rights; counter-terrorism measures; issues relating to the administration of justice; asylum and extradition; and a brief list of potential other topics for guidelines.

5.   The Sub-Commission responded favorably to this initial start, and in its decision 2004/109 entitled "Guidelines and principles for the promotion and protection of human rights when combating terrorism", called for a sessional working group at its fifty-seventh session, with a mandate to "elaborate detailed principles and guidelines, with relevant commentary, concerning the promotion and protection of human rights when combating terrorism, based, inter alia, on the preliminary framework draft of principles and guidelines contained in the Working paper prepared by Ms. Koufa."

6.   While not able to provide analysis of specific counter-terrorism measures during the course of her mandate to prepare her study on terrorism and human rights, the [Coordinator][Special Rapporteur] did form the view that there were a number of such measures that gave her great concern due to their apparent incompatibility with long-established human rights and humanitarian law norms. Some areas of concern were addressed in her study, as well in a number of other reports of, or comments raised by, United Nations and regional procedures and bodies, non-governmental organizations and national legal associations about both specific and general counter-terrorism measures. As noted in her working paper, she chose the issues to more fully develop in her study that presented the most difficulties,

distinguishing terrorists from combatants, for example, to establish a better foundation for guidelines.[1] Certain other issues were merely mentioned or only minimally addressed (distinguishing terrorist crimes from ordinary or non-terrorist crime, for example) as they were already under concerted review elsewhere, especially in the course of deliberations of the United Nations treaty bodies and at the regional level. The [Coordinator][Special Rapporteur] did not address some issues at all (such as the root causes of terrorism) as these were, in her view, better addressed in separate studies due to their vastness, complexity and the need to draw on a number of disciplines other than law to be useful.

7.   The [Coordinator][Special Rapporteur] nonetheless recognizes that guidelines, if they are to be useful, must be comprehensive: they must address all issues relative to human rights and terrorism whether fully addressed in her study or not. The Working group, therefore, faces the daunting task of formulating guidelines in areas that have not been fully addressed at the Sub-Commission or, in some cases, anywhere else. Thus, at this stage, the [Coordinator][Special Rapporteur] considers it essential to identify some areas where additional work would be helpful, with a firm hope that members of the Sub-Commission, whether on the Working group or not, consider them and perhaps prepare topic papers or commentary on them to be submitted to the Working group.[2] These include, but are not limited to: (1) distinguishing ordinary crime from terrorist acts; (2) the degree (or lack thereof) of effective interaction between terrorist groups and organized crime: are there genuine points of convergence or merely parallel operations;[3] (3) what is it about terrorist acts that is different from ordinary crime—even especially violent ordinary crime?;[4] (4) the effectiveness of counter-terrorism measures;[5] (5) generating fear of terrorism out of proportion to the actual threat of terrorism for political purposes;[6] (6) further elaboration of the procedural rights at risk: the issues of denial of counsel; indefinite detention (with no notice of charges); interrogation methods and strategies (for example, removal to a torturing country); evidence and sources of evidence (including unreasonable searches); cross-examination rights; sentencing; selective prosecution; conditions of detention; denial of defense witnesses; persecution of counsel, to name a few; (7) privacy rights and property rights; (8) compensation for victims;[7] (9) reducing the risk of terrorism, including the need to more fully understand the root causes of terrorism; and (10) countering State terrorism. The [Coordinator][Special Rapporteur welcomes any suggestions for other topics not fully addressed in her study for consideration by the Working group.

8.   At the risk of usurping the Working group's efforts, the [Coordinator] [Special Rapporteur] respects the urgency of the Sub-Commission's directive

but recognizes that the task will not be completed in one session of the Sub-Commission. Therefore, she has reworked her draft principles and guidelines in the hope that this will contribute to the adoption of principles and guidelines by the Sub-Commission as quickly as possible, giving due respect to other members of the Working group and the Sub-Commission as a whole. This draft draws mainly on all of her work in the course of her study, as well as review of treaty bodies, regional human rights bodies, and other guidelines or statements of principles, whether already adopted or in progress. She has also taken the liberty to provide some brief comments, recognizing that the Guidelines require sound bases in existing law. Her comments seek to avoid duplication of the Digest issued and recently updated by the Office of the High Commissioner for Human Rights. Accordingly, the [Coordinator] invites the Sub-Commission to read this draft with that Digest in mind. She submits, then, this expanded framework draft of principles and guidelines to provide a basis for further action by the Sub-Commission and its Working group on this topic.

A FRAMEWORK DRAFT OF PRINCIPLES AND GUIDELINES CONCERNING HUMAN RIGHTS AND TERRORISM

General Principles

1.   All international, regional and national action concerning terrorism should be guided by the United Nations Charter, all general principles of law, all norms of human rights as set out in international and regional treaties, and all norms of treaty-based and customary humanitarian law. Due attention should be paid to United Nations or regional treaty bodies, in particular to comments, commentary, guidelines or sets of principles on specific treaty articles or issues.

2.   International and regional treaties and agreements relating to terrorism that do not specifically address human rights and humanitarian law should be interpreted and acted upon, as necessary, to conform with all universally binding norms of these bodies of law.

3.   International action to combat terrorism should, to the degree possible, focus on the development and imple-mentation of forward-looking strategies rather than being responsive or reflective of individual acts or series of acts of terrorism. International action to combat terrorism must focus heavily on prevention of terrorism.

Comments: Action relating to terrorism must be firmly based in existing law. Paragraph 2 is self-evident and reflects, inter alia, the principles of "pacta sunt servanda" "jus cogens", "erga omnes." Paragraph 3 reflects the [Coordinator's] concern about hasty and

*over-reaching measures that do not help in addressing terrorism
and eventually have to be curtailed or eliminated.*

Duties of States regarding terrorist acts and human rights

4.   All States have a duty to promote and protect human rights
of all persons under its political or military control.

5.   All States have a duty to protect and promote the safely and
security of all persons under its political or military control.

6.   All terrorist acts result in violations of rights, whether
committed by States themselves or sub-State actors.

7.   All States have a duty to promote and carry out national and
international policies and practices to eliminate the causes of
terrorism and to prevent the occurrence of terrorist acts.

8.   All States have a duty to refrain from producing undue fear
or apprehension of terrorist acts among their citizens or residents
out of proportion to the real threat.

9.   There shall be no impunity for States engaging in State
terrorism or sponsoring international terrorism.

*Comments: This section is largely based on the Charter, the
Universal Declaration of Human Right (especially Article 28), and
principles, such as "due diligence," set out in the study. The
provision of the duty to refrain from producing undue fear is
essential to guarantee citizen confidence in actual counter-
terrorism measures so as to prevent measures that undermine
human rights and humanitarian law norms. The work on
guidelines relative to impunity, initially undertaken by Sub-
Commission members Mr. L. Joinet and Mr. E. Guisse, recently
up-dated, consolidated, and presented to the Commission by the
[special representative of . . .] will provide guidance in this regard
and will not be duplicated here.*

General principles relating to counter-terrorism measures

8.   All counter-terrorism measures must comply fully with all
rules of international law, including human rights and humanitarian
law, as interpreted by treaty bodies, experts of Charter-based
bodies, regional human rights bodies and all other sources of
international law. Special attention should be paid to insure that
all laws, acts and policies in this regard reflect the right to non-
discrimination on any basis and are not carried out in a way that
fosters racism, xenophobia, religious intolerance, or any undue
social unrest.

9.   There shall be no reprisals by the effected State, or any
other State, directed at any people or nation in response to a

terrorist act committed by either State or sub-State actors. There shall be no military operations by the effected State or any other State against a State accused of carrying out a terrorist act unless there is a clear showing of imminent military attack by the accused State against the effected State or the explicit approval of such actions by the Security Council.

10.   As terrorist acts by sub-State actors might only in an extremely rare circumstance threaten the existence of a State, State may not invoke derogation clauses of human rights agreements in response to a terrorist act by a sub-State group unless a clear case of such a threat is demonstrated by the known facts.

Counter-terrorism measures and the definition of terrorism

11.   Counter-terrorism measures shall directly relate to terrorism and terrorist acts, not actions undertaken in armed conflict situations or acts that are non-terrorist crimes. Definitions of terrorist acts must be very carefully drawn so as to clearly set out their elements. Due attention should be paid to what are elements of the acts that support the term "terrorist" when applied to a crime.

(a) Military operations undertaken in times of armed conflict shall be evaluated in light of all existing rules relating to such operations. Military operations that are not prohibited shall not be treated as terrorist acts. The use of force undertaken by a people with the right of self-determination shall not be treated in general as terrorist acts or the group using such force as a terrorist organization: only a particular act that meets the definition of a terrorist act shall be considered as such. Acts that constitute terrorist acts in an armed conflict, regardless of the type of conflict, must be acted upon, as all other violations of humanitarian law, in strict conformity with the rules set out in humanitarian law instruments and not by any other means.

(b) States shall not use either the issue of terrorism or the existence of a terrorist act in the conduct of an armed conflict as an excuse to deny the right of self-determination of a people or to avoid application of humanitarian law in situations of civil wars, wars of national liberation or international armed conflicts.

(c) Crimes not having a quality of terrorism, regardless of how serious, shall not be subject to counter-terrorism exceptions or derogations, even when carried out by a suspected terrorist or terrorist group. Definitions of terrorist crimes must be in conformity with all applicable international norms such as *nullum crimen sine lege* or the principle of individual criminal responsibility. In particular, definitions should clearly set out what elements of the crime are terrorist.

Comments: This article addresses the two biggest definition problems: separating terrorism from armed conflicts and terrorist crimes from ordinary crime. The study focused more on the armed conflict definitional problem, but important principles discussed in the report such as "nullum crimen sine lege" and the principle of individual criminal responsibility, apply mainly in the criminal law field. This article largely draws these parts of the study as well as the norms of humanitarian law relied on in the study and jurisprudence regarding terrorist crimes. Especially relevant are the many comments, cited by the [Coordinator] in her study, made in UN and regional bodies expressing concerns with over-broad definitions of terrorist acts. As the [Coordinator pointed out in her study, great specificity is required because a charge or conviction of a terrorist crime may be used to justify, for example, denial of bail or enhanced sentences or special penalties.

Exceptions and derogations

12.   Any exceptions or derogations in human rights law in the context of counter-terrorism measures must be in strict conformity with the rules set out in the applicable international or regional instruments. A State may not institute exceptions or derogations unless that State has been subjected to terrorist acts that would justify such measures. No State may use attacks on another State to justify exceptions and derogations in its national law. Additionally, counter-terrorism measures must not abrogate any existing norm of *jus cogens* (peremptory norms), whether set out in applicable derogation clauses or not. In particular, States shall not invoke derogation clauses to justify taking hostages or to impose collective punishments.

(a) Given the sporadic occurrence of sub-State terrorist acts, great care should be taken to ensure that exceptions and derogations that might have been justified because of an act of terrorism meet strict time limits and do not become perpetual features of national law or action.

(b) Given that most acts of sub-State terrorism are carried out by small groups, great care should be taken to ensure that measures taken are necessary to apprehend actual members of terrorist groups or perpetrators of terrorist acts in a way that does not unduly encroach on the lives and liberties of ordinary persons or on procedural rights of persons charged with non-terrorist crimes.

(c) Given the fact that sub-State groups are not usually able to be a threat to a State as a whole that would justify exceptions or derogations, exceptions and derogations undertaken following a terrorist incident should be carefully reviewed and monitored by national and international authorities. Such measures should be subject to effective legal challenge in the State imposing exceptions or derogations.

Comments: In general, only certain mercenary groups, not terrorist groups, have the capacity to threaten the existence of a State, and then only a small or poorly defended one. This sections draws on the report prepared by Sub-Commission Special Rapporteur Questiaux (E/CN.4/Sub.2/1982/15), and General Comments 5 and 29 of the Human Rights Committee. The final report on human rights and states of emergency (E/CN.4/Sub.2/1997/19 and Add.1) of Sub-Commission member Mr. L. Despouy is also instructive in this regard. Additionally, this issue has been frequently addressed in all the regional bodies as set out in the Digest.

13.   Any person or class of persons unduly affected by counter-terrorism measures, as well as groups who advocate for rights, should have the right to an effective remedy against the State implementing those measures, regardless of the nationality of the affected persons or class of persons. States may establish expedited procedures, especially for vulnerable groups such as children, elderly, infirm or disabled, or for non-citizens.

Comments: Because of the potential for significant social harassment and human rights violations as well as encroachment into long-established procedural rights, persons unduly affected by such measure should be able to challenge them offensively and on an expedited or priority basis. Similarly, interested groups seeking to challenge, for example, overly broad or vague definitions need to have legal standing in this regard. Such undue effect, for example, could arise were a State to cordon off a neighborhood for a long period of time, or mandate that all adult men of a certain ethnic background report to the local law enforcement agency once a month, or that no person of a certain national origin is able to purchase property near a military base. Sub-Commission member Mr. T. van Boven's guidelines on compensation, now under review and amendment at the Commission, provides the standards in this regard and will not be repeated here.

Specific principles relating to arrest, detention, trial and penalties of alleged terrorists

No person shall be arrested for a terrorist act unless there are reasonable grounds to support the arrest. No person may be detained solely on the bases of race, colour, national origin, ethnicity or any other factor. Evidence used to justify the arrest of a person must meet all international standards. Abduction and hostage taking are prohibited in all circumstances.

(a) No person shall be arrested based on evidence obtained by means of a search that violates international standards. While in certain circumstances area-wide searches may be undertaken or restrictions on freedom of movement imposed to facilitate seizure of evidence, there must be sufficient grounds of the presence of terrorists or evidence to justify them, and they should be undertaken in a way that least varies from international standards. Forcible transfers of persons on the pretext of securing evidence without compelling grounds permitted under international law constitute crimes against humanity.

(b) No person shall be arrested based on evidence obtained under torture, or cruel inhuman or degrading treatment.

(c) No person shall be arrested solely on evidence provided by a person already detained.

Persons detained under suspicion of engaging in or planning terrorist acts at all times have the right to know the charges against them. A charge of being a terrorist is insufficient, and must be accompanied with charges of specific acts.

Persons detained under suspicion of engaging in or planning terrorist acts at all times have the right to counsel from moment of arrest.

Persons detained under suspicion of engaging in or planning terrorist acts at all times have the right to the presumption of innocence.

Persons detained under suspicion of engaging in or planning terrorists acts have the right to remain silent. Exercise of the right to remain silent shall not carry with it any penalties or presumptions.

Persons detained under suspicion of engaging in or planning terrorists acts and held in administrative detention must be brought before competent legal bodies promptly, generally within four days.

Persons detained under suspicion of engaging in or planning terrorist acts may not be subjected to torture, cruel, inhuman or degrading treatment. No evidence obtained under these conditions may be admitted into evidence or in any way be used to support a conviction. Persons detained for trial in one State may not be transferred to any other State for interrogation purposes and any evidence obtain in these circumstances shall not be admitted into evidence or used in any way to support a conviction.

All international and national norms relating to legal proceedings must be followed in any case involving persons charged with terrorist acts. In particular, fundamental requirements of fair trial must at all times be respected. States may limit media or public presence at such trials if the interest of justice so demands. However, there must be some mechanism for observation or review of any trial with limited access of the media or general public to guarantee the fairness of it.

The use of military tribunals should be limited to trials of military personnel for acts committed in the course of military actions. The use of military tribunals to try a person accused of terrorist acts must meet all requirements of international humanitarian law for such tribunals.

The right to submit writs such as *habeas corpus* and *amparo*, as well the legal means to prepare and submit these writs, may not be denied to any person arrested and charged with a terrorist act.

No person can be convicted of a terrorist act unless that person has been able fully to present witnesses and evidence in his or her defense, cross-examine witnesses and evidence against him or her, and unless the trial has had all other elements of fairness, impartiality or other requirements of fundamental legal principles.

Penalties for convicted terrorists shall conform with all international and national rules, especially those relating to the death penalty and life sentences without possibility of parole. While participation in a terrorist act may be grounds for evoking "special circumstances" that can be used to justify higher penalties, no penalty may be cruel, inhuman or degrading.

No person convicted of a terrorist act can be denied the right to appeal, including to relevant regional or international tribunals or mechanisms.

Conditions of detention, whether pre-trial, during trial or post-conviction, must conform to all international standards, except that in exceptional circumstances, provided for in conformity with international and national law, persons accused or convicted of terrorist acts may be detained in facilities apart from persons accused or convicted of ordinary crimes, provided that rules relating to the prohibition of prolonged solitary detention are obeyed. Under no circumstances may a person be held in either unacknowledged or incommunicado detention.

Comments: This section draws largely on non-discrimination principles from many international and regional human rights treaties and on related principles in humanitarian law, Article 15 of the Convention Against Torture and commentary of the Committee against Torture, on the General Comments 5, 8, 21 and 29 of the Human Rights Committee, the directives of the Working group on arbitrary detention and the jurisprudence of regional human rights bodies. While there is some variance in the regional human rights bodies regarding the length of time persons may be held in administrative detention, the European Court of Human Rights is quite firm that persons detained for terrorist-related offenses (or any other charges) — must be brought before a judicial officer within four days. Brogan and Others v. the United Kingdom, *ECHR, 29 November 1988, (para. 62). The Human Rights Committee, in its General Comment 29, indicates that the prohibition of unacknowledged detention is absolute due to its status as a norm of general international law. General Comment 29, para. 13 (b). This rule is further supported by obligations regarding both POW's and civilian detainees in humanitarian law. The Geneva Conventions contain explicit fair trial requirements that are not subject to derogation. The Human Rights Committee sees no reason for derogation from them in other emergency situations falling short of war. General Comment 29, para. 16. The Committee, while not mentioning any particular writs (such as habeas corpus or amparo) declares that the legal means to challenge the lawfulness of a detention is essential to protect non-derogable rights. Humanitarian law, and Article 7(1)(d) and 7(2)(d) of the Statute of the International Criminal Court address the absolute nature of the rule against deportation or forcible transfer. The Guiding Principles on Internal Displacement (E/CN.4/1998/52/Add.2) also address this point, as does Sub-Commission member Mr. P. Pinheiro in the guidelines he is developing on the right to housing (E/CN.4/Sub.2/2004/22 and Add.1.) There are many international instruments relating to the conditions of detention, such as the Standard Minimum Rules for the Treatment of Prisoners, Body of Principles for the Protection of All Persons under Any form of Detention or Imprisonment, and United Nations Rules for the Protection of Juveniles Deprived of their Liberty. The Digest cites many decisions in the regional human rights bodies on these issues.*

Asylum, forcible transfers, and extradition

All national policies involving asylum, extradition, and forcible transfers must conform to international, regional and national law. In particular, there must be full respect for the principle of *non-refoulement* and full regard to laws relating to the death penalty or other harsh sentences. No person shall be transferred or deported to any State unless there is a verifiable guarantee that there will be full protection for all human rights in the receiving State. Until the transferred person's status is fully settled in accordance with all applicable international and national law, the transferring State remains liable for that person. A transferring State must seek the return of any transferred person whose rights are at risk. Mass deportation is a crime against humanity.

Forcible transfers undertaken in the context of a terrorist act must meet all international, regional and national law. Prolonged forcible transfer unjustified by the exigencies of the situation is a crime against humanity.

As extradition is a major procedure in counter-terrorism agreements and measures, all States should endeavor to elaborate extradition rules that are compatible with the rules of other States and with international law.

Extradition requests should not be granted when there is reasonable cause to believe that such a request is motivated by prejudice, discrimination or other impermissible bias or when there is any reason to believe that the person for whom extradition is sought would not have a fair trial in conformity with all rules of international law relating to the administration of justice, or would be subjected to conditions of detention that fully meet all international standards. In particular, States sending a person should affirm that there are no unjustifiable exceptions, limitations or derogations in place in the receiving State. A transferring State remains liable for any extradited person until that person's status is determined in full conformity with international standards. A transferring State must seek the return of any extradited persons whose rights are at risk.

Comments: This section draws on the Human Rights Committee's general comment 31, basic rules of asylum law, relevant provisions of humanitarian law (especially articles 45 and 49 of Geneva Convention IV), the above-mentioned section of the Statute of the International Criminal Court, the Torture Convention, the report of the OAS's special rapporteur on migrant workers (OEA/Ser.L/V/II.111, Doc.20 rev.16 (2001) and the OAS report on terrorism and human rights (OEA/Ser.L/V/II.116, Doc.5 rev.1corr.(2002).

Privacy and property rights

All rules relating to privacy and property rights shall be in strict conformity with international human rights and humanitarian law norms. States shall not encroach, either electronically or by any other means, on correspondence or other private communications, without warrants issued with sufficient cause. Property may not be seized as part of counter-terrorism measures without warrants issued on the basis of sufficient cause. All persons or groups whose property has been seized or whose assets frozen have the right to challenge this through full and fair legal proceedings, which, owing to the gravity of seizing property or freezing assets in democratic societies and the principle of the presumption of innocence, shall be preemptory.

Comments: The Human Rights Committee, in its General comment No. 16 on the right to privacy, provides basic rules relating to privacy. Property rights are guaranteed in the Universal Declaration of Human Rights, Article 17. Regional human rights declarations and conventions must also be consulted in determining what is sufficient cause. The European Court of Human Rights has ruled that some "secret surveillance" might be allowed during genuine emergency situations, but this is not unlimited. The Klass case, European Court of Human Rights, judgment of 6 September 1978, Series A No. 28. The issue of housing rights is relevant, and the above-mentioned guidelines in process by Mr. P. Pinheiro on the right to housing will provide that framework.

Compensation for victims of terrorist acts

Victims of terrorist acts committed by States are entitled to full remedies for the violations of their rights in conformity with international law relating to effective remedies and reparations. National legislation should also provide means by which victims of sub-State terrorism can receive full remedies.

Comments: As stated above, the standards for compensation are evolving at the Commission and will not be set out here.

ENDNOTES

[1]   E/CN.4/Sub.2/2004/47, para. 2.

[2]   The [Coordinator][Special Rapporteur] prepared a considerable amount of text for some of these areas, but then, for reasons stated in the course of her mandate, in the end did not include it or included it in reduced form.

[3]   This topic also should address, for example, whether mere trafficking in drugs is "terrorism."

[4]   Elaborating on the "terror" of "terrorism" is essential for the formulation of the elements of terrorist acts in national legislation or in extradition agreements in keeping with the principle of *nullum crimen sine lege*.

[5]   This topic addresses, inter alia, on the utility of using counter-terrorism measure to combat ordinary crime rather than focusing resources on actual terrorism.

[6]   This topic concerns not only using unreasonable fear of terrorism to facilitate counter-terrorism measures that violate human rights, but also using that fear to stifle dissent. Each act of terrorism generates great pain, but as the [Coordinator][Special Rapporteur] pointed out in her study, the numbers of terrorist acts committed by sub-State groups are few in comparison to acts carried out by States engaging in State terrorism or by common criminals. Using the United States Department of States figures for the past year, the number of persons killed by sub-State terrorist groups equaled the number of persons killed by lightening.   —

[7]   The Sub-Commission, and especially its expert Mr. von Boven, elaborated principles in this regard that are now advancing at the Commission level. The [Coordinator][Special Rapporteur] assumes that issues relating to compensation and other remedies for victims of terrorist acts will follow these principles, especially in relation to victims of State terrorism or State-sponsored terrorism.

NILS ANDERSSON

INTERNATIONAL HUMANITARIAN LAW AND TERRORISM

THE NEED TO DISTINGUISH BETWEEN COMBATANTS AND MURDERERS

For centuries, no attention has ever been given to the condition of armed forces—and even less to that of civilians. However, as a consequence of the slow evolution of the moral code, of the relation between societies and death, of the notion of the winner and the defeated, of barbarity or civilization, the second half of the 19th century witnessed the establishment of international rules of humanitarian law that have to be applied in armed conflicts, as stipulated in the Geneva Conventions, in the United Nations Conventions, in the European Conventions, in the American States Conventions, and/or in the Rome Statute.

Yet when the perpetrators of war crimes have to be prosecuted—of whatever country they may be citizens, and whatever their current or past bench warrant might be—these rules are not respected and are even openly violated by established democracies. This is what happens when some nations yield to the pressures applied by the United States (interruption of economic help, suppression of some accustomed benefits, etc.) and sign bilateral agreements with Washington in order to withdraw from international justice those American citizens who are under suspicion of having committed war crimes;[1] or when we witness European states releasing—in absolute illegality—suspects to the CIA in order for them to be transferred to countries where they can be tortured with impunity.[2]

As Karen Parker stressed, documents from the Office of the United Nations High Commissioner for Human Rights and from the Sub-Commission on the Promotion and Protection of Human Rights urgently remind us that "nations have to ensure that any measure taken to fight terrorism respects the obligations incumbent upon them by virtue of international law, and in particular of the international tools that relate to human and refugees rights, as well as to humanitarian law." These reminders are null and void: cases of non-respect and of severe violations of humanitarian law are often observed and are justified by the fight against terrorism (military courts, discriminatory laws, measures of racist nature—and this on a national level as well as on a regional or even international level).

These violations are also committed under the cover of a judicial deficit, such as when international instruments are neither adapted to the evolution of the means of destruction, nor to new war strategies (often because of obstruction by Great Powers): hence these "commonly known insufficiencies of international law" as emphasized by Monique Chemillier-Gendrau, inadequacies that are obviously observed in the current conflicts. Humanitarian law is not, and cannot be, a fixed matter; therefore the obligation to reinforce the rules that govern the way wars are waged has to be added to the exigency of its application (for which the practice of the law of universal jurisdiction is a means). In this sense, one of the questions that stands out with some acuity is the definition of terrorism in terms of international humanitarian law. This question does not appear as an object of consideration in the aforementioned documents.

While raising this question, let's already set a proviso: we all wish for a world at peace that would banish war but, because of oppositions between nations, because of geopolitical purposes, of imperial or regional ambitions, of the intent to dominate populations or of these populations' longing to free themselves from a colonial domination or from a dictatorial regime, the resort to war is a reality.

Why should one define terrorism?

A preliminary distinction has to be made between, on the one hand, criminal law which does not have to take into account the motivations but determines what are antisocial behaviors and their corresponding penalties, and on the other hand, the international conventions and documents which define war crimes and crimes against humanity in armed conflicts, and take motivations into account, for example through the recognition of the right to independence or through the condemnation of vengeance, and distinguish between combatants and civilians, between partisans and mercenaries.

An ubiquitous subject in political discourses and in the media is the latent danger of slaughters that do not recognize any frontier. Beyond the violence it represents and the sufferings it breeds, terrorism leads to a worldwide surveillance of people that becomes increasingly onerous, while containing the risks of a totalitarian drift. Since 09/11, in the spirit of the

American Patriot Act, and on all the continents, a net of "anti-terrorist devices" has been displayed—the European Union has nominated a coordinator of anti-terrorist policies placed under the political responsibility of Javier Solana. The new NATO strategic concept stresses that "the security interests of the Alliance could be jeopardized by other risks of a more general nature, including acts relating to terrorism"; the UN has set up a Comittee Against Terrorism, and on May 2, 2006, its secretary-general presented a report entitled "Uniting Against Terrorism: A Recommendation for a Worldwide Anti-terrorist Strategy". The terrorism syndrome cannot be ignored or obscured.

The transnational nature of terrorist acts justifies the institution of these internationalized devices, but while conventional wars, guerrillas and civil wars (conflicts during which the belligerents resort to terrorism)[3] are judicially defined, there is no operative judicial definition of terrorism, and therefore of the fight against terrorism. Hence, without having defined what is a terrorist act or what is a terrorist, it suffices to qualify an act as "terrorism" for this act not to be recognized either by custom or by international law as an act of war, and for it to be acknowledged as a crime. This allowed, for example, the US Government to open the camp of Guantanamo in spite of all the rules of international law—which led soldiers to humiliate, rape or torture, in the prisons of Abu Ghraïb, Bagram or elsewhere, those they consider as deprived of rights.[4]

The Convention on the financing of terrorism, in accordance with the rules of humanitarian law, characterizes as terrorist "any [...] act meant to cause death or serious bodily injury to any civilian, or to any other person not taking an active part in the hostilities in a situation of armed conflict", a definition which anyone would approve of. However, this very same document switches to another position by considering an act as terrorist "when the purpose of such an act, by its nature or its context, is [...] to compel a government or an international organization to do or to abstain from doing any act". Such an extension allows the consideration of any resort to violence in response to violence as a terrorist act. If one accepts this interpretation, the sheer fact of opposing Montoire[5] politics by arms becomes a terrorist act since the purpose was to obligate a government—the Vichy government—not to accomplish its collaborationist politics. The danger resides in the certainty that "the law is what it is, that any other so-called law is not law."[6]

The importance of defining terrorism can also be justified because of the extreme diversity of actions that the word covers. Thus, the suicide bombing against the World Trade Center, the actions of the Algerian FLN, of the death squads in Latin America, of the Basque ETA, of the Peruvian Shining Path, of the Stern Gang and Irgun in Palestine, of the Red Hand in France, of the Lebanese Hezbollah, of the Contras in Nicaragua, of the Vietnamese FLN, of the Weathermen in the USA, of the Red Armed Faction in Federal Germany, of the Aun Sect in Japan, the bombings of Lockerbie and of the train station of Milan, the murder of Letellier (one of Allende's ministers), the bombardments of Dresden, Tokyo or Coventry or that of Marwahin in Lebanon, the Korean airplane shot down by the Soviets, or the acts of resistance against Nazism,[7] have been or could be qualified as terrorist acts.

That very incomplete enumeration highlights, if needed, the complexity of the problem posed by acts undertaken with political and ideological, religious, or ethnic motives, and stresses the necessity to distinguish the revolutionary act from the factious act, the operations resulting from state terrorism from those resulting from insurrectional terrorism, the attacks that belong to a military strategy from isolated attacks, mass terrorism from individual actions. This is why no fewer than 212 definitions of terrorism have been enumerated in English!

Then, what is a terrorist? The bombardment of Dresden meets Raymond Aron's definition: "A violent act is termed terrorist when its psychological effects are out of proportion to its purely physical results". The dropping of a bomb in a public place corresponds to that of Paul Wilkinson,[8] to whom terrorism is "the systematic use of political violence by small groups of conspirators whose purpose is to influence political positions more than materially defeat the enemy". If one refers to Thomas Aquinas' principle: "war can only result from public power, otherwise it is a crime", then only state terrorism is legitimate. These quotes prove that if one wants to avoid confusion, what matters in order to authorize a definition is to distinguish in every war the type of conflict, the fighting forces, the military means in use, as well as the aims and the motives of the parties at war.

What Differentiates Terrorist Acts

It is therefore useful, in order to choose one's position, to pose the question by starting with concrete facts, with acts that correspond to the etymological definition of terrorism: the will to sow the seed of terror. That was the case for the atomic bomb launched on Hiroshima and for the bombing of the Milk Bar during the Battle of Algiers—two examples chosen on purpose because they do not belong to current conflicts and do not bear the same level of intensity. How comparable are they? How different are they? And beyond that, how are they treated in regard to humanitarian law in the absence of a definition for the word terrorism?

In the first case, what is in question is an act of war committed by a national army with the military, financial, technological and scientific resources of a great power. The operation has been conducted as a result of a presidential decision, not in order to destroy any military or strategic objective, but deliberately targeting civilian populations with, according to President Truman's own declarations, the objective of abridging the course of the war in the Far East and, while acts of retaliation are forbidden by the Geneva Conventions, the intention of avenging Pearl Harbor and the treatment inflicted by the Japanese on prisoners of war.

In the second case, the operation was driven by a clandestine movement which, facing a modern army, was unable to wage a conventional war. Instead, they resorted to guerrilla warfare. If the movement, that is to say, the Algerian FLN, benefited from huge support among the population, its military resources were obsolete. By perpetrating bombings, they achieved three objectives. Because of inequalities between the military forces, the first one was to support the resistance by moving the struggle from the countryside to the cities. The second objective was to respond to the repression by the colonial state and to the attacks by paramilitary groups by striking the colonial community. The third was to use the media coverage of the attacks as a weapon in order to internationalize their struggle. A last distinction to take note of is that these actions were not decided by a constituted power, nor by a military hierarchy but, because of the rules of clandestinity, because of the lack of a communications medium and because of the surveillance of the country by the enemy, the decisions were taken by isolated leaders.

These two events, whether concerning the human consequences, the impact of the strike upon the enemy, or the influence of the operation on the evolution of the conflict, cannot be compared in any way. Hiroshima was an act of war, in a high-intensity conflict that opposed nations and regular armies, and that would re-enforce the capitulation of Japan. The Milk Bar corresponded to the only possible level of operation by the weakest camp from a military point of view, in a so-called asymmetric war, an operation which, as everyone knew, would not lead to victory over the enemy.

With these differences underlined, the two cases are terrorist acts, in the sense of the Geneva Conventions, and can be considered as war crimes. The first case could even be qualified as a crime against humanity. However, if the person who dropped the bomb at the Milk Bar is called a terrorist, it seems unconceivable to use this same term for those who launched the bomb on Hiroshima. The handling of these two acts of war by the international jurisdiction is also radically different. Neither the crew of the Enola Gay (the plane that delivered the atomic bomb) nor the political and military leaders who ordered the launching of the bomb incurred the risk of being judged for the war crime that the launching of Little Boy (the code name of the atomic bomb) represented. In addition, if the airplane had been shot down on the way back, the crew were wearing military uniforms and would have benefited, as war prisoners, from the protection of the Geneva Conventions, contrary to the bombers who would have been excluded from the Geneva Conventions and the rules of international humanitarian law since they did not openly carry arms and were devoid of any given distinctive sign noticeable from a distance, and therefore could not be considered as fighters, but as criminals.

The "legitimacy" of Little Boy rests on the fact that it concerned a war between two nations and two conventional armies, whereas the "illegitimacy" of the Milk Bar comes from the fact that the bomb was not set by a regular army but by a clandestine branch of a national liberation movement, instead. And that in spite of the fact that the Milk Bar bombers can call upon a double legitimacy: the first one, that cannot be denied, is that their country was occupied by a foreign force—and the right of resistance of a people subdued by a colonial or foreign domination has been recognized in the United Nations instruments; the second one is of a military nature— these men and women were fighting with the weapons they had at their disposal. The answer given by Larbi Ben M'Hidi, leader of the Wilayat of Algiers, to the French officers after his arrest and before he was assassinated is worth attention. Asked whether or not he was ashamed to use women to get bombs out of the Casbah by hiding them in their baby bassinets, Larbi Ben M'HIdi answered: "Give me your airplanes and I will give you my bassinets", thus revealing the essential question in the case of an asymmetric war, that of the unevenness of the resources between the warring parties.

Why a Legal Definition of Terrorism Is Difficult to Achieve

On one hand, the trivialization of terrorism as a war strategy is the consequence of political, economic and social situations. This was underlined by the General Assembly of the United Nations as early as 1987 when it noted, "acts of violence that originate in despair, frustrations, injustices and hopelessness, and that lead some people to sacrifice human lives, including their own, in order to try and provoke some radical changes". On the other hand, it is the consequence of reasons of a military nature that reside in the generalization of so-called asymmetric wars.

Hence a first interrogation: since launching an atomic bomb and committing an attack with a handcrafted bomb are both terrorist acts that international law differentiates, one being absolved, the other condemned, what means of action can an armed revolt resort to during an asymmetric war in order not to be qualified as terrorist? Angelism would offer pacific means, but the Three Monkeys of Wisdom cannot change in the slightest our reflection stemming from a reality become tragically routine, to which it is necessary to respond—save to propose that there is only one logic, that of the strongest, that of preventive and punitive wars.

It is nowadays obvious that the criminalization of terrorism without distinction leads to the spiral of repression/terrorism, the repression bringing forth terrible frustrations and also bringing forth the risk of a worldwide destabilization. This is acknowledged by Kofi Annan's report for a reform of the United Nations in March 2005, in which one can read: "the struggle against terrorism has a very important side-effect: by fighting against terrorism we run the risk of a very heavy sacrifice on the side of human rights, of democracy, and of good governance".

The Geneva Conventions, their additional Protocols and the United Nations Conventions for the repression of acts of terrorism may provide a working basis to distinguish criminal acts and acts of war in "what is usually referred to as terrorist acts". This is true in particular for the additional Protocol I and its articles 43 on armed forces, 44 on combatants and war prisoners, 45 on the protection of persons who took part in hostilities, 37 on the prohibition of perfidy, or possibly 47 on the definition of mercenaries. But the work of distinction should abandon the ambiguity which often characterizes these documents, and hence opens the way to various interpretations, always to the benefit of the victors and strongest parties.

The legal approach to terrorism has indeed to be accompanied by an interrogation on the resort to terrorism as a military strategy as well as on its military or political effectiveness or ineffectiveness; a judgment should also be made about its "ideologization" and about its sacrificial drift (by putting morality in perspective in any act of war, I will avoid asking about terrorism and morality). These are incontrovertible questions, but still, the right to revolt of a population suffering from the violence of a repressive, dictatorial, colonial regime or that of a foreign occupation, and to oppose violence by violence, remains. Refusing these populations that right is going against the Declaration on the Granting of Independence to Colonial Countries and Peoples voted by the General Assembly of the United Nations on December 14, 1960, that specifies in its point 1: "The subjection of peoples to alien subjugation, domination and exploitation constitutes a denial of fundamental human rights, is contrary to the Charter of the United Nations and is an impediment to the promotion of world peace and co-operation". That declaration goes as far as to demand in its point 4 that "All armed action or repressive measures of all kinds directed against dependent peoples shall cease in order to enable them to exercise peacefully and freely their right to complete independence, and the integrity of their national territory shall be respected". Of course this document, buried in the archives of history, deals with another kind of struggle between dominated and dominating than the one known nowadays; however, no one can contest it.

The rules of international humanitarian law are meant to protect the injured military, the war prisoners and the civilian populations; they do not deny the realities of wars but aim to codify them in order to alleviate the sufferings they inflict. As a concrete illustration, if one applies these rules to the letter of the law, actions mounted by liberation movements against occupying armed forces, against representatives of the power or against collaborators—excluding attacks deliberately targeting civilian populations— should be considered as acts of war as long as, during such operations, their authors, in addition to wearing a given distinctive sign noticeable from a distance, would openly carry arms. Once again, considering the asymmetric nature of many conflicts, these demands would only lead to making them designated martyrs.

In order to act effectively against a fanatic and blind terrorism, which is "a terrible feature of globalization", one has to get away from the unique discourse of the law of the strong, of preventive wars and of continued repression. Laws are constantly evolving; the matter here, as a form to define, is to stipulate the conditions allowing those who fight occupying armed forces, representatives of power or collaborators, to be given the title of combatant even if they do not bear a given distinctive and noticeable sign and do not openly carry arms. Everyone knows that such actions cannot be undertaken without a real military capacity, without implantation inside the population and without reliable sources of information. By refusing to look for an accurate definition (however great the difficulty), one breeds the blind terrorism that aims exclusively or indistinctly at civilians, and that is deservedly condemned by international humanitarian law.

Some will argue: would that not amount to legalizing factious terrorism? In international humanitarian law, a distinction is made between members of a regular army, fighters for a national cause, and mercenaries; the same could be done in the definition of terrorism. Others will argue that it would amount to legalizing state terrorism; the latter is a reality and its impunity remains quasi general in spite of the dispositions of humanitarian law: here, it is the moralization of the powers that is at stake.

The main argument still has to be evoked: the very search for a definition of terrorism boils down to yielding to terrorism, to legitimizing it. The question may be raised, but what answer can be given to those who say, "this is the only option we have" as an insurrectional strategy? What answer can be given to those who mention resort to terrorism by regular armies benefiting from an absolute military superiority, bringing into play commandos, paramilitaries, mercenaries or agents who operate without any given distinctive and noticeable sign, and without openly carrying arms, and are moreover protected by a penetration cover and by optimal retreat possibilities? Or above all, what answer can be given to those who are facing the great powers that clamp their political, economic, financial and military domination without limits and with arrogance, and who resort to—using Clausewitz definition—"modern total war in all its crushing energy"? One of the oldest precepts of war is to always keep an escape opening for the enemy, in the absence of which he would become enraged. Societies ponder the problems they have to resolve; for the reasons that were enumerated in this text, the need for a judiciary definition appears as a substantial problem that has yet to be solved.

As the means of extermination improve and slaughters become more and more rational, if the aim is to fight against blind and fanatical terrorism, it is necessary to break with the democratic discourse that is accompanied by an imperialistic politic; it is necessary to stop using the terrorist weapon as in Fallujah, that Guernica of the Iraq war,[9] and prohibit "the excuse of the loopholes in the law", denounced with such pertinence by Barbara Delcourt, as a cover for barbarity.

This will never atone for the horror "beyond understanding" that is embodied by the deathly sacrifice that echoes "Kill them all and God will distinguish His people" reserved for the Cathars during the sacking of Béziers. Faced with this triumph of irrationality, one has to weave the threads of understanding, one of these threads being humanitarian law, whose mission is to regulate wars. In 1864, the first Geneva Conventions recognized that "the injured or sick militaries would be rescued and treated"; for this to come true, one more slaughter had been needed: Solferino. Today, and this is a disturbing, a shocking but an unavoidable question that nonetheless has to be asked concerning terrorism: how many civilian slaughters are needed before the law will be able, not to put an end to these acts, but to settle the rules that would allow the distinction between murderers and combatants?

The danger is the assurance that "the law is what it is, any other pretended law is not law". We are all depositaries of humanitarian law and, "for the universality of the facts to harmonize with the universality of principles", we should not only demand its application but also make sure it is constantly improved and reinforced: this should be part of our responsibility as citizens.

ENDNOTES

[1] In 2003, according to the FIDH, 32 countries, having refused to sign such an accord, were the object of economic sanctions, while 65 states have signed these bilateral impunity accords with the United States.

[2] See the report for the Council of Europe prepared by Dick Marty, counsellor to the States (Switzerland), June 2006.

[3] UN General Assembly Resolution 3314, December 1974, and Optional Protocols I and II of the Geneva Conventions, 1977.

[4] Such a denunciation could naturally be heard concerning the acts committed in Chechnya, in Palestine, in Lebanon, in Darfur and numerous other places.

[5] Site of the meeting between Hitler and Petain sealing the collaboration of the Vichy regime with Nazism.

[6] Jacques Bidet, *Explication et reconstruction du Capital*, p. 253, P.U.F, 2004.

[7] Some of these terrorist acts had been committed by heads of states and sitting governments or by leaders who, after having been qualified as terrorists, acceded to power.

[8] Director of the Department of History and International Relations at University of St. Andrews, Scotland.

[9] At Fallujah, the bombing of civilian populations, the use of fragmentation or white phosphorous bombs caused, according to American scientist, Les Roberts, 100 000 deaths. See his contribution in *La science et la guerre*, under the direction of D. Iagolnitzer, L. Koch-Miramond and V. Rivasseau, eds. L'Harmattan, 2005.

[10] *La conquete des droits de l'homme*, preface by Federico Mayor, Secretary-General of UNESCO, 1988.

PHILIP GRANT

LAW VERSUS
THE NATIONAL INTEREST
THE ROLE OF NGOS

In the battle for the respect of human rights, NGOs (nongovernmental organizations) have long played a major role within the international system. NGOs, and more particularly NGOs from the United States have largely been responsible for the explicit mention of human rights in the Charter of the United Nations as one of the main purposes of the Organization. NGOs also played a crucial role in the negotiation and then adoption of the Rome Statute of the International Criminal Court. Some of them are active in gathering information and proofs on the ground, which will then serve in the prosecution of the gravest crimes before criminal tribunals. Others are specialized in the representation of victims and the preparation of the files to be submitted to national or international tribunals, to cite only these examples. Even though it is limited, the NGOs have a major role to play in the battle for the respect of international humanitarian law in a large sense, in particular in the battle against impunity for international crimes, war crimes, genocides and crimes against humanity.

The title of this contribution, "Law Versus the National Interest: the Role of NGOs", is a wink to an association, active in the '90s, animated by Olivier Russbach. This association, Droit contre raison d'État, had indeed succeeded in opening many doors, notably of tribunals, due to a great capacity of judicial imagination to bring major questions of international law before ordinary judges.

For example, it brought a request for reparation against the company Thomson-Brandt Armaments before the Paris Tribunal de Grande Instance, in view of the illicit character in international law of the delivery of military material to Iraq, even though it had been authorized by the French government. For the Paris Tribunal, "deliveries of military material to Iraq were undoubtedly contrary to the respect of international humanitarian law". Why should we mention this story which took place more than seventeen years ago? More than its actual result, the interest of this procedure is due to the fact that an association, representing merely itself, was able to bring a problem before an ordinary tribunal which was requested to apply the law, and not merely commercial law but public international law, the resolutions of the Security Council, international humanitarian law and the jurisprudence of international authorities.

This example, which does not directly concern the United States, illustrates the cultural revolution which has emerged in the world of the NGOs, and also in the academic world and in the wider public. Namely, law is useful only if one makes use of it, and mainly if it changes and develops, even quickly. For instance, immunities considered over a very long period as obvious and necessary, or even absolute, should no longer prevail against the demands for justice by the victims of international crimes; the territorial field of application of conventions on the matter of human rights should be extended whenever troops are sent abroad; a civil or military superior should not necessarily be relieved from his responsibility, even though he did not order the commission of a crime, but "only" omitted to repress it. And that is not all. Huge fields of action open for human rights militants with the possible civil responsibility of industrial companies or banks, or even their criminal responsibility for acts of complicity committed abroad.

But one has to be able and to know how to act. And here, the ways of approach are varied. Let me give some examples. On the question of nuclear weapons, some NGOs, convinced of the illicit character of the use and stockpiling of these arms, have launched an important campaign for the recognition of their illicit character. Through intense lobbying, this large coalition of NGOs has first convinced the World Health Organization, then the United Nations General Assembly, to solicit an Advisory Opinion from the International Court of Justice, the main judicial organ of the United Nations. This was done in 1996: the Court did essentially declare that the use of nuclear weapons was prohibited, apart from some exceptional cases which in practice cannot probably occur.

NGOs also had the merit of bringing tens of cases of disappearances, torture, and extrajudicial executions before the European Court of Human Rights, in order to break the vicious circle of impunity in Turkey and more recently in Chechnya. This was done with intelligence and success, through alliances between victims, human rights militants, lawyers and personalities from the academic world.

If May 1968 in France had "imagination in power" as its slogan, one might today adopt "imagination in court" as our slogan. In fact, the main problem today in the battle against impunity is not so much to be obliged to battle for the creation of judicial rules: the development of international criminal law and international humanitarian law during the last ten years is just huge. The problem is rather to find the way to bring this law to reality, to request— to demand—its application. For some people, in the present state of international relations, there exists no supranational authority having the legitimacy to sentence violators of international law. For this approach, sometimes close to cynicism, the international criminal tribunals which have been created since the '90s (for ex-Yugoslavia and Rwanda, but also the Special Court for Sierra Leone, the tribunal for the judgment of persons responsible for the genocide in Cambodia or the experiments of justice in Kosovo, Timor or presently in Bosnia-Herzegovina, which all take place in a more or less international context), must be definitely rejected as the expression of the justice of victors. There is some truth in this statement. The Tribunal for ex-Yugoslavia did not prosecute the crimes committed by NATO during the 1999 military intervention. The Tribunal for Rwanda did not prosecute any official of the Rwandan Patriotic Front. These examples are indeed a scandal. They correspond to the state of force relations within which these new courts act. But rejecting the very idea of international justice by arguing that it would merely be an expression of the will of powerful States is an insult to victims who do not care if the bombardments against them are due to the United States and their allies or not, and retain an inalienable right to obtain reparation and to see the authors of the crimes judged, regardless of the ideological color of the war criminal.

This rejection is also a strategic error: the development of the battle against impunity is precisely due to the existence of international justice. It allows the mobilization of public opinion, the participation of media, the activation of NGOs. What would the state of the debate on the very theme of this conference be today, without the International Criminal Court, the special tribunals for Rwanda or ex-Yugoslavia, the Pinochet case? Without these important successes, the case against Rumsfeld in Germany, the complaints against some members of the French military force in Rwanda, or other similar cases would be unimaginable.

The NGOs therefore make a different bet. Instead of throwing the baby out with the bathwater, rather than refusing to accord any legitimacy to the attempts at universal justice, most of them, while criticizing everything that does deserve it, have decided to use available mechanisms to point out the contradictions which still exist between prosecutions of the weak and of the powerful. It is indeed preferable to live with this very basic troublesome contradiction, which lets the rulers of the world escape justice, and will still do so for some time to come, rather than getting rid of this contradiction by simply throwing away any international justice. In fact, there is no possible popular or associative mobilization without the very idea of justice, embodied in the procedures against the Pinochets, the Milosevices or the Charles Taylors. In the final instance, getting rid of any international justice would open the way to the flowering of impunity for both the weak and the powerful.

The world of NGOs has therefore clearly chosen to accompany this movement and use it with patience and inventiveness, so that the powerful might also be obliged to account for their acts some day, maybe not today, but certainly in ten, twenty years from now. And it is precisely here that imagination must play its role. As illustrated by previous examples, it is the role of militants, of defenders of human rights, of lawyers, of members of the academic world, to find a way to bring cases before the judge, for the affirmation of the law and, if possible, sentences, to oppose justice to *raison d'état*.

At that point, we come to the case of the United States.

One first clearly has to get rid of some ideas. Historically, no other country has had such a positive attitude towards international justice. Already by 1789, the US Congress had adopted the "Alien Tort Claims Act", a law on the basis of which many civil procedures could be carried out in the United States, including some against companies of that country. Their leadership role in the establishment of the Nuremberg and Tokyo Tribunals, their support (often more important than that of European countries) for the special Tribunals for ex-Yugoslavia and Rwanda, as well as for Sierra Leone, may also be mentioned.

Of course, we are not so naïve as not to see that this support to international justice is at least conditional. The hostility towards the International Criminal Court (ICC) clearly shows that, when prosecutions of nationals of the United States can be envisaged, the attitude of the US administration is totally different. Given the enormous power of military intervention of the United States outside its borders, the risk of prosecution for war crimes and (as soon as it is defined, in principle in 2009), for crimes against the peace, does exist. The reason why the United States rejects the ICC in such a way is the independence of the Prosecutor: he may already today (at least theoretically) initiate investigations against members of the US military force for acts committed e.g. in Afghanistan (which ratified the ICC Statute in 2003), and this is an unacceptable idea. This fear justifies a veritable guerrilla war against the ICC at the risk, if not of destroying it, of weakening for a long time an institution whose main objective, everyone has to be reminded, is to take care of situations of crimes against humanity or of genocide, be it in Darfur, in the Democratic Republic of Congo or in Uganda, or elsewhere. One may express the notion that due to United States' weakening of the Court and lowering of its capacity to prosecute these crimes, the civilian populations of these countries, or possibly others, can be put on the long list of collateral damages caused by the United States. Once this is said, is it really possible to go beyond the record of impunity of the powerful, so often observed? What are the tools at our disposal?

Obviously judicial activism is possible only when some judicial routes are available. This is often not the case for the United States (which has launched a campaign, with some success, to conclude tens of international agreements with other countries according to which these countries will not hand nationals of the United States over to the ICC). Nevertheless, some possibilities exist and deserve to be explored. The United States is, for instance, party to the International Covenant on Civil and Political Rights of 1966. This treaty applies in particular to occupied territories, as confirmed by the July 9, 2004 Advisory Opinion of the International Court of Justice on the consequences of the construction by Israel of a wall in the occupied Palestinian territory. It thus protects civilian populations against attacks on their right to life, to physical integrity... The problem is that the United States did not ratify the Optional Protocol to this treaty allowing private persons to bring a case before the United Nations Human Rights Committee (individual cases can indeed be brought before this Commttee, whose role is to control the way States apply their obligations with regard to the Covenant, but only if the State involved has ratified this additional protocol, as over 100 States did). However, and this is of interest for what will follow, the United States did accept the provision according to which a State party to the Covenant may initiate what is called an Interstate Complaint before the Commission of Human Rights. This mechanism has never been used so far (at least before that Commission—it has been used before the European Court of Human Rights, by Ireland against the United Kingdom, or by many States against Turkey). Nevertheless, it must in its conception allow a State, or a group of States—which need not be Cuba or Venezuela, but might be Sweden, Belgium, Switzerland, Norway, individually or collectively—to bring a complaint for non-respect of the provisions of this convention by another State party, the United States in the present case. This is a track that NGOs should explore, putting pressure on certain progressive governments so that a symbolically strong measure along these lines might be undertaken.

The United States is also a party to the 1984 United Nations Convention against Torture. However, in contrast to France or Switzerland, it did not authorize persons to bring a case before the Commission Against Torture of the United Nations. It at most accepted that a case might be brought before this Committee by another State, here too through the mechanism of Interstate Complaint.

What are the other authorities to which cases could be submitted, either against a person or against the United States as a State? There are not too many possibilities. A complaint has for example been lodged against the United States before the Inter-American Commission on Human Rights following their invasion of Grenada in 1983 and the bombardment of an asylum for mentally sick persons (the case was concluded to the satisfaction of plaintiffs). This is an interesting avenue to explore (there is also a process ongoing concerning the bombardment of an hospital in Fallujah, Iraq, by the US troops). On the other hand, after they were condemned by the International Court of Justice in the famous Nicaraguan case (June 27, 1986) for military and paramilitary activities against Nicaragua, the United States has withdrawn its acceptance of the jurisdiction of that Court.

As already mentioned, the United States not only refuses to ratify the Statute of the International Criminal Court, but has launched a campaign to weaken the Court, notably through agreements of immunity with tens of countries according to which their nationals will never be handed to the ICC.

The picture that results concerning international institutions is that of a quasi-total retreat, in some sense a desertion from the battlefield. It is not really possible today to prosecute the United States, or their nationals, before a regional or international authority for violations of international law, except possibly the Inter-American Commission on Human Rights.

What about internal procedures in the United States? To my knowledge, there have been only a few procedures for violations of international humanitarian law. Following the slaughter at My Lai in Vietnam, in which almost 500 civilians were executed by the Baker Task Force, Lieutenant William Calley was sentenced to hard labor for life (and was discharged after three and a half years). And Captain Ernest Medina, Calley's superior, was simply acquitted. In spite of several attempts, former Secretary of State Henry Kissinger was never brought before a judge in France or in the United Kingdom for his responsibility in the illegal and secret bombardments of Cambodia, or those of Vietnam, or for the authorization given for the invasion of Eastern Timor and the subsequent support to Suharto, for the coup by Pinochet in Chile, and many other cases. To my knowledge, no procedure has followed the invasions of Panama or Grenada in spite of the many civilian deaths.

Similarly, no serious investigation has been completed after the first Gulf War. There was also no prosecution for the bombardment of Serbia in 1999 and its many flaws. The Tribunal for ex-Yugoslavia was obliged to produce a report, which was very criticized, whose conclusions allowed the Prosecutor to get rid of this cumbersome problem. The report, which is not credible according to NGOs and a majority of the academic community, concluded there was no basis for prosecution against NATO forces, mainly US forces. There has been nothing about Guantanamo whereas Paul Wolfowitz, who benefited from immunity as president of the World Bank, or General Miller largely deserved to be put under investigation and probably judged for grave breaches of the Third Geneva Convention.

That leaves Iraq, Abu Ghraib and the proceedings against a few soldiers considered as having acted alone, such as Charles Graner or Lynndie England. A few investigations against some soldiers or lower level superiors may also be mentioned, following the many deaths of prisoners in Afghanistan or murders or rapes of civilians in Iraq, but all that remains very limited (according to Human Rights Watch, over 600 persons would be implicated in detainee abuse in Iraq, Afghanistan and Guantanamo). These investigations (and sometimes proceedings) have concerned only subordinates and never superiors at a higher level. So, what about people like Donald Rumsfeld, Alberto Gonzales, Tommy Franks? Of course, one should not be under any illusion that these loyal servants of the Empire would one day face an inquest at home.

This does not mean that nothing is possible. On the contrary, many NGOs battle in a very courageous way before tribunals for the application of international humanitarian law. One should, for instance, pay homage to the role of local NGOs such as the Center for Constitutional Rights in New York, not only for the defense of prisoners in Guantanamo, but also for a series of proceedings aiming at the disclosure of documents which compromise the Bush administration.

That said, it remains embarrassing to cite the instances in which NGOs could have initiated proceedings in the United States or before international institutions for war crimes committed by civilians or members of military forces, apart from the few cases cited above. This observation of impunity has led some NGOs, groups of victims, or isolated lawyers to submit cases to national tribunals having a priori no link with the crimes committed, on the basis of what is called universal jurisdiction. Arguing that justice would never be obtained in the United States itself, complaints have been lodged against Tommy Franks, George W. Bush, Colin Powell and others, for instance in Belgium, Canada and Switzerland. These proceedings unfortunately had harmful consequences, at least in Belgium. Under pressure from the United States, which threatened to remove NATO headquarters from Belgium, the Belgian authorities were obliged to empty a very progressive law of a large part of its substance, in order to avoid the repetition of such problems. In Switzerland, the Ministry of Public Affairs considered that George W. Bush had immunity against any proceedings as Head of State, something that any first year student in law knows very well. The same occurred in Canada.

The complaint lodged in Germany at the end of 2004 against Donald Rumsfeld and nine civilian or military officials, including General Ricardo Sanchez, George Tenet, former boss of the CIA, and simple soldiers, is more interesting. Proceedings were initiated by four Iraqis and the Center for Constitutional Rights on the basis of acts of torture committed in Abu Ghraib prison. To mention only Donald Rumsfeld, he was accused of having directly issued illegal orders relative to the methods of questioning that had led to war crimes against detainees or, as a hierarchical superior, of having tolerated such acts without punishing their authors. Arguing that German law allows the investigation of international crimes and the opening of proceedings even if the person suspected is not in Germany—which is true—the plaintiffs argued that Iraqi justice would never be active on such a case—which is also true—and that Germany therefore had to act. This action was also supported by the presence in Germany of two units which had been involved in Abu Ghraib. German justice unfortunately replied that nothing proved that proceedings would not be opened in the United States itself against the persons involved—which is obviously false, at least for the hierarchical superiors. The NGO transmitted new elements to the German justice and called its attention to the fact that, after its first decision, no action had been taken by the justice of the United States against the persons involved.*

All this may seem very frustrating, but is merely the consequence of the existing power relations at play. Authorities from countries which, according to their domestic legislation, might at least initiate investigations of United States officials, to say nothing of rendering judgments, in general have little motivation to intervene. The only case which went beyond the lodging of a complaint, the case of Tommy Franks in Belgium, gave rise to the pressures already mentioned.

What we can do therefore is sketch out some routes which NGOs might pursue in the future. We have already mentioned the possibility that one or several States might lodge a complaint against the United States before the United Nations Human Rights Committee, for instance in a case where some nationals of that or these States would have suffered violations of their human rights by US troops. This would be a first at the United Nations. It has never been done to date. But it would allow one of the main United Nations organs in matters of human rights to make a statement on the obligations of the United States in its military operations. Some associations might also mobilize their governments on concrete cases. It would also be useful for NGOs to get a better understanding of the way some obscure working groups of the United Nations function, such as that on arbitrary detention. Such working groups would certainly deserve to be activated e.g. on Guantanamo. Or it would also be useful to establish links with the Special

---

* *[Editor's Note]* As Philip Grant indicated above, Germany adopted universal jurisdiction in its 2002 Code, for crimes close to those defined in the Statute of the International Criminal Court. A first complaint was lodged in 2004 against Donald Rumsfeld, then US Secretary of Defense, and other US officials for crimes committed in Iraq. However, the complaint was rejected: the German judge considered that the US justice was taking care of these problems... A new complaint was then lodged at the end of 2006 by the CCR and the FIDH, after Donald Rumsfeld left the US government (and therefore arguments based on possible "diplomatic immunity" of persons during their official functions could no longer be used). A large number of organizations were associated with this new complaint. It has again been rejected. The central argument for dismissal was that the facts did not directly concern Germany: this is very surprising since Germany had specifically adopted universal jurisdiction in its 2002 Code and the judgment would amount to saying that this law cannot be applied... There has been an appeal.

A further complaint in France against Donald Rumsfeld in October 2007 has also been rejected: see details in the last part of Section 3 in the contribution by D. Iagolnitzer to this book.

Rapporteurs of the Council on Human Rights, such as the Rapporteur on Torture, who might intervene, though in general with limited means of action. The actions in relation to the Inter-American Commission on Human Rights should also be reinforced.

On the other hand, wild complaints against George Walker Bush are not only stupid as it relates to international law, in view of the immunity of a president in office from actions put before internal jurisdictions of other States, but they are also unfortunately counterproductive. One has to be more clever and have more modest objectives. And one should not forget that the threat of judicial procedures can nevertheless have some effect. The fear that criminal complaints in France or in the United Kingdom might yield embarrassing questioning have in the past led Henry Kissinger to quickly leave his hotel in Paris, or Israeli General Doron Almog to stay in his plane at Heathrow airport in London and to immediately return to his country for fear of being arrested.

In view of everything that we have said, it is difficult to conclude on an optimistic note or to propose concrete actions. But this should not prevent NGOs from trying to find imaginative ways to use the judicial means at our disposal in order to try to obtain some successes in the battle against impunity for international crimes. In fact, the law changes, as do mentalities. And what seemed impossible yesterday sometimes becomes possible tomorrow. Who could imagine that in 1998 two policemen would enter into the room of an old man in a London hospital to tell him: "General Pinochet, you are under arrest"?

The NGOs will not stop their work for law and justice. We have to imagine, to innovate, to struggle in order to modify power relations in the judicial field as well. This is the only way to ensure that sometime the Rumsfelds and the Kissingers will also have to account for their actions.

JEAN BRICMONT

RIGHT OF INTERVENTION OR INTERNATIONAL LAW

In the absence of a genuine international force, the only thing that could limit the impunity of powerful states is the action of their own citizens. However, this action is often inhibited by the dominant discourse that constantly calls on those states to intervene militarily in the internal affairs of other states. The goal here will be to discuss some of the most frequent arguments in favor of this "right to intervene".[1] I shall first defend the principles of international law, as it exists today, and then discuss the way that the events of the 1930s and '40s are used to legitimize "preventive wars".

1. The defense of international law

As is very well explained by the Canadian professor of international law, Michael Mandel, contemporary international law has as its aim, to cite the preamble of the United Nations Charter, to "preserve future generations from the scourge of war".[2] And to achieve that, the basic principle is that no country has the right to send its troops into another country without the consent of its government. The Nazis did so repeatedly, and the first crime for which they were condemned at Nuremberg was initiating a war of aggression, which, according to the 1945 Nuremberg Charter, "is the supreme international crime, differing only from other war crimes in that it contains within itself the accumulated evil of the whole."

The "government" whose consent is required does not need to be an "elected government" or one which "respects human rights", but simply whoever "effectively controls the armed forces", because that is the factor which determines whether crossing the border leads to war. It is easy to criticize this basic principle, and human rights defenders do not fail to do so. For one thing, it is often the case that the borders of states are arbitrary, having resulted from totally undemocratic processes which took place in the distant past, and that they are considered unsatisfactory by various ethnic minorities. Moreover, nothing ensures that governments are democratic or even minimally concerned with the welfare of their populations. But international law never claimed to solve all problems. Like practically all law, it seeks simply to be a lesser evil compared to no law at all. And those who criticize international law would do well to explain by which *principles* they want to have it replaced. Can Iran occupy neighboring Afghanistan? Can Brazil, which is at least as democratic as the United States, invade Iraq in order to install a democracy? Can Congo attack Rwanda in self-defense? Can Bangladesh intervene in the internal affairs of the United States in order to impose a reduction of greenhouse gases so as to "prevent" the devastation with which it is threatened by global warming? If the "preventive" American attack on Iraq was legitimate, why wasn't the Iraqi attack on Iran, or on Kuwait, also legitimate? Worse still, why wasn't the Japanese attack on Pearl Harbor a legitimate preventive attack?[3] When one asks such questions, it quickly becomes clear that the only realistic alternative to the existing law, other than widespread chaos, would be for the most powerful state in the world to intervene wherever it pleases, or else, in some cases, to authorize its allies to do so.

Now, all of liberal thinking since the seventeenth century is based on the idea that there are essentially three forms of life in society:

- the war of all against all,
- an absolute sovereign who imposes peace by force,
- and third, a legal, democratic order, as the lesser evil.

Dictatorial regimes, denounced by human rights defenders, have the advantages of the absolute sovereign: the ability to preserve order and avoid the war of all against all, which is illustrated today by the situation of so-called "failed states". But the drawbacks of such a sovereign are well known: he acts in accordance with his own interests, his authority is not accepted in the hearts and minds of his subjects, and this provokes an endless cycle of revolts and repression. This observation is the very foundation of the argumentation in favor of the third solution.

All that is considered banal when it is a matter of the internal order of democratic States. But now let us turn to the international order. The sovereign, should we abandon the existing principles of international law, would inevitably be the United States. The United States is a great power which obviously pursues its own interests. Let us note that the advocates of humanitarian intervention do not always deny that fact, but then they argue, by recourse to a very selective reading of history, that the rest of humanity gains more benefits than harm from that pursuit. I have already tried to explain why I do not share that conclusion, but however that may be, the backlash linked to the exercise of that absolute power is exactly what classic liberalism predicted.[4]

Examples are easy to find. Osama bin Laden is a product of the support provided to the Mujahiddin in Afghanistan during the Soviet period. By selling weapons to Iraq, the West inadvertently provided a precious aid to the present Iraqi resistance.

In 1954, the United States overthrew Arbenz in Guatemala. For Washington, it took little effort, and apparently involved little risk. However, the United States thereby also contributed to the political education of a young Argentine doctor who happened to be there and whose portrait today adorns millions of T-shirts throughout the world: Che Guevara.

After the First World War, a young Vietnamese came to the Versailles Conference to plead the cause of self-determination for his people to Robert Lansing, Secretary of State of the President who presented himself as the champion of self-determination, Woodrow Wilson. He was shown the door; after all, he was harmless.[5] He then left France for Moscow to complete his political education and became famous. His name was Ho Chi Minh.

Who knows what the hatred being produced today by the policies of the United States and Israel will give birth to, tomorrow?

In the international order, the third solution, the liberal solution, would mean more democracy at the world level through the United Nations. Bertrand Russell compared discussing who was responsible for the First World War to discussing who was responsible for a car accident in a country without traffic regulations. The mere awareness of the idea that international law should be respected and that it should be possible to control conflicts between states through an international entity in itself marks a major progress in human history, comparable to the abolition of the power of the monarchy and the aristocracy, the abolition of slavery, the development of freedom of expression, the recognition of trade unions and women's rights, or the concept of social security.

At present, it is obviously the United States, as well as those who support its actions in the name of human rights, which is opposed to strengthening that international order. And there is every reason to fear that the reforms of the United Nations currently under consideration will lead to a greater legitimization of unilateral actions. The problem with the idea of using human rights to undermine the international order is that, at every meeting of the non-aligned countries, and at every summit of Southern countries, which represent 70% of humanity, all forms of unilateral intervention, whether embargos, sanctions or wars, are condemned, and not only by "dictatorships".[6] The same thing occurs during votes in the UN General Assembly concerning the US embargo against Cuba, for example. The democracy argument—if what one means by that is taking into account world public opinion—weighs massively *against* the right of unilateral intervention. In the last analysis, the liberal imperialists, that is, most of the US Democrats and a large part of European social democrats and greens— who defend democracy on the domestic level but call for intervention, that is, the dictatorship of a sole country or small group of countries, on the international level—are perfectly incoherent.

Finally, when, as often happens, people complain of the United Nations' lack of effectiveness, it is necessary to recall all the treaties and all the agreements on disarmament or on prohibition of weapons of mass destruction, opposed primarily by the United States.[7] It is the great powers who are most hostile to the idea that their trump card—recourse to force— might encounter legal opposition. But just as, on the domestic level, nobody suggests that gangsters' hostility to the law is a good argument for abolishing it, the sabotage of the United Nations by the United States is not a valid argument for discrediting the world organization.[8]

But there is one more argument in favor of international law, perhaps even more important than the others: it is the paper shield that the Third World believed could protect it from the West at the time of decolonization. People who use human rights to undermine international law in the name of the "right to intervene" forget that, all through the colonial period, no border and no dictator was there to prevent the West from making human rights prevail in the countries it had subjected. If that was what had been the intention, the least one can say is that the colonialized peoples failed to notice. And here is probably one of the main reasons why the right to intervene is so strongly condemned by the countries of the South.

2. "Anti-fascist" fantasies.

Unfortunately, the problem is not only a matter of good and bad arguments, but also of non-arguments, that is, of frequently repeated ideas whose consequences are rarely made explicit, but which nevertheless produce a certain demobilizing effect within anti-war movements. A main source of such non-arguments is the history of the Second World War.

When Lebanon was invaded in 1982, an Israeli opposed to that war, Uri Avnery, wrote an open letter to Menachem Begin, entitled: "Mr Prime Minister, Hitler is dead."[9] Because Begin, of course, claimed to be attacking the "new Hitler", meaning Arafat, entrenched in Beirut. Ever since the Suez Canal crisis, when Nasser was "Hitler on the Nile", every adversary of the West—Saddam, Milosevic, the Islamists—is a "new Hitler", "green fascist", etc. One can observe that whenever the comparison is turned around (Bush or Sharon equals Hitler), clumsily in my opinion, it is met with accusations of trivializing Nazism. Of course, before there was Hitler, each new enemy—the Germans during the First World War, for example—were the new Huns, led by a new Attila. This type of rhetoric can simply be dismissed as low level war propaganda.

Nevertheless, beyond this rhetoric, there is a vision of the Second World War which plays a major role in legitimizing war. The general idea is that the West, by cowardice or indifference, waited too long to launch a preventive war against Hitler which would have saved the Jews. This argument is psychologically particularly effective, and particularly vicious, when it is used against people of the generation that grew up in the 1960s and felt that the crimes committed against the Jews had not been sufficiently recognized immediately after 1945.

New wars are repeatedly justified by analogy with that situation: we must save the Albano-Kosovars, the Kurds (in Iraq, but not in Turkey), Afghan women, etc. During the Kosovo war, I constantly ran up against that argument—but shouldn't we have declared war on Hitler in 1936?—even from political militants whose supposedly "Marxist" background should have led one to expect more lucidity. The Kosovo example is an illustration of how the use of analogy often enables people to dispense with informing themselves seriously about the realities of a given situation.

We may observe in passing that in the view of classic political liberalism, war strengthens the powers of the state and should be avoided except in cases of extreme necessity. Trade, negotiations and cultural exchanges are far preferable to war or to embargos. The whole ideology of the "new Hitlers" goes against these liberal ideas, and thus is more often adopted by ex-revolutionaries who have renounced their past, retaining only a certain anti-liberal sympathy for violent change. This ideology gives intellectuals a role to play, mobilizing public opinion "before it's too late".

There are two answers to this argument, one conceptual, the other historic. The conceptual aspect, that is, the defense of international law in the face of legitimization of preventive war, which constitutes the principal aspect of the response, has already been mentioned. The historic aspect has to do with what really happened before and during the Second World War. It deserves to be recalled, inasmuch as the reference to those events to justify military intervention is symptomatic of a widespread ignorance, or of a radical revision, of history. Here we shall be brief, since a treatise on history is beyond the scope of this article.

"Better Hitler than the popular front" was a slogan that expressed the attitude not only of the defeatist segment of the French bourgeoisie, frightened by the success of the left in the mid-1930s, but also, each in its own way, of a good part of the British aristocracy, of the American capitalist class, and of the dominant social classes throughout Europe. If there was no war against Hitler, it was, among other reasons, because the "social achievements" of fascism—eliminating left-wing parties and disciplining the workers thanks to corporatism and nationalism—won the admiration of the dominant social classes everywhere, the very counterparts of those who today call for preventive wars against new Hitlers. This being the case, a defensive alliance against Hitler—such as the one that fought in 1914-1918, but with the Soviet Union replacing Tsarist Russia—capable of preventing World War II altogether by dissuading aggression, was out of the question precisely because of the anti-communism of the ruling circles in the West. Moreover, avoiding war is what would have made it possible to save most of the Jews, since it was only after the war was well underway that they were massively killed. Western government aid to the Spanish Republic, whose victory, had it taken place, might well have served to dampen the ambitions of fascism, was impossible for the same reasons. It should be emphasized that neither a defensive alliance nor aid to a legal government violates international law, in contrast to a preventive attack. Moreover, the Munich agreement that allowed Hitler to seize the Sudetenland was not merely a matter of cowardice, but was also due in part to hostility toward Czechoslovakia, the European country most favorable to an alliance with the Soviet Union.

The discourse on the "new Hitlers" is inevitably accompanied by the more or less explicit identification of today's pacifists with Daladier and Chamberlain. But apart from misrepresentation of the motivations of the "appeasers", the logical lesson from Munich is not that we should plunge madly into war on all sides to defend minorities, which was precisely what Hitler claimed he was doing. For in fact, Hitler legitimized his wars as the necessary way to protect minorities, first the Sudeten Germans in Czechoslovakia and then the Germans in Danzig. Note also that at the end of the Second World War, the United Nations was set up precisely to ban "preventive war", a notion which Eisenhower, for example, viewed as essentially Nazi.

The logical lesson of Munich is that the great power gambit of using the discontents of minorities to destabilize weaker countries is extremely dangerous, at least for world peace, even when the minorities in question welcome such great power intervention, as the Sudeten Germans welcomed Nazi Germany in 1938 and the Kosovo Albanians welcomed NATO in 1999. The fact is that "liberating" the Sudeten Germans encouraged Hitler just as "saving" Kosovo gave American imperialism a huge bonus in legitimacy.

The catastrophe of Hitler's victory over France in 1940 finally led part of Europe's ruling circles to fall back on an alliance with the Soviet Union, but too late to avoid the war, too late to avoid the suffering it inflicted on the victims of aggression, and too late to avoid paying the political price that inevitably resulted from the fact that the victory over fascism was primarily due to the Red Army and the sacrifices of the Soviet people. The visionaries who attack "pacifists" by harping on the 1930s would do well to study those years a bit more thoroughly.

Defenders of humanitarian war in Iraq stress the inconsistency of those who oppose such a war in Iraq when they agreed to it in Yugoslavia.[10] They are obviously right on this point, and therefore one of the main reasons to oppose the 1999 war was precisely that, by agreeing to it, one was *de facto* legitimizing an indefinite number of other wars. The endless war in which we are involved today is in part the consequence of the euphoria brought about by the easy victory over Yugoslavia in 1999.

Finally, if one wants to play the little game which consists in saying, once one knows how history turned out, "ah, if only at such and such a time one had done this or that" (for instance, launch a war against Hitler in 1936), one might as well ask whether it wouldn't have been a good idea to avoid the *First* World War. In those days, there was neither Hitler, nor Stalin, nor Milosevic, nor Saddam Hussein. The world was dominated, as it still is today, by governments which are imperialist in their foreign policy but relatively liberal in domestic policy. Nevertheless, this liberalism in no way prevented an accumulation of weaponry on all sides, secret treaties, colonial wars. A spark in Sarajevo, and Europe was plunged into a war that dragged the world after it, whose unexpected results included the emergence of both Bolshevism and fascism. Those who ceaselessly decry the "tragedies of the twentieth century" would do well to reflect on their origins and on the similarity between the interventionist policies and the search for hegemony that they advocate today and the policies that led to the catastrophe of the summer of 1914.

It can be suggested that if World War I is largely forgotten, this is not only because it took place farther back in time than World War II. Indeed, the more time passes, the more the Second World War seems to gain importance—in any case, as presented through the dominant interpretation discussed above (sixty years after the end of the First World War, we were in...1978. Who in 1978 was still thinking about the First World War?) The fundamental reason is no doubt that the First World War was the very epitome of a totally absurd war. There was no valid reason to wage it in the first place, and the "victory" only gave birth to new problems. The Versailles Treaty, mainly sought by French leaders to protect France by crushing Germany once and for all, is a perfect example of human passions producing the opposite result of the one intended: Germany relentlessly took its revenge, which led to France's defeat in 1940 and the beginning of the end of its role as a great power. In contrast, thanks to Hitler's unilateral aggression, the Second World War was the most justifiable of all wars, at least for the countries he attacked. As a result, constant reference to the Second World War is used to strengthen the case for war, whereas lucid reflection on the First would rather be an incitement to pacifism. This partly explains the difference between the way the two are treated.

3. Conclusion

The Western movements and individuals who claim to be progressive should first of all ask themselves if their view of the world is not too *Western*. Instead of jumping on the bandwagon about alleged fascism in the Third World or in movements like Hamas, they should try to help Westerners understand the way the rest of the world sees us and oppose everything that strengthens our feeling of superiority and of moral purity.

What the world needs today, alongside the human rights organizations, would be an observatory to report on imperialism, a sort of "Imperialism Watch", whose job would be to denounce not only wars and war propaganda, but all the economic pressures and various other maneuvers, thanks to which injustice prospers and endures. Such an observatory could also try to counter the mass of disinformation and rewriting of history which characterize Western perceptions of the relations between ourselves and the rest of the world.

Following their victory in the Cold War, the United States and the ruling classes that it supports became dizzy with success: their reign, covered with the rhetoric of democracy and free markets, was extending to infinity. But this may be a misunderstanding of the direction of history. Let us look at it in the long term. At the beginning of the twentieth century, all of Africa and part of Asia were in the hands of European powers. The Russian, Chinese and Ottoman Empires were helpless in the face of Western interventions. Latin America was more tightly controlled than today. Of course, not everything has changed, but with the exception of Palestine, colonialism has at least been relegated to the ashcan of history, at the cost of millions of lives. This end of colonialism no doubt constitutes humanity's greatest social progress of the 20th century. Those who want to revive the colonial system in Iraq, even with what Lord Curzon described, in the days of the British-controlled monarchy, as an "Arab façade", are dreaming.[11] The 21st century will be that of the struggle against neo-colonialism, just as the 20th was the century of struggle against colonialism.

ENDNOTES

[1]   For more details on these questions, see Jean Bricmont, *Humanitarian Imperialism*, Monthly Review Press, New York, 2007.

[2]   Michael Mandel, *How America Gets Away With Murder*, Pluto Press, London, 2004.

[3]   In 1940, the year before Pearl Harbor, U.S. Air Force General Chenneault recommended using flying fortresses "to burn out the industrial heart of the Empire" by dropping incendiary bombs "on the teeming bamboo ant heaps" of Japan, a proposal that "simply delighted" Roosevelt. Saddam Hussein never expressed such warlike intentions against the United States. See Michael Sherry, *The Rise of American Airpower*, Yale University Press, New Haven, 1987, Chapter 4, and Noam Chomsky, "The Manipulation of Fear", *Tehelka*, July 16, 2005, available on: http://www.chomsky.info/articles/20050716.htm.]

[4]   See Chalmers Johnson, *Blowback: The Costs and Consequences of American Empire*, Metropolitan Books, New York, 2000, for a warning, before September 11, from someone who had worked as a CIA consultant, as to the risks to the United States itself of its empire.

[5]   *The Washington Post*, September 14, 1969, p. A25, cited by William Blum, *Killing Hope*.

[6]   For example, consider the following statement, made on the eve of the US invasion of Iraq: "The Heads of State or Government reaffirmed the Movement's

commitment to enhance international co-operation to resolve international problems of a humanitarian character in full compliance with the Charter of the United Nations, and, in this regard, they reiterated the rejection by the Non-Aligned Movement of the so-called "right" of humanitarian intervention, which has no basis either in the Charter of the United Nations or in international law." Final document of the Thirteenth Conference of Heads of State and of Governments of the Movement of Non-aligned Countries, Kuala Lumpur, February 24-25, 2003, Article 354. (Available on http://www.bernama.com/events/newnam2003/indexspeech.shtml?declare).

[7] See William Blum, *Rogue State*, for numerous examples. See also Stephen Zunes *Tinderbox: U.S. Foreign Policy and the Roots of Terrorism*, Common Courage Press, Monroe, (Maine) 2002, for an account of how José Bustani, who directed the Organization for prohibition of chemical weapons, was fired under United States influence the moment he wanted to have both American and Iraqi sites inspected, which might have had the disadvantage of allowing a peaceful resolution of the conflict.

[8] "The Bush administration has withdrawn from the Kyoto Protocol, opposed the International Plan for Cleaner Energy, withdrawn from the International Conference on Racism, refused to join 123 nations pledged to ban the use and production of anti-personnel bombs and mines, opposed the UN Agreement to Curb the International Flow of Illicit Small Arms, refused to accept the 1972 Biological and Toxin Weapons Convention, refused to join the International Court of Justice, withdrawn from the 1972 Antiballistic Missiles Treaty, rejected the Comprehensive [Nuclear] Test Ban Treaty, among other matters. It is developing more refined nuclear weapons for more practical use, is pursuing space-based weapons stations, and has announced a right to engage in preventive war at its own discretion." Edward S. Herman, "Michael Ignatieff's Pseudo-Hegelian Apologetics for Imperialism", *Z Magazine,* October 2005. See also Richard Du Boff, "Mirror Mirror on the Wall, Who's the Biggest Rogue of All?" for a more complete and detailed list of the treaties and accords rejected by the United States. Available on http://www.zmag.org/content/ForeignPolicy/boffroguebig.cfm.

[9] See Robert Fisk, "The Wartime Deceptions: Saddam is Hitler and It's Not About Oil", *The Independent*, January 27, 2003.

[10] See for example, Thomas Cushman (ed), *A Matter of Principle: Humanitarian Arguments for War in Iraq*, University of California Press, Berkeley, 2005.

[11] "[We need] an Arab facade ruled and administered under British guidance and controlled by a native Mohammedan and, as far as possible, by an Arab staff.... There should be no actual incorporation of the conquered territory in the dominions of the conqueror, but the absorption may be veiled by such constitutional fictions as a protectorate, a sphere of influence, a buffer state and so on." Memorandum of Lord Curzon, "German and Turkish Territories Captured in the War", December 12, 1917, CAB 24/4. Cited by William Stivers, *Supremacy and oil : Iraq, Turkey, and the Anglo-American world order, 1918-1930*, Cornell University Press, Ithaca, 1982.

PEDRO A. GARCIA-BILBAO

THE RIGHT TO INTERFERE IN A CONTEXT OF IMPERIAL IMPUNITY

Law is the attempt to subject the reality of human conflict to a certain degree of control in order to bring solutions in the least traumatic way possible; but human conflicts go beyond the boundaries of law, and more is required to fully comprehend them. In order to apprehend the social reality where our lives are played out, it becomes necessary to combine different social science disciplines which, let us not forget, rely on each other.

Some years ago now, Raymond Aron, in studying Max Weber's contributions to the study on social reality, brilliantly explained that knowledge is vital for action, and that knowledge of society requires a profound comprehension of the human activity dynamic, its internal future and the factors which explain it. To be able to act on the problems of our time, it is not enough to draw up a deed of the facts before a notary. It is not enough to describe them, or to reconstruct them in their time sequence. This is necessary, but not enough. We must also ensure that these facts bring an internal, profound comprehension of the processes. In order to seek solutions, we must first understand the dynamic which explains the appearance of problems.

It is essential that we know and have fair responses to false questions. We must ask the right questions after having analyzed reality. This is the first step to be able to move forward. We live in a time where economic and political pressure groups finance tailor-made studies, and where much of what we propose as objective knowledge is in fact only pure ideology. We must preserve professional independence and judgment as far as possible, and defend public spaces in the academic field. Unlike the think tanks of the United States and their subsidiaries spread over the world, we, ourselves, are disposed to submit our analyses and conclusions to the appraisal of academics.

This is a necessary task. We dream that even the title of our Paris Conference—International Justice and Impunity: The Case Against the United States—might already be causing changes in opinions. There is no shortage of people who state that the United States of America is not committing crimes against international law, but the simple reality is that it is in the process of going even further than this phase. In recent years, significant political figures in the American administration have publicly stated that their country will act on the international scene in defense of its supposed interests, irrespective of what the international institutions and international law dictate. Should the two coincide, they will respect the rules. However, if they do not, they defend the argument for action even if this means violating the rules established by the international community. We are witnessing an enormously serious qualitative leap in view of the fact that crimes have always been committed, but today they are openly justified and legitimized, or disguised by appealing to the state of need which arose after September 11. Since then, that power publicly states that international law has ceased to count in its present form, that international obligations are only valuable if they serve its own interests, and then acts in full impunity… in such a case we are just a step away from barbarity.

In fact, in these first years of the 21st century, we are observing a painful reality. The development of international law relating to humanitarian rights, conventions on war and violence, and attempts to make conflicts less inhumane, is being subjected to harsh attacks on several sides. The fact that crimes which are classified as serious under international law are being committed is cause for concern; but repeated impunity is even worse. We live in a time where brute force has become the main source of legitimization, where we face a claim to impose the rights of the strongest, and where barbarity is disguised with words like democracy, freedom and human rights.

In order to defend democracy, we are creating special laws and powers immune to all external control; to defend freedom, we are restricting individuals' rights and denying collective rights; to defend human rights, we are legalizing, or we are claiming to legalize, torture… It is true that this is not the case everywhere, that all countries are not witnessing such a degradation of freedoms in the same way, but this said, it is no less true that a large part of the world's countries are living under regimes where freedoms have never known better times. In the European Union, perhaps because of our own past experience of war, our societies are rejecting any political move which legitimizes violence and reinforces power over freedoms. Europeans know that wars are lethal and that suffering spares no one. European society fiercely rejects war and force as political tools, and our governments must take this factor into consideration. However, while this is the situation in continental Europe, unfortunately we cannot say the same about the Anglo-Saxon world, where the particularities of the political system and the very different collective memory of the war phenomenon allows fractions which are currently in power to establish a practice and objectives where the resort to violence has almost been a constant in recent years.

How have we been able to arrive at such a situation, in which a state claims its so-called right to attack and destroy another state as a preventative measure, and moreover where it has been done with impunity?

At this moment in time, more so than in the past, it is already clear to everyone that decay can spill over to the heart even in an international system, and that this can no longer be hidden or disguised. We know the dangers faced in the past, including those which were borne out of internal contradictions, but what do we perceive of the new dangers we face today?

It is continually repeated to us that the main threat to freedoms and our western lifestyle come from international terrorism. I am not saying that international terrorism is not a real threat to life and security for all, whoever is behind this "international terrorism". Such a claim would be false; the deaths in New York, Madrid and London testify to this. But when, using the excuse of the fight against international terrorism, we limit the American firefighter's right to trade union activity—allow me to use this as an example—and we threaten the activists of the United States peace movement, this shows that some things, many things, are not right. Without doubt, freedom and democracy are in danger; however, the main threats do not come from outside the system, but rather from its very heart. International terrorism which has been developed, encouraged and protected by states which were well established to fight the soviets and the progressive forces in Afghanistan, is only one threat more, when there is no excuse for other kinds of crimes. What a terrible realization for the victims of international terrorism—that the weapons which caused so much pain and misfortune were supplied not long before by the governments of their own countries! Need we remind ourselves here, today, who the director of the CIA was at the time when fundamentalist terrorism was protected and sheltered by those who call themselves the "champions of the free world"?

I am going to try to be a little more direct: we have to analyze, expose, and debate specific cases where the protagonist is a specific state, the United States of America. And the reason for this is obvious: it is the state which most repeatedly, and during the longest period of time, has acted both against and outside of the attempts of the international community to subject conflicts between states to the rule of law, in the clearly established goal of avoiding war and protecting rights and human dignity.

The sad history of the 20th century, with its terrible world wars, made international law and the international institutions necessary in order to avoid the sourge of modern war between states. It is therefore surprising that there are countries which voluntarily and consciously place themselves outside of the obligations conceived to defend the values that these same states use in their speeches to defend their constitution and their foundational tradition itself. Unfortunately, this is not just speculation: it is a true reality. It is true that this contradiction is not restricted exclusively to any one country, ideology, or religion: humans have also killed each other in the name of nearly everything that is good (the homeland, the common good, freedom, Christianity, socialism) and everything that is terrible (ethnic cleansing, devastation, fascism).

Of this terrible history of the 20th century, one conviction, perhaps predominantly, has remained: war is the supreme evil and must be avoided; the supreme crime against humanity is a war of aggression. All constructions from the international community, law, and institutions must set their sights on the supreme goal: to end the global reality of war. It is this conviction which I would like to address, saying that Europeans, as a majority, reject war and treasure hope in the law and the international institutions.

However, there are many who say that the international community, drawn up in the heart of the United Nations, as well as all constructions of international law, have failed, since they have not avoided conflicts and have not succeeded in preventing wars. But those who say this are forgetting that the United Nations and its internal power structure emerged, among other reasons, to prevent, or at least render more difficult, a war between the Superpowers, by offering new and different means of resolving conflicts—an objective which, quite obviously, has been achieved.

The balance of nuclear threat, deterrence, is one factor which prevented war between the powers. The other has been the existence of international institutions which have helped end conflicts. Today, the so-called balance between the powers has been shattered, and only one superpower is visible in the international order. Some call it the "hegemon" and here see a phenomenon which has resulted for the first time in history. The disappearance of the Soviet Union meant a loss in balance between the Powers and, just as gas fills an entire space by expanding, the surviving superpower, the United States, has done the same. Some of its university students and intellectuals serving power groups openly develop the theory according to which all international policy is the subject of internal interest for their state. International policy no longer figures on the agenda of the superpower: everything is now brought back to the realm of interior policy. The only external mechanism to slow the expansion of its power designs (to employ the imperial "design" concept created by Washington during the Cold War to characterize the soviets) is the current existence of international law.

That is to say that the written law is a way of subjecting power and human relationships to a certain objective, external control, for a power which wishes to exercise power without restraint will not accept arbitration and will not submit to it if it is possible to avoid it. We are facing a clear conflict. As you are aware, the subjects of the international community are States, and

States have their own characteristics which distance them from individuals, as they are subjected as citizens or subjects.

International law demands respect for the rules, but those who hold power seek to avoid any form of control. In the United States, the association of economic and political power is severely distorting the democratic order. If, at the internal level, the controls are dying and are subjected to what we have called "designs" of power, the international institutions and international law are, in some extreme cases, an external source of control and limits which the emerging imperial power is rejecting and fighting against.

The problem is extremely complex because this power which seeks to escape all control is not exclusively State power, because this State is, first and foremost, a tool in the hands of the social class which holds the economic power. If the individuals who form part of the economic elites can determinedly condition political State action, even in a "democratic" society, the emergence of these new public subjects, the large companies and megacorporations, means that the weight on the state is greater every day. "Leviathan" is not a danger to itself in a society which really exists at the moment; "Leviathan" is becoming increasingly dangerous because every day it is more clearly serving private interests, not just people constituting an identifiable social class by different criteria which we could list, but also megacorporations and large companies, which could condition the entire representative political order and direct the specific policies of the people who govern.

As citizens, not necessarily part of the university community, but simply as informed citizens, we have been witnesses to military attacks in recent years, with an indiscriminate use of force against countries which were far from representing a real threat to world peace. We have seen how these countries were, and still are, subject to the ravaging of military occupation forces, without any excuse and beyond any form of legality.

The example of Iraq is paradigmatic. Setting to one side the nature of the regime prior to the occupation, action against this state brought war, immense destruction, and the loss of hundreds of thousands of lives of completely innocent women, elderly people and children. This action was taken outside of the international legal system created to prevent war and avoid major evils. This war still continues today, atrocious crimes are continually committed against the civilian population, and also against those who fight the occupation. Iraq today is a country which has been destroyed, where the entire population is suffering at an even greater level than it had to bear in any previous situation: the degree of destruction in the country, the intensity of violence and its consequences on the people´s lifestyle confirm this statement.

How have we come to the stage that wars of aggression can be engaged in with the declared purpose of plundering a nation, without anyone being able to prevent it? How is it possible that lies and manipulation can be used as evidence and that nothing happens, that the events and drama which they represent simply follow their course and that the crimes against humanity continue to take place with complete impunity?

During the years that we called the Cold War, those years of so-called imbalance, crimes against humanity were also committed, but at least we disguised them externally. Now we justify them, similarly using lies and deception, but when some of these lies are seen for what they are, as manipulation, quite simply ... nothing happens!! One of the distinctive traits of fascism was that it did not hide its crimes, because they were considered justified and legitimate. Nowadays, when we blitz and kill the civilian population in some countries subjected to an illegal military occupation or to wars of aggression, when we justify and defend the need for torture, when we legalize mercenaries, we are beginning to do it openly. We still use ideas which legitimize, we preserve the big words (justice, freedom), but we use them in conjunction with ancient horrors such as torture and deportation. The two extremes are polluted.

Aggression towards Iraq, for example, was neither justified nor supported by any decision on behalf of the United Nations. This is how the United Nations institutional spokespeople, prestigious personalities from the legal and university world, and of course, almost all associations of professionals from international law, express themselves. On the alleged reasons for the conflict, the infamous Weapons of Mass Destruction, it was soon proved that they were simply an excuse. And in the end, this truth was openly recognized by the President of the United States. In effect, there were no such arms, "but there could have been", and this justified the intervention, according to his own view of reality. Therefore, where have law or collective morality gone?

All this leads us to the concept of the right to interfere. In a context where international relations were governed by a group of shared values, such as the rejection of war and respect for human rights, values expressed specifically by a series of legal tools—those to which states would voluntarily submit—and institutions for international collaboration, the Right to Interfere would have a completely different meaning than in a situation where international law is questioned and where the law of the stronger dominates.

We began to talk about the right to interfere, in the contemporary sense of the expression, towards the middle of the '90s, after important crises—famines and ethnic massacres—from Somalia to Rwanda to Burundi. The general public is once again being assaulted by terrible images of hunger and desolation, and we are beginning to talk seriously about the need to "do something" even at the risk of compromising the principle of state sovereignty. In certain media we were told that we perhaps needed to review the principle of non-interference in state sovereignty in order to be able to put an end to catastrophic situations, of human suffering as a result of wars and famines.

But, we ask ourselves… has this principle of non-nterference really been respected over history?

The contemporary form of State prerogatives concerning independence from external powers comes, as we know, from the model resulting from the Peace of Westphalia. There we put an end to the period of great wars in Europe on the basis of the principle that no state could interfere in another, nor in its internal dynamics, the state being sovereign over its interior and other states having no right to interfere. Any threat towards other states was henceforth considered a crime, and interference in another state without its consent was not only disapproved, but fought. States had territories which were under their influence, as well as market systems in the international order, but in which the interference of one state in another became something which was expressly prohibited.

Curiously, it was these same states which, having dictated the conditions of Westphalia, years later, after the Napoleonic crisis, at the Congress of Vienna, agreed on the right to interfere in other states to defend the power imbalance. Vienna was the symbol of conservative reaction to the changes spread by the laws of the French Revolution. That is to say: no interference if it would mean tampering with the sovereignty of a state based on the Ancien Régime, but if a state, employing its sovereignty, threatens the balance of world power by proclaiming an end to the Ancien Régime, then interference was approved. The Place du Trocadéro in Paris is a painful reminder of what I am saying, because the name of this place refers to a battle in Spain between the constitutional and liberal Spanish forces and the French troops serving absolutism, who were sent to Spain by the Congress of Vienna in 1823.

The answer is obvious: the principle of sovereignty was respected if the interests of the Superpowers accepted it. International law did not exist; there were agreements between Powers, treaties and alliances. We sought peace or war through alliances. All parties believed war to be a political tool. By the beginning of the 20th century, we knew the outcome of all this.

At the moment—I know I should say "not yet"—a "right to interfere" in the affairs of other states does not exist; relations between states are regulated by the principle of sovereignty and the respect for it. Since the creation of the United Nations after 1945 there have been some reservations about the principle of sovereignty, and the limit is war: no state has the right to declare war, or initiate a war outside of the international order which was organized to ensure peace. No state, having accepted the United Nations Charter, has the right to violate it, and all are bound to respect the obligations imposed by the International Treaties they have signed.

With regard to the United States, we could mention several cases where the principles of the Charter were clearly violated, and observe that we risk legitimizing, counter to all legislation, a so-called right to interfere, even on a military basis, in other countries if one's own security is threatened or if we suppose that it could be. In other words, according to the practice of the United States, the only thing which can guarantee that a country does not become the object of an aggression is a unilateral decision from the American government itself. The concept of "preventive war" represents the end of the international order based on maintaining peace as the supreme good, the end, too, of a conception of the international community as an order articulated on the basis of law. The United States promotes the notion that the change in the international situation after the disappearance of the Soviet Union demands a change in the international relations model; based on one fact, its military power, and on one ideological consideration, its so-called "exceptional" character, it is claiming to reconstruct the international community in step with its national interests.

The issue of the right to interfere therefore does not carry only the possibility of humanitarian intervention. It is not only about law for states or for the international community facing a serious crisis to step outside of national sovereignty to stop a catastrophe or a flagrant violation of human rights. Without doubt, this is a relevant discussion. It is currently being debated at the heart of organizations as important as the International Committee of the Red Cross, among others, as well as in the university fields. But reality goes far beyond the issue of knowing if the right to humanitarian intervention is desirable: the right-to-interfere hypothesis is currently being used to disguise aggressions. Using the excuse of national security and the fight against terrorism, aggressions have taken place; crimes have been committed, which have brought war and devastation.

We need to combine different facts in one analysis. We cannot speak about international relations and security in the world today without evaluating certain facts. We are well aware that it is not "politically correct" to name certain things, and to mention them publicly; however, some questions must be asked out of moral obligation.

I will pose these questions:

How can the existence of the Project for the New American Century affect national defense? How can the existence of this Project affect the collective security of the international community?

Not long before the fraudulent presidential elections which gave power to George W. Bush, a neo-conservative research center, consisting of people linked to the previous Reagan and Bush administrations, and to the military-industrial pressure groups, produced a series of documents claiming to show the need for the United States to follow an imperial course. Resort to the army and technological superiority, together with economic and cultural penetration, were to be implemented in order to ensure that the 21st century would be "the new American century". The United States was to follow the clear destiny which made this nation a state elected by God. The shining city on a hill found itself legitimized to impose its view on the entire world. This could just have been a fantasy of the extreme right, an impossible plan developed by a group of rich people with time to waste and reviving the nostalgia of their years in the government during the Cold War—but this is not the case.

The project for a new American century is underway. The members of this pressure group (one more in the galaxy of the American extreme right linked to the industrial-military lobby) are now in the government and are imposing their program step by step to the shock of the rest of the world. Their objectives involve a full revision of the old alliances and a restructuring of international relations on a new basis.

Such is the context in which the most recent attacks against international law are in the process of being produced, a context where the genocidal occupation of Iraq is following its course. Crimes are not isolated facts; they are the necessary consequence of an aggressive exterior policy course, marked by a new strain of imperial policy which has broken all the former balances.

We can easily understand that impunity stimulates a particular effect in a criminal. Crime debases, repeated impunity reinforces the crime, it leads the criminal to believe in his individual right, it can make him think that the morality and ethics which rule human relationships are made for others, not for him. Repeated impunity leads the criminal to believe himself to be an "exceptional" person, someone for whom the rules which were created for everyone do not apply. In the case of crimes against international law, impunity has similar effects.

In the context of implementing the "New American Century", the danger is not that the unpunished crimes against international law continue. The danger is that we are claiming to re-write international law, and that what is a crime today will become law tomorrow.

VINCENT RIVASSEAU

TOWARDS AN INTERNATIONAL AGENCY FOR THE EVALUATION OF SUFFERINGS DUE TO ARMED CONFLICTS

In every sufficiently developed civilian society, justice tries to establish the facts with precision. To achieve this aim, judges or police officers who are in charge of criminal investigations can rely on the help of highly specialized services, those of forensic medicine and related experts. These experts use the most advanced scientific tools (autopsy, ballistic studies, DNA analysis...) to establish the exact nature of the crime and identify its authors.

But nothing of this kind exists to date at the international level for humanity's worst crimes, namely war crimes and crimes against humanity. There is no specialized body of experts in charge of the precise, systematic, and scientific study of sufferings due to armed conflicts, in order to establish causes and responsibilities. It is true that many non-governmental organizations perform part of this work. They do inform and alert world opinion, but objective evaluation of sufferings is not among their primary missions. The United Nations does publish some estimates in this domain. The International Committee of the Red Cross or ICRC does observe all conflicts, in particular the treatment of prisoners, but it has to keep a low diplomatic profile in order to remain in contact with all parties. Some pioneers, such as Les Roberts and his team for the Iraq war, do investigate the situation on the ground, but without any official mandate, and with inadequate means. All these efforts are very useful, sometimes worthy of our admiration, but they are far from sufficient. Note that well-organized armies, such as those of the United States, document with great precision each of their casualties, dead or wounded. This is *a priori* a good thing. However one cannot rely on them for an unbiased objective evaluation of the sufferings caused by the wars in which they take part.

In 2005, these questions and the action of Les Roberts were among the topics discussed at the Paris International Conference on International Humanitarian Law and the Impunity of Powerful States: The Case of the United States. Motivated at least in part by this event, I would like to propose here the creation of an independent international Agency with an adequate budget and the most advanced means of investigation. This Agency would have as its sole mission the systematic evaluation of all the sufferings which are the consequence of any armed conflict. Since I am not an expert in international law and institutions, I shall limit myself in this contribution to briefly sketch the motivations for the creation of such an Agency, together with some necessary conditions and some possible difficulties along the way. I hope that this idea will be endorsed, developed, and ultimately carried out by many other people.

I would like to start by observing that in the absence of unbiased serious data, various very different figures circulate about the casualties due to armed conflicts, even the most recent. These figures are then exploited politically in various dishonest ways. Moreover, it seems to me that establishing the facts seriously and scientifically is a very difficult task, with potentially momentous political consequences. Therefore one cannot simply put individuals or even nongovernmental organizations, no matter how excellent, in charge of such a delicate, complex, and sensitive mission. Only the United Nations and the International Committee of the Red Cross seem invested with a sufficiently universal authority to become the godfathers of such an undertaking, and ensure its credibility and ultimate success. Do they then have to assume this task directly by creating a new internal department charged with this task? I am not sure this would be the optimal road to follow. First, the United Nations or the ICRC could be criticized for diverting some part of their energy from their main mission, which is much wider. Let's recall that this primary mission is nothing less than for the United Nations to maintain peace, and for the ICRC to enforce the Geneva Conventions. The question of evaluating sufferings is narrower and more specialized. And again, this evaluation mission involves very particular technical aspects. For both reasons, it would be preferable to give this mission to a specific international Agency. It seems to me that this Agency should work under the aegis of the United Nations, with upstream links to the ICRC and downstream links in particular to the International Criminal Court.

This *International Agency for Evaluation of Sufferings due to Armed Conflicts* would be in charge not only of "counting bodies" of military and civilians killed by the armed forces, but also of measuring precisely any of the related sufferings. It would use all current modern scientific means of investigation, joining together in a comprehensive way various types of demographic, health and environmental studies together with significant research on the ground. It would in this way try also to identify the causes of each type of sufferings in the best possible way. It would be requested to provide reliable and accurate estimates of the number of dead and wounded people in each conflict for at least four categories of victims, namely: the soldiers or members of the armed forces on each side, the civilians directly killed or wounded by these forces, the civilians killed or maimed in other violent actions related to the war (for instance, those due to the increase in criminality), and finally the middle and long-term victims due to hunger, epidemics, and environmental destruction in direct relation to the conflict. Of course this last category of victims requires some patient long-term studies for a complete picture to emerge. This picture finally emerged only after several decades in the case of the victims of the Hiroshima and Nagasaki atomic bombs. The questions of material destruction and economic damage, which require a different kind of expertise, could be entrusted to an auxiliary institution.

Two main positive consequences of the creation of such an Agency may be expected. First, world opinion would be correctly informed as to the true human costs of armed conflicts. Political manipulations of any kind in this domain would become more difficult. Secondly, essential elements would be gathered which would help considerably in investigating responsibilities and adequately prosecuting the authors of war crimes or crimes against humanity. Bear in mind that trials of such criminals should not be held mainly as a retaliation but also, and above all, in a pedagogical way. Their main goal should be to prevent the repetition of such crimes.

Let us now develop each one of these topics

1. Better Information to Prevent Manipulation

By using precise and standardized methods, the Agency proposed here should permit the swift clarification of the current cacophony characterized by the inaccurate figures that everybody throws out at political opponents about Iraq, Afghanistan, Darfur, Chechnya and so on. Estimates of casualties often vary by a multiple of ten or even one hundred. It is clear that double standards are the rule rather than the exception. Let us pause briefly here for a few typical examples voluntarily chosen from various political sides.

During a recent visit of Bush to Vietnam, one could read in US media that the Vietnam war, besides killing about thirty thousand US soldiers, also killed *tens of thousands of Vietnamese people!* This is an understatement by a factor of about one hundred!

Concerning Cambodia, around one million deaths are now attributed by most experts to the Khmer Rouge regime. This is obviously an horrendous figure, but still significantly smaller than the truly enormous figure of about three million deaths in a total population of six to seven million. The latter figure was nevertheless common belief for a long time. Indeed it was circulated by both Vietnam and its ally, the Soviet Union, to justify its military intervention in Cambodia, and widely reported in the West to dissimulate the more numerous victims of the French and US wars in Indochina (which probably killed around four million people).

In a completely different register, during the military coup (of course without excuse) of Pinochet in Chile, the European left-oriented media widely talked about tens of thousands of victims killed. Current estimates are now much lower (between 3,000 and 5,000).

Concerning the conflicts of the 20th century in Asia or in Africa, the great uncertainty on the true figures for victims is accompanied by many specific additional difficulties in distinguishing what is due to wars, to genocides, to the consequences of the colonization and decolonization cycles, or even to plain poverty. It has been claimed, for instance, that the genocide perpetrated by the Belgians during their colonization of the Congo at the beginning of the 20th century may have been the worst of that century in terms of the total number of victims... although it is obviously much less known than the genocide of Armenians by Turks, not to mention the Shoah.

Let us now come back to the recent and so controversial case of the precise mortality due to the current war in Iraq. The United States media today still talk about a few tens of thousands of civilian victims, when other studies ahd already concluded long ago that the conflict had cost at least many hundreds of thousands of Iraqi lives. Very recently, similar studies have shown that the Iraq war has claimed more than a million Iraqi lives, hence that this war is by far the deadliest of our starting 21st century.

How is this discrepancy possible? We have first to come back to the different methodologies, which have been explained in detail by Les Roberts. To simplify and summarize, it is possible to count a certain number of bodies clearly killed by soldiers or insurgents. On the other hand, it is possible to perform an active statistical survey among the population: a significant sample of people is questioned and the result is then extrapolated to the whole population. None of these two methods is bad in itself, but one has to be aware that, in a war, many bodies are neither found nor counted. Communications are difficult and reporting deaths to authorities may not be safe or easy. As a result, statistical surveys will in general provide much higher figures than body counts. A discrepancy factor of five to ten between both estimates seems perfectly possible, at least for a while. Both methods, if they are used in a honest and rigorous way, should as a matter of fact progressively converge to the truth. But the main political manipulation in the United States and in Europe occurs in the following way. In the case of wars in the underdeveloped world (for instance in Africa), the Western media are fed with the very high figures of the statistical surveys. However when the West itself is implicated in a war, as in Iraq, the same media use the low figures of body counts, and sometimes even figures of the most strict and biased kind. Statistical surveys such as those of Les Roberts are discredited publicly at the highest level. Bush or Blair declare they are wrong, without even trying to offer any scientific evidence for their claim. In this way, public opinion in the West is kept believing that military interventions of their leaders all over the world are clean and enlightened, when in contrast Africans, for instance, remain stuck in cruel and dirty wars.

Such political manipulations might become much more difficult if a truly independent Agency would publish accurate figures allowing each citizen to know the sufferings inflicted by any war and to better compare, understand, and evaluate the responsibilities of each side. Applying the same standards everywhere would also indirectly fight the fundamental inequalities which govern our world today: although they are never explicitly formulated (except perhaps by airline companies?), the life of a single Westerner is considered as roughly equal to that of one hundred Africans or Iraqis.

2. To contribute to a credible international justice

The objective establishment of the facts is a prerequisite to any fair trial. It is also a prerequisite to any just evaluation of the material and moral reparations owed to the victims or to their families and heirs. Concerning the first issue, in the recent case of the Saddam Hussein trial, there is great frustration. Saddam Hussein has not been judged for any of his main crimes, at least none of those that were presented as such before the invasion of Iraq.

Neither starting the war against Iran (by far the costliest act in terms of human lives) nor the use of chemical weapons, including against a fraction of his own Kurdish population, nor the invasion or Kuwait, nor the repression of the insurrections which followed it, were judged. Saddam has been condemned for the relatively obscure killing of 148 Shiite villagers in Dujail in 1982. His hanging in rather undignified settings created a deep embarrassment. The eight-year war against Iran killed about one million people or more (again, no precise figures are available...). Why is it that this war was never at the center of the trial? The will to cover the responsibilities of Western nations seems obvious. They were the ones who pushed Saddam towards this war of aggression, supported him, and even armed him with the chemical weapons so much touted later. A few days after Saddam's hanging, the dictator Pinochet, installed by a military coup orchestrated by the United States, quietly died in his bed. Which observer of this state of affairs can believe that an unbiased system of international justice exists today? In the future, a truly independent evaluation of war crimes and of crimes against humanity must be a key element of a whole array of tools in the service of an international justice worthy of its name. Otherwise, even the notion of such a justice will be totally discredited.

The trial of a head of state is certainly a cathartic and spectacular moment. But we must not forget the even more important question of the reparations due to the victims or to their heirs. This is a more positive action, which is oriented towards the future. But, concerning these war reparations, what is striking is not so much their absence as their enormous bias. This issue has dramatic consequences, since war wounds remain open instead of healing. For instance, the enormous reparations that the winners attributed to themselves after the First World War ("Germany will pay...") did not allow reconciliation of the European peoples and played some role in the disastrous ascent to power of Hitler. Closer to our time, what should we think of the indecent billions attributed to the major oil companies after the first Gulf war, if we compare them to the complete absence of any US reparation to Vietnam for the indiscriminate civilian bombings and the enormous areas devastated by Agent Orange? Here also, there is an urgent need for a fair and independent evaluation of the long-lasting damage to the health and environment of the Vietnamese people, as is demanded by groups of victims.

To summarize, the unbiased systematic evaluation of all sufferings due to all armed conflicts seems essential to correct the many deformations of history, largely written by the winners to serve their selfish interests. Let us finally mention another positive fallback. If facts are established in a fair, uniform way beyond any reasonable doubt, no revisionism of any kind can come back to insult the victim's memory.

3. Some difficulties not to be underestimated

We should not harbor any illusions on the difficulties which await the proposed creation of such an Agency. In the short term, it will garner neither the support of powerful states nor that of weaker states. The current government of the United States is opposed to any new extension of humanitarian and international law (not to mention previous treaties). It perceives the whole subject as a potential obstacle to its worldwide domination. It alone can, of course, prevent the creation of this Agency. Other powerful states also want to preserve their freedom of maneuver in their respective regional areas of influence. They do not want to see their corresponding actions scrutinized too closely. Poor or weak states, discouraged by recent evolutions, may be tempted by cynicism. They have indeed many reasons to fear being again the only ones to be criticized. The leaders of all states (no matter how large or small) that are currently engaged or might be engaged in armed conflicts fear that a more precise evaluation of the sufferings caused by these conflicts, especially to civilians, might involve their responsibility and lead to their trial in international courts. This means many strong enemies for this Agency, even before its birth!

In the middle term, however, we think that our proposal could receive the support of many medium-sized states whose societies are, on average, much better organized, more democratic, and more prosperous than in the recent past. They have a growing say in world affairs and do ask for more international justice. World opinion, due in particular to the new media such as Internet, is now also a powerful factor. Inside the wider subject of international law and humanitarian rights, let us also remark that the specific question of the evaluation of sufferings in recent wars, and in particular the Iraq war, has led to such intense political controversies that it seems difficult to pull it back under the rug for much longer. This subject played a heavy role in the last 2004 presidential campaign in the United States. We already recalled that Bush himself was essentially forced to enter the arena, in order to deny the figures of Les Roberts, without providing any scientific argument or counter-estimate. These questions will not fade away and should surface again in the next presidential campaign, that of 2008. After Bush leaves the US presidency, it is quite possible that the idea of such a precise evaluation may progressively make its way forward and finally succeed. If I am allowed to indulge briefly in some political fiction, this may, for instance, occur in the following way: a new Democratic administration might, for instance, ask a national agency to evaluate Iraqi civilian casualties precisely, in order to hasten the end of that unpopular war. Then, in due course, another president might, for instance, support the creation of an independent international agency similar to the one proposed here, so that not only US conflicts but also those of other countries as well should be scrutinized in detail. Other scenarios are, of course, possible.

Without waiting for such prospects, if we agree with the idea, we should discuss it with the citizens of our respective countries and inform them about the benefits that this Agency could bring, as explained above. Let us review briefly some of the arguments that could be opposed to our proposition and some possible answers.

We do not yet have enough doctors to save lives during wars and yet you propose a better count of the dead

Of course ordinary medicine, that which saves lives, is the essential one. It must be endowed with much greater means than those of forensic medicine. However, as long as crimes do exist, should we get rid of forensic medicine? Is this medicine not essential to correctly inform justice and public opinion about the facts? The same argument at the international level seems even more forceful when applied to wars, and especially to war crimes. Besides an international humanitarian medicine endowed with rapid action capacities adapted to present tragedies, no matter whether they are wars or natural disasters, we should also support the creation of an officially recognized international forensic medicine.

Again another costly and bureaucratic agency!

If it remains entrusted to the good will of some particular states, of some non-governmental organizations, or even of some individuals, the international forensic medicine proposed here will have neither visibility nor credibility. Hence some means must be devoted to this agency. But I suggest, at least as a beginning, that a light institution could be started out of existing structures, for instance, the structures in charge of investigation on behalf of the two Special International Courts, the one on former Yugoslavia and the one on Rwanda, which otherwise should be dismantled within two or three years. The cost of such a light structure would in any case be only an incredibly tiny fraction of the giant current military budgets, which a truly effective international justice should contribute to deflating. Let us recall that the cost of the first study of mortality in Iraq by Les Roberts' team was about US $40,000. Even multiplying this figure by one hundred, who, for that prize, could propose something better for peace?

The United Nations Organization today is no longer credible. We must first reform it in depth before entrusting it with any new mission.

Certainly many people (including me) believe that the United Nations Organization must be deeply renovated and made more democratic. However, this reform will be long and difficult. To demand it as a prerequisite to the creation of the Agency proposed here would deprive us for an indefinite period of a much more modest but useful project. One should, by the way, make some distinctions in the ONU galaxy. Some institutions under its aegis, such as the United Nations High Commissioner for Refugees, have performed groundwork that should be saluted. They have been able to relieve great numbers of refugees and to raise public awareness of their problems. The Agency proposed here, however, would be of a much more technical nature, such as the International Atomic Energy Agency (IAEA). This comparison underlines, in fact, both its interest but also some of the limitations and possible dangers to be avoided. Indeed, the IAEA trained teams of competent experts who have gathered objective data in many cases, but one can regret that this institution works on a single aspect of the treaty of nuclear non-proliferation. They try to check that non-nuclear States parties to the treaty do not acquire the atomic bomb. This places the IAEA *de facto* exclusively in the service of the powerful nuclear States and of their historical advantages.

To prevent nuclear proliferation is a good thing, but not at the cost of completely ignoring the nuclear disarmament which was promised by the powerful nuclear states as the other side of the treaty. To avoid similar snags, the proposed new Agency must absolutely remain truly independent, in the service of all humanity, not just one more tool for the strong states to better impose their will on the weaker ones.

It is much more important to prevent wars rather than to evaluate them!

This last argument can be applied of course to the whole domain of international humanitarian law. We must pay attention to it, and it will in fact lead us to our conclusion. Why indeed should we spend so much effort to humanize or to evaluate what should be purely and simply suppressed? To definitely eliminate war is, of course, our true goal, indeed. It was also the dream of all humanists before us. So we must ask: why did they all fail? This is because the elimination of war is an extraordinarily complex problem which cannot be solved by general statements, no matter how well intended, nor by such or such particular technical tool, were it even a powerful and reformed organization of United Nations. Humanity will be able to eradicate the madness of war only through a giant network of patient, clever, coordinated actions maintained over time. These actions must not only address the problem of war but have also to eliminate all the injustices and inequalities which are at its root. They should raise the resources and education for all, especially in poor countries. They should make any military aggression more and more difficult and costly, with punishment more and more certain for all persons responsible for wars, no matter how powerful. It is only inside this extraordinarily complex network of actions that our proposal for a specific *International Agency for Evaluation of Sufferings due to Armed Conflicts* makes sense. It is only one element of that network, even a quite modest one. One day, we hope, this agency will no longer be needed. Today its creation seems necessary, and even urgent.

NILS ANDERSSON, DANIEL IAGOLNITZER
AND VINCENT RIVASSEAU

WHAT CAN WE DO TODAY?

The analyses presented in the various contributions to this book are overwhelming as it concerns most United States governments from the time of the Hiroshima bombing to our day, where the present administration pursues a politic of aggression and of violation and flouting of international humanitarian law. This law, for all humanitarian oranizations, is a fundamental instrument in the struggle against war crimes, and without it, the situation would probably have been much worse. Even the United States is obliged to take international humanitarian law into account to a certain extent. All consider, in consequence, that it is better to bring this to public attention, to work for improvement, and to make the U.S. a "good citizen", to denounce all serious violations that are committed, and to struggle against the impunity of all those who are responsible. How can this be achieved ? A first general difficulty is well known: impunity can sometimes aid in the re-establishment of peace. But can there be a true peace without justice? For example, can there be a true peace in the Near and Middle East without the end of the interventions of the United States in that region *and* its recognition of the crimes committed? We mention below other problems and points of view tied more specifically to the case of powerful states, and more particularly, the United States. We will then provide our own conclusions.

• Universal jurisdiction linked to the Geneva Conventions and Protocols, or international jurisdiction? Universal jurisdiction concerns the sovereignty of each people to the extent that the most serious war crimes concern the whole of humanity. It can, however, be used in an improper or selective way (e.g. for political reasons), or also in a way which may be considered as inappropriate (for example, is it best to have those Africans responsible for crimes being judged in those countries which in the past colonized their country, e.g. in France which granted an amnesty to those responsible for torture and other crimes during the Algerian liberation war)? International jurisdiction can then appear to be a better approach. However, the present jurisdictions, ad hoc tribunals established by the Security Council of the UN or the International Criminal Court are submitted to the influence (or to the right of veto) of the most powerful states. Further, the definition of war crimes given by the ICC with regard to attacks capable of causing grave civilian losses is being watered down in comparison with that of the 1977 Geneva Protocol, and the ICC is not able, or does not really wish so far, in any event, to judge the crimes of the most powerful States, such as the United States.

Large-scale murders, rapes, and the enlistment of children are rightly prosecuted by the International Criminal Court in several African countries. Are violations of basic human rights, killing and destruction through the use of planes, missiles and other sophisticated arms more acceptable?

• Numerous countries have ratified the Geneva Conventions and Protocols or the Statute of the International Criminal Court, but, contrary to their obligation, still to this day have not adapted their national legislation in such a manner as to put into force the undertakings to which they have agreed. In relation to the Geneva Conventions and Protocols, the International Criminal Court has the advantage of also dealing with other crimes, including in times of peace (genocide, crimes against humanity…) but is retrograde in relation to the Geneva Protocol I as it relates to attacks and bombardments against civilian populations: this opens the way in practice to interpretations conducive to exonerating the leaders of powerful states such as the United States from their responsibilities in this domain. Must we resign ourselves to this, in favor of at least the adoption of the Statute of the International Criminal Court with the risk that the situation be thus congealed, and that a major part of the war crimes by powerful states and their leaders thus remain unpursued?

• Is it better to put the accent on the more plausibly successful struggle against the impunity of those responsible from weak countries or the vanquished, for which the support, or at least the agreement of the United States, can be useful? With regard to the United States itself, an approach would be to denounce its violations of humanitarian law, but without putting in question its "democratically elected" leadership while hoping that the affirmation of the principles and the action taken inside the country will permit a positive evolution in the future. Or must we demand judgment of all those responsible for the gravest war crimes, including the leadership of powerful states, such as the present president of the United States, at least after they leave office, if diplomatic immunity is considered to apply while they are in office?

We share with others this latter point of view. International justice can only lose all credibility, with grave consequences which are already present today, if on the one hand we pursue, albeit in a manner very largely justified, the crimes committed in Congo, Darfur, or those of the former Khmer Rouge leadership in Cambodia, while on the other hand, those responsible in the United States for crimes from Hiroshima to Iraq and Guantanamo, in Indochina and South America, continue to benefit from total impunity. The idea that the application of international justice in weaker countries will lead to a positive evolution of powerful States remains itself doubtful: we witness the establishment of a justice in a unique direction. In international meetings, the present president of the United States is the first one to claim that those responsible for crimes must be pursued and punished…e.g. in Darfur. The problem is that, for him and other leaders of powerful States, the criminals are the others, the "terrorists" (including all those who resist to them) or those savages in Africa. Their own bombardments and other actions are self-regarded as almost "humanitarian".

It seems to us that these conditions suggest that we coordinate juridical actions according to the actual possibilities and that we appeal to public opinion. While attending a change in the direction of the world—illusory in the short term—that would permit an authentic international jurisdiction, even limited juridical actions can be undertaken on the basis of universal jurisdiction. They must, in our view, target in priority, in western countries, the directors of powerful states, and in particular the United States. The recent complaints against Donald Rumsfeld in Germany and France, albeit so far rejected, are an example. The opening towards and parallel appeal to international public opinion appears indispensable. This can be done by public tribunals, citizens' inquests, etc., and one can also conceive of a massive appeal to public opinion in our countries that the international treaties be respected, that the Geneva Conventions and Protocols be more effectively put into force, and that all those responsible for transgressions be pursued, including the present president of the United States, on the basis of the principle of universal jurisdiction. If it is illusory in the short term to arrest high officials of powerful countries, pursuits in various other countries will be able to prevent their entry into those countries: this in itself is a strong signal against impunity and, as it concerns the United States, a support for the citizens of that country who struggle courageously against their current administration.

CONTRIBUTORS

Honorary Presidents of the Paris Conference

Théo Van Boven was the representative of The Netherlands to the UN Commission on Human Rights, then Director of the Human Rights Division of the United Nations from 1977 to 1982. He presently teaches law atthe University of Limbourg.

Pierre Vidal Naquet, historian, militant against torture and against the Algerian War, specialist in Greek history, has also directed numerous works on modern and contemporary history, and taught the sociology of ancient Greece at the French School for Advanced Studies in Social Sciences.

Contributors

Tadatoshi Akiba, Mayor of Hiroshima, has inspired a powerful upsurge in anti-nuclear activism. As president of the Mayors for Peace, he has increased by one-third the number of member cities. In November 2003, the Mayors for Peace, supported by the cities of Hiroshima and Nagasaki, launched an Emergency Campaign to Ban Nuclear Weapons. This campaign has since received strong endorsements in resolutions passed by the European Parliament, the Conference of U.S. Mayors, International Physicians for the Prevention of Nuclear War (IPPNW), and Abolition 2000. Mayor Akiba and Mayors for Peace won a Global Citizen Award from the Nuclear Age Peace Foundation in 2005. As a part of this campaign, Akiba led a delegation of 19 mayors and deputy mayors from 12 countries to the NPT Preparatory Committee Meeting at UN Headquarters in New York. Akiba has recently travelled to India, Pakistan, England, France, Germany, Russia, the U.S., Canada and China to make personal appeals to university presidents and professors concerning the Hiroshima-Nagasaki Peace Study Project. Several institutions of higher learning (many universities in Japan; American University in Washington, D.C.,Tufts University in Boston, where Akiba taught, and Illinois Wesleyan University in the U.S.; Berlin Technology Institute and Paris Institute of Political Studies in Europe) have already begun offering courses or seminars, and many more are in the planning stages. Mayor Akiba is a respected leader in the most critical movement of this decade: the campaign to eliminate nuclear weapons.

Nuri Albala, lawyer, has carried out numerous observation missions, both judicial and for the defense of human rights, notably for the International Association of Democratic Lawyers (Association Internationale des Juristes Democrates); and has worked on problems of international law and the place of the United Nations, as well as on economic, social, and cultural rights in globalization. He has published numerous articles on these questions. He is a founding member of Observatoire de la Mondialisation, President of the Commission, Fundamental Rights and Globalization, and an international director of DROIT-SOLIDARITE (AIJD).

Samir Amin is an Egyptian professor of political economics and development. He has written more than 30 books including *Imperialism & Unequal Development, Specters of Capitalism: A Critique of Current Intellectual Fashions, Obsolescent Capitalism: Contemporary Politics and Global Disorder, Maldevelopment,* and *The Liberal Virus.* His memoirs were published in October of 2006 He is Director of the Third World Forum in Dakar, and President of Forum Mondial des Alternatives.

Nils Andersson, journalist, former editor, founder of La Cité Editeur in Lausanne, has published numerous works denouncing torture during the Algerian war. He contributed to a number of anthologies and reviews on questions of war in the Balkans and Iraq, and on the UN system. He is a founding member of the ADIF and member of the French Committee of the Helsinki Federation on Human Rights and of the Advisory Scientific Committee of the Institut de Documentation et de Recherches sur la Paix.

Amy Bartholomew is an Associate Professor of Law at Carleton University, Ottawa. She was an expert witness at the BRussells Tribunal in April 2004, part of the World Tribunal on Iraq, and on the panel of advocates at its culminating session in Istanbul in June 2005. She is the editor of, and a contributor to, *Empire's Law: The American Imperial Project and the 'War to Remake the World'* (London: Pluto Press). She has written on human rights and legal and political theory and is currently completing a manuscript on 'justice without guarantees'.

Abraham Behar, physician, honorary professor of biophysics at the University of Paris VI, is a specialist in nuclear medicine and radiobiology and a former president of the Nobel Prize winning International Association of Physicians for the Prevention of Nuclear War (IPPNW). He is presently president of its French section and member of the UN Disarmament Commission in Geneva.

Antoine Bernard is a specialist in international public law (human rights and fundamental freedoms) and consultant at the United Nations Centre of Academic Studies He has been the permanent representative of the International Federation of Human Rights at the United Nations, then executive secretary and is now Executive Director of this organization (since 1995). He is also associate professor at the University of Paris X.

William Blum left the State Department in 1967, abandoning his aspiration of becoming a Foreign Service Officer because of his opposition to what the United States was doing in Vietnam. His book on U.S. foreign policy, *Killing Hope: U.S. Military and CIA Interventions Since World War II*, has received international acclaim. Noam Chomsky called it "far and away the best book on the topic." He is also the author of *Rogue State: A Guide to the World's Only Superpower* and *West-Bloc Dissident: A Cold War Memoir*. His books have been translated into 15 foreign languages.

Pascal Boniface is a specialist in geopolitics, Director of IRIS (Institute of International and Strategic Relations, and professor at the Institute of European Studies of the University of Paris VIII. He is chief editor of *La revue internationale et stratégique* and *L'Année stratégique*, member of the Advisory Committee on Disarmament of the United Nations, administrator of the Institut des Hautes Etudes de la Défense Nationale, and member of the support committee to the Académie diplomatique africaine.

Jean Bricmont is professor of theoretical physics at the University of Louvain (Belgium). He has been active in the anti-war movement since 2002. In 2004, he participated in the BRussels Tribunal, which was the first session of the World Tribunal on Iraq. He is the author of a book (in French) about the "humanitarian" justifications of wars.

Robert Charvin is professor of law, honorary president of the University of Law and Economic Sciences at Nice-Sophia Antipolis. He is a former member of Executive Committees of several NGOs, some of which hold an advisory role at the United Nations (ECOSOC): the International Association of Democratic Lawyers (Brussels) and North-South (Geneva). He is presently member of CETIM (Geneva), of the committees of the journals *Recherches Internationales* (Paris), *Utopie Critique* (Paris) and *Droit Ouvrier* (Paris). He is the author of several books on international relations, law and globalization, human rights and individual freedoms.

Monique Chemillier-Gendreau is an honorary professor at the University of Paris VII-Denis Diderot, specializing in public law and political science. She has participated in many procedures before various tribunals and before the International Court of Justice, has been involved in a number of international conflicts, in particular in Asia (Laos-Thailand, Vietnam-China,...), and has been a consultant for UNESCO. She is a regular collaborator with the French journal, *Le Monde Diplomatique*.

William Ramsey Clark served in the United States Department of Justice as the Assistant Attorney General of the Lands Division, and as Deputy Attorney General. He was director of the American Judicature Society (1963) and president of the Federal Bar Association (1964-65). He then became active in the American anti-war movement, and has become globally known and respected for his continuing advocacy against and for civil and human rights political causes. He is founder of the International Action Center, and with it, one of the more prominent American peace organizations, International ANSWER (Act Now to Stop War and End Racism). He has served as defense counsel to, inter alia, Philip Berrigan and the Harrisburg Seven, Slobodan Milosovic, Saddam Hussein, David Koresh, and US deserter Camelo Mejia. He is a recipient of the Gandhi Peace Award.

Barbara Delcourt is a professor of social, economic and political sciences, member of the Institute for European Studies, and associated member of the Center of International Law and Sociology applied to International Law at the Free University (Brussels). She has worked in particular on the relations between international politics and international law on the basis of the European management of the Yugoslavian crisis. Her present research work is oriented on the external and security politics of the European Union, a subject she teaches, and on questions of security.

Rudolf El-Kareh is Professor of Social and Political Sciences and Epistemology, writer and essayist. He is Associate Professor at the ULB (Brussels), member of the "Center for International Cooperation and Development Studies" (Brussels), and member of the "Center for Contemporary Orient Studies" of the University of Paris III-Sorbonne Nouvelle. He was also professor in the Lebanese University (Beirut) and the Institute for Political Studies of Aix-en-Provence (France). He also is an international consultant for development in Europe, the Arab World and the Mediterranean area. He published hundreds of studies and articles and contributes regularly to *Le Monde Diplomatique* and the French *Journal of Palestine Studies*. Among the books he published on conflicts and geopolitics is *Informe sobre el Conflicto y la Guerra de Kosovo*.

Pedro A. García-Bilbao is a writer and Professor of Sociology at the University Rey Juan Carlos URJC, Spain. He was a member of the Refugees Department, then Coordinator of the Spanish Red Cross Program during the European Year against Racism and Anti-semitism. He is a specialist in forced displacements of populations, in the military sociology of defense, and in the Republican historical memory. He won the Prize for fantastic literature of the Catalan Polytechnical University for his book *Fuego sobre San Juan*, an ironical history of the US-Spanish 1898 war.

Philip Grant is a lawyer in Geneva, and a specialist in particular in international humanitarian law. He is the author of several scientific publications and editor of the book *The struggle against impunity in Swiss Law* (in French). He has founded and is president of TRIAL (Track Impunity Always), a Swiss Association against impunity.

Stèphane Hessel, born in 1917, resistance fighter to the German occupation during World War II, was deported to Buchenwald and Dora. After the war, as a diplomat, he worked along with René Cassin in drafting the Universal Declaration of Human Rights. During his long diplomatic career, as a close collaborator with Pierre Mendès-France, he was accorded the title of Amassador of France in 1981. Representing France at the United Nations World Conference on Human Rights, he is today strongly engaged in defending the rights of the homeless.

Daniel Iagolnitzer is a former professor of physics, founding member and co-president of the ADIF. He is the author of the book *International Law and War: Evolution and Present Problems* (in French).

Jan Myrdal, writer and essayist, has lived in different European countries and in Afghanistan, China, India, and Mexico He has published some ninety volumes: novels, plays, political commentaries; literary and art criticism; sociology, books on Afghanistan, Central Asia, China, India, and Mexico. He has produced feature films and documentaries. His exhibitions and art-books (together with Gun Kessle) inter alia on Romanesque art in Norway and France, on Buddhist cave art along the Silk Road, on French political graphic art. He holds an honorary Ph.D. from Nankai University China (for *Report from a Chinese Village*), and Honorary Doctor of Literature from Upsala College N.J. USA (for *Confessions of a Disloyal European*).

Michael Parenti received his Ph.D. in Political Science from Yale University. He is an award winning author and activist who has published some 250 articles and 19 books, including *Superpatriotism* (2004), and *The Assassination of Julius Caesar* (2003) which won the Book of the Year Award (non fiction) from Online Review of Books, and *The Culture Struggle* (2005). Various works of his have been translated into some twenty languages. He lectures frequently in North America and abroad, and has appeared on many radio and television talk shows.

Karen Parker is an attorney from the United States (San Francisco) who specializes in human rights and humanitarian law. She is co-founder of the Association of Humanitarian Lawyers. She has represented NGOs at United Nations human rights fora for over 20 years, and has made substantial contributions to special UN reports such as those on economic sanctions, weapons (including weapons containing depleted uranium), and human rights and terrorism. She is the attorney on a case at the Organization of American States brought by the Association of Humanitarian Lawyers against the United States for attacking medical facilities in Falluja.

Vincent Rivasseau is a professor of physics at the University of Paris XI. He is involved in various actions in relation to human rights and international humanitarian law, and to the scientific development of Africa. He is a member of the Executive Committee of the African Institute for Mathematical Sciences (South Africa).

Les Roberts has a Masters degree in public health from Tulane University and a Ph.D. in environmental engineering from Johns Hopkins. He did a post-doctorate fellowship in epidemiology at the Centers for Disease Control and Prevention where he worked for 4 years. In 1994, he worked as an epidemiologist for the World Health Organization in Rwanda during their civil war. He was Director of Health Policy at the International Rescue Committee from Dec. 2000 until April of 2003. He is presently a lecturer at the Johns Hopkins University Department of Geography and Environmental Engineering where he teaches each fall, and teaches in the Columbia Program on Forced Migration and Health each spring.

Geneviève Sevrin is president of the French section of Amnesty International

Roland Weyl is a lawyer and is vice-president of the International Association of Democratic Lawyers (IADL).

INDEX OF AUTHORS